Self-Reliant

PILOT

Alaskan Style Training

William A. (Bill) Quirk, III

PO Box 221974 Anchorage, Alaska 99522-1974
books@publicationconsultants.com—www.publicationconsultants.com

ISBN 978-1-59433-564-8
eBook ISBN 978-1-59433-565-5
Library of Congress Catalog Card Number: 2015943913

Front Cover: Ski-equipped taildraggers
on the Kenai Peninsula's Spencer Glacier

Manufactured in the United States of America.

Dedication

This book is dedicated to the distinguished Alaskan pilots who have provided a captivating influence in helping fledgling aviators become the best pilots they can be.

Contents

Acknowledgements

I must first honor Chuck Keim, professor in the University of Alaska's Department of Journalism and former dean of the College of Arts and Letters. Although my academic career is in the biological sciences, I veered off track and enrolled in Chuck's introductory college course in writing short articles. This was when I was in residence at the university in Fairbanks, Alaska in the early 1970s. Chuck was such an influential teacher that most of his students would go away from that experience knowing that they were capable of writing meaningful narratives. Of course there is no substitute from being a prolific writer to improve your journalistic talents. We were all required to write a short piece to turn in at the end of the semester. I wrote on hunting Mearns quail in Arizona with my clever and multi-talented Weimaraner (Gray Ghost) that could wind, trail, point, and retrieve the birds. I have also benefited in improving my writing skills by being a voracious reader ever since my high school days.

Bill Diehl is a long time aviator that has made significant contributions to aviation in Alaska. Bill recognized the Interstate S-1B1 airplane manufactured by the Interstate Manufacturing Company based in El Segundo, California for its dependable flying characteristics and its durable construction. He believed that it would make a useful bush plane for Alaska. Bill purchased the Type Certificate and tooling from Interstate in the late 1960s and created the Arctic Aircraft Company in Anchorage, Alaska. Arctic Aircraft transformed the Interstate S-1B1 into a bush plane by upgrading structural elements of the fuselage, landing gear, and wings. The redesigned aircraft was designated the Interstate S-1B2 and has come to be known as the Arctic Tern. A Type Certificate for the Arctic Tern was issued by FAA in 1975. Bill produced 31 Arctic Terns in his factory near Anchorage International Airport between 1975 and 1985. Ten additional Arctic Terns were built in the factory by converting Interstate S-1B1s to Terns. Bill also has designed and built 4-place Arctic Terns called Privateers. He has built five Privateers.

There was nothing that prepared me for the consequences of meeting so many pilots in Alaska. The camaraderie has been fulfilling and it has helped me create a highly inspired learning and flying experience in Alaska. Below is a listing of pilots that I have met along my aviation journey.

Glen Alsworth, Bret Andersen, Tyler Andrews, Walt Audi, Jim Bailey, Jay Balwin, Thomas Beckman, Gary Bishop, Paul Boots, Bob Breeden, Bill Brown, Mark Brown, Bill Bullard, Glen Burkheimer, Wally Butts, David Calkins, Terry Cartee, Dan Case, Scott Christy, John Claus, Paul Claus, Sam Cole, Bert Crowley, Dick Davidson, Ray Davis, Sean Davis, Steven Dawson, Tony Dawson, Phil Dean, Dee Deoudes, Eugene Desjarlais, Bill Diehl, Michael Dolan, Vicki Dombe, Darlene Dubay, Jeff Duft, Greg Endsley, Mark Faires, Eddie Farmer, Winthrop Faulkner, Ron Fullerton, Jeff Garness, Tom George, Damon German, Lars Gleitsmann, Charles Goentzel, Peter Goldberg, Andrew Granger, Bill Granger, Rick Grant, Lee Griffin, Robert Haggerty, Bill Hamm, Mark Hamm, Chet Harris, Dorothy Harris, Steve Harvey, Arthur Hoag, Gary Hofstrand, Terry Holliday, Dan Hollingsworth, Herb Hubbard, Cliff Hudson, Jay Hudson, Oren Hudson, Ray Huot, James Johnson, Zachary Johnson, Wolfgang Junge, Larry Kaniut, Jo Ann Keller, Matthew Keller, David Krall, Tim LaPorte, Paul Larson, Dr. Scott Laudon, Tom Laughead, Dr. Finn Lunoe, Dr. Leif Lunoe, Clinton MacArthur, Dave Machado, Bob Magnuson, Dr. Michael McNamara, Mike Meekin, Joe Mets, Alfred Meyer, Scott Mobley, Kris Ogonoski, Joe Pazsint, Perry Pearce, Kellie Peirce, John Peterson, Richard Reiley, Jim Richmond, James Rood, Bill Roth, Heidi Ruess, Danny A. Sanchez, John Schoen, Marshall Severson, Ed Sharpe, David Slenkamp, Alex Stanionis, Calvin Stephens, Greg Stoddard, Dick Sutliff, Evan Swensen, Robin Sylvester, Sean Sylvester, John Thorsness, John Toenes, Randy Tyler, Vern Ulmer, Charles Vandergaw, Robert Vanderpool, Ernie Walker, Art Warbelow, Charlie Warbelow, Ron Warbelow, Dave Wartinbee, Billy Weidekehr, Adam White, Artic Wikle, David Wilks, Kenneth Wolter, Paul Woodward, Eric Yould, Patricia Yould, Mike Zaidlicz, Doug Zweifel.

Warning and Disclaimer

This book provides basic knowledge on strategies and techniques that Alaska's elite pilots employ while flying in the Great Land. Please note that serious injury or death may occur from attempting to duplicate any of the techniques described in this book. This especially applies to pilots without the proper experience, skill levels, judgment, and common sense. Do not attempt any of the book's techniques without weighing the risks to you, your passengers, and your airplane. The author and the publishers of this book are not responsible for any reader's negligence, ignorance, or downright stupidity.

The basic theme in this book is self-training. If any techniques discussed in this book are attempted, it becomes the sole responsibility of the pilot to make the decision to proceed with the undertaking. You will be proceeding on your own terms, on your own risk, and with your own assurance that you can safely perform the task at hand. None of the decisions to train in your aircraft are implied in this book.

Preface

Alaskan style training will provide enormous benefits in becoming a self-reliant pilot. The training to become a self-reliant pilot is the most potent that exists and it will provide the simplest, safest, and most effective way to fly an airplane. A self-reliant pilot has learned skills and strategies that become an art and are far superior to what General Aviation (GA) pilots obtain from conventional advanced training. Alaskan style training is based on learning in your own aircraft to become the best pilot you can be. The flying strategies and techniques are selected from two aviation spheres—the first is the Federal Aviation Administration's (FAA's) instructions and directives from their handbooks and certificated instructors and the second is the elite Alaskan pilot's unwritten aviation domain. The best strategies and techniques are selected from both of these aviation spheres and incorporated into the pilot's flying skills. Becoming a much improved self-reliant pilot is one of the most cherished events in a pilot's aviation career.

Over half of GA aircraft accidents are occurring during the takeoff and landing phase of flying while the largest number of fatal and serious injury accidents occurs from stall/spin accidents. The aircraft accident rate for these operations is way too high and all aviation groups agree that it should be reduced. The FAA and the National Transportation Safety Board (NTSB) have been working diligently in the past decade to help reduce these aircraft accident rates by holding Safety Seminars and by issuing Safety Alerts. These determined efforts have not provided beneficial results in reducing the aircraft accident rate to an acceptable level. This provides mounting evidence that the quality of the flying techniques is closely tied with and is reflected in the accident rate. Making positive gains in reducing the GA accident rate for these flying operations will require abandoning the weak and inadequate flying techniques and replacing them with more effective ones.

The distinguished Alaskan pilots have developed *Precision Landings* that can perform a double bonus in substantially reducing both of these elevated accident rates to an acceptable level. *Precision Landings* are amazingly easy in performance and provide a high degree of accuracy and consistency. This technique was developed in Alaska many years ago for safely landing airplanes in challenging off-airport short field operations. Short field landings in Alaska could not be accomplished without using *Precision Landings* as there would be a continuous and unlimited number of aircraft accidents. GA pilots that adopt *Precision Landings* will also receive the same useful benefits by substantially lowering their aircraft accident rate to acceptable levels. GA pilots landing on airports with runways that are longer than necessary are provided little safety from landing accidents caused by aircraft overloaded with kinetic energy by applying FAA's 1.3 Vso Rule. *Precision Landings* requires the pilot to land the airplane on a selected target at initial stall speed removing every bit of excess kinetic energy prior to touching the wheels down. This will prevent most landing accidents that are caused by the mismanagement of kinetic energy. Landing at stall speed on every landing will also provide sufficient training that will allow pilots to never unintentionally stall their airplane. Both of these elevated aircraft accident rates by GA pilots can be substantially reduced by applying *Precision Landings* developed by Alaska's extraordinary pilots.

Introduction

Self-Reliant Pilot was written to inform, educate, and familiarize aviators with the extraordinary Alaskan pilots who fly extreme and challenging short field operations in the Great Land. This aviation niche is very small when compared to the FAA's immense realm. Nevertheless, it has global significance for its uniqueness and for its practical benefits to GA pilots. This small aviation sphere is tied to some of the world's most innovative and distinguished pilots. They have advanced their own flying strategies and techniques to become the most capable pilots that are possible. This is the roots for developing Alaska's amazing self-reliant pilots. GA pilots can greatly improve their flying careers by adopting strategies and techniques from Alaska's elite pilots. These strategies and techniques will provide the best advanced training possible and it will substantially reduce their aircraft accident rate.

Self-Reliant Pilot serves as a primer for providing aviators precisely what is required to reach their goal for learning to become an innovative and self-reliant pilot. The book shows the invigorating flying in Alaska's stunning mountain and glacier landscape, it highlights winter ski flying operations, the camaraderie of flying Alaska, and shows features on Alaska's magnificent wildlife. It scrutinizes the elevated aircraft accident rate in Alaska and provides practical ways to lessen the problem.

The mid-section of the book includes a compendium of 32 color images by the author to fully display Alaska's incomparable flying environment.

The last part of the book contains 75 brief narratives covering aviation topics and flying adventures in Alaska's remote and scenic backcountry. The narratives provide detailed explanations of the joy of flying Alaska.

Part 1:
Becoming Your Own
Self-Reliant Pilot

Alaska's Flying Environment

The locale where pilots are flying is an important factor in pilot development. To evolve into the best pilot you can be, it is essential to have natural aviator talents and an intense passion for flying. These attributes are essential for further pilot progression. Often overlooked is an inspiring and motivating flying environment. Alaska offers among the best flying environments a pilot could ever hope for, especially in Southcentral Alaska when flying out of Anchorage. Having all three of these elements in your flying background will contribute to the highest possible level and sustainability of pilot development. The stimulation will propel your aviation career to new and higher levels. There will be no dull moments and boredom from flying in Southcentral Alaska.

What makes Southcentral Alaska's flying environment so invigorating? Why it's the sheer beauty of the sculpture (shape and form) of the magnificent mountains, glaciers, fjords, the wilderness character of the terrain, the spectacular wildlife to be found here, and the freedom experienced flying over an unpeopled land. All these unusual experiences are rare to find today in such a developed world. We are fortunate in Alaska that we still have these natural unspoiled frontiers.

Mountain ranges within an hour's flying time in all directions from Anchorage offer a wide choice of landscape diversity. The Chugach Mountain Range rises above Anchorage and continues eastward for 250 miles to Valdez, Cordova, and beyond. The massive Stevens Ice Field is found here along the north side of Prince William Sound. To the northeast of Anchorage are the Talkeetna Mountains with small glaciers near the highest mountain peaks, which are in the neighborhood of 8,000 feet. Northwest of Anchorage in the Alaska Range are Mount McKinley and the other gigantic mountains surrounded by massive glaciers up to 45 miles in length. To the west of Anchorage is the southern end of the Alaska Range with spectacular mountains and glaciers around perpetually snow-covered Mount Gerdine and Mount Spurr. To the south of Anchorage across Turnagain Arm of Cook Inlet is the legendary Kenai Peninsula. The Kenai is approximately 150 miles in length oriented northeast–southwest and from 50 to 100 miles in width consisting of 6,425,320 acres. The enchanting snow-capped mountains rise from sea level to over 6,000 feet and surround the massive *Harding and Sargent Ice Fields*. The Kenai Peninsula replicates, in miniature, all of Alaska's stunning landscapes. It also provides world-class salmon and halibut fishing. The inspiration from flying in these pristine mountains and glacier environments is off the charts. It will sustain your flying adventures forevermore.

Alaska has some of the best weather for flying. Although the mountains in Alaska reach high elevations, the valleys are usually low in elevation. The days are cool in summer and cold in winter. This makes for excellent flying weather with great lift in summer when day temperatures are in the 50s and 60s Fahrenheit. This contrasts with high temperatures (from 80 to over 100 degrees Fahrenheit) and miserable flying conditions (greatly reduced lift) in the Lower 48 states in the summer months. Density altitude is rarely a problem in Alaska; we can fly anytime without worrying about high density altitude conditions. Alaska can have very windy days, low ceilings (fog), and other serious flying weather problems that can be challenging. However, there is ample good weather and sufficient flying conditions for many days in Alaska in both summer and winter. The Alaska snowpack is sufficient for excellent ski flying during the winter months. The colder winter flying days (10 degrees Fahrenheit or lower) are the best. They not only provide better lift but the snow conditions are enhanced for landings. The hills with plateaus above tree line (higher than 3,000 feet) make excellent landing places in winter due to powder snow and a deeper winter snowpack. Glaciers and ice fields provide some of the best ski landing areas. These areas being at higher elevations maintain powder snow conditions as the glacial ice keeps uniformly low snow temperatures throughout the winter.

Alaska's Extreme Flying

We have the extraordinary pilots in Alaska that are legendary for performing challenging short field landings in natural terrain both in the summer on Alaskan Bushwheels and in the winter on skis. These short field landings are made all over remote Alaska without any infrastructure. Many of these landings are the shortest short field landings for small taildraggers that exist. Special Alaskan pilot skills are necessary to perform these operations consistently and without accidents. Canada has a limited and far fewer number of off-airport operations where pilots land their taildraggers in challenging natural terrain. Other places in the world such as Australia, Africa, and Idaho in the Western United States also fly aircraft into remote regions and land them in off-airport locations. However, most of these landings are on improvised or makeshift landing strips. Landing on these partially improved strips can be challenging. Nevertheless, after learning the proper flying techniques these landings become routine and can be performed with little or no difficulty. Selecting a short field landing site in natural terrain from the cockpit of your airplane is significantly more complex. It requires *edge of performance* flying skills. These skills are substantially more complex, varied, and difficult when compared to landing on unimproved airstrips. These landings in Alaska are referred to as off-airport short field landings in natural terrain or extreme flying in Alaska's backcountry.

Alaska has had a long history and necessity for unique pilot development for increasing capabilities for landing airplanes in extreme conditions. The first use of airplanes in Alaska was for carrying passengers and freight to remote places with no infrastructure. When the pilots arrived at their destination, there were no landing strips available. The pilot had to improvise and find a suitable landing place close to the drop-off point. Often these landings were made in natural terrain such as gravel bars along rivers.

Alaska has developed a tourism industry during the past 50 to 60 years that has shown rapid expansion each decade to the present time. The current influx of outsiders brings in 2 million visitors a year with a $4 billion economic impact. Visitors are drawn to Alaska by two distinct factors—wilderness and wildlife. Outdoor pursuits in Alaska for tourists include hunting, fishing, backpacking and trekking, bear viewing, mountain climbing, kayaking pristine rivers and saltwater, cross-country skiing, and many others. Alaska's aviation industry is a necessity for providing access in the State for these visitors. Most flights will leave from airports and are likely to have unimproved airstrips for the first flight to a lodge or camping site. Further access to more remote wilderness areas will require flights in small taildraggers often landing in extreme conditions in natural terrain (airstrips are usually not available).

Hunters and fishers come to Alaska to pursue the State's world-class game which includes Alaska's fabulous big game animals, salmon, and native rainbow trout. This has been a key driver in requiring substantial numbers of Alaskan pilots for accessing remote areas in the State. Nonresident hunters from the Lower 48 States are required to have a licensed Alaskan guide to hunt brown bear, Dall sheep or mountain goat. Nonresident aliens from foreign countries are required to be personally accompanied by a licensed Alaskan guide to hunt any game animal in Alaska—brown and black bears, bison, caribou, Dall sheep, deer, elk, moose, mountain goat, muskox, wolf, and wolverine. These Alaskan guide requirements create a substantial number of clients. Many of the guides are also licensed pilots with the extreme flying skills necessary to access Alaska's big game animals. These guides have established a lucrative business making large sums of income. Examples of guided hunts on the high end in Alaska are $18-25K for a 9-10 foot brown bear; $10-18K for trophy moose; $10-16K for trophy Dall sheep; $6-10K for caribou; and $10K for mountain goat. Each guide / outfitter usually has 6-15 hunters booked for each hunting season. Flights for brown bear viewing from selected sites on the ground can cost from $1,000 to $3,000 per day. Fishing lodges in world-famous Bristol Bay top out on the high end at $8,000 or more per week. The huge sums of money have made the difficulty and high cost of providing extreme flying in Alaska to support the clients possible.

Fishers travel to remote parts of Alaska on fishing trips. Most are flown into lodges or temporary camps in float planes. Many of the lodges have float planes parked at the lodge to take fishers out to productive areas on a daily basis. Again, most of this remote access is by float or amphibian airplanes. This requires much greater flying skills and advanced training beyond *Private Pilot and Commercial License* skills. The fishing lodges and camps require many highly trained pilots to carry out these missions. These operations perpetuate extreme flying in Alaska to a certain level. However, it is to a much lesser degree than landing in natural terrain on wheels.

The many Super Cub pilots over the years that are big game guides are the ones that are primarily responsible for developing the extreme flying so prevalent in Alaska. They have constant difficult challenges like few other pilots. They are sustained by having a long-term business as a well-paid guide. There are enough of these pilot-guides all over the State to perpetuate extreme flying. They could not earn their huge incomes without being able to deliver their hunters to the remote places where the big game animals are found. They are constantly challenged with heavy loads and landings in new and difficult places in all kinds of weather—they have to land where they find the big game animals. The unique strategies and techniques that these pilots have developed are passed on to the younger generation of pilots that go into being future big game guides. These techniques are also distributed to many other pilots in Alaska included many General Aviation (GA) pilots. GA pilots pickup these techniques and learn how to incorporate them into their flying routine because off-airport flying and landing in natural terrain is one of the most challenging and revering of all aviation pursuits. Another affirmation for the joy of off-airport flying small taildraggers in Alaska is the many Airline Transport Pilots (ATPs) after retiring from their professional airliner profession relocate to Alaska. They buy a Super Cub and fly it on many occasions in the summer on Alaska Bushwheels and in the winter on skis to Alaska's scenic locations in the mountains, fjords, glaciers, and vast ice fields. Many of these pilots are hunters and fishers and use their airplanes in the pursuit of wildlife. Others used their airplanes to access their remote cabins.

In Canada fewer GA pilots learn extreme flying strategies and techniques. The primary reason for this is that the middle-class in Canada is far less well off when compared to Alaskans. Canadian pilots simply do not have the time and funding to support this endeavor. That leaves Alaska as the lone center in the aviation world where extreme flying has been dominant for years and continues to flourish to this day.

Extreme flying in Alaska is a very small niche in the exclusive realm of aviation. Nevertheless, its uniqueness and significance is the reason for disseminating its originality to the GA community. Its strategy and training is based on the highest level of innovation and creativity to develop the most proficient self-reliant pilots. It is in a far different aviation sphere when compared to the standardized Federal Aviation Administration (FAA) program.

Nonetheless, pilots with knowledge in both aviation spheres will be in a position to choose the best of both worlds for improving pilot proficiency and reducing the rate of aircraft accidents. Alaskan flying procedures have been adopted for advanced training by a substantial number of GA pilots after receiving their Private Pilot License. It offers among the best available approaches for a continuation in training. The advanced training will be challenging, joyful, useful, and practical. The pilot will become a much-improved aviator and his/her aircraft accident rate will be greatly reduced.

Alaska's Elite Pilots

Alaska's elite pilots are able to fly light aircraft safely in and out of short and natural terrain landing areas that would be regarded by most pilots as marginal, too dangerous or impossible. This type of flying is a highly skilled art. It is important to provide the background for Alaska's elite pilots as the training style and many of the strategies and techniques for becoming an exceptional self-reliant pilot were developed by them. Below are all-inclusive insights in the Alaskan pilot's flying environment and details of their exceptional capabilities in flying short field operations in natural terrain.

The era of the traditional Alaskan pilots flying unreliable aircraft without radios across uncharted territory has ended. Nevertheless, modern-day pilots in Alaska are still flying into the backcountry. One of the most unique and rewarding experiences of living in Alaska is a continuation of this type of flying. Pilots regularly land tail-equipped aircraft (taildraggers) in remote, road-inaccessible or so-called backcountry areas in every part of the state. The landing apparatus on the small fixed-winged aircraft consists of wheels, skis, and floats to serve every season. There is no place where off-airport flying is as important and no place where it serves such a vital role in providing the transportation link as in Alaska. There is no place where the taildragger is revered more than by pilots flying in the Wilds of Alaska. And there is no place where the camaraderie of taildragger flying is more alive and well than in Alaska. All these features are what make backcountry flying in Alaska unique from routine flying elsewhere.

The type of aircraft, the terrain that is flown over and the skill level of the pilot characterize the uniqueness of backcountry flying in Alaska. The taildragger is of historic importance as it was the originally manufactured aircraft in this country. The modern tricycle aircraft is now universally used throughout the world both in commercial and recreational aviation. The Alaskan backcountry pilot is a throwback and flies a taildragger because it is the type of aircraft that is the most versatile under the broadest range of conditions in accessing the more remote and undeveloped areas. Backcountry pilots take off from airports such as Merrill Field in downtown Anchorage,

Alaska but the next landing will be on remote lakes and rivers, gravel bars, sandy beaches, mudflats, grass-covered sod, tundra, glaciers, ice fields, and on the winter snowpack. Many landings are first-time events with no visually marked landing areas. The pilot selects the landing site while airborne and then goes in and lands.

The terrain flown over is typically remote wilderness. Often the terrain is mountainous and capped with large glaciers and ice fields. Many of the river valleys are intensively forested. Coastal plains are often covered with vast areas of wetlands. The Alaskan backcountry pilot not only flies over undeveloped terrain but mostly over unpopulated lands. There is no one out there to rely on for help or for anything else. Alaskan backcountry pilots are not deterred by this handicap but are energized by this rare type of freedom and independence that is almost impossible to find elsewhere in the modern world.

The skill level and training time necessary for a proficient Alaskan pilot are substantial. It requires hundreds of hours practicing on natural terrain to hone the skills that make competent Alaskan backcountry pilots. The pilots who go through these exhaustive drills are richly rewarded for they are the most skilled pilots in knowing the finer nuances of their aircraft and being able to obtain the maximum flying performance under the most difficult conditions. They become masters of *edge-of-performance* flying skills that are required for safe flying operations in remote country. There are many pilots in Alaska with the highest skill level that is attainable for backcountry flying. These pilots are characterized as unusual, extraordinary, and unorthodox. They are far beyond the ordinary measure or limit of the instructor-trained pilot. They have amazing proficiency due to their many hours of flying time with their highly innovative self-training procedures.

Flying taildraggers and being highly competent for off-airport landings in natural terrain is not about landing on backcountry airstrips. Alaska's elite pilots would consider this no more difficult than a routine landing on the gravel strip at Merrill Field in downtown Anchorage. This is about a pilot having the capabilities of selecting short, challenging landing areas while airborne and going in and landing on curving gravel bars, sloping ocean beaches, grassy tundra, mountain saddles and ridges, and other natural terrain areas. This is a *first-time* landing event—no pilot has previously landed here. The skills needed to perform these difficult and challenging landings are marvelous to watch. It is close to unbelievable just how good an Alaskan backcountry pilot can be. You cannot overstate the incredible ability of the pilot to land and take off in such places. They can do it safely over and over again.

Taylor and Piper built nearly 40,000 production airplanes that qualify for the name Cub. Of these, approximately 10,000 are still on the U S Civil Register and Alaska has more than 3,000 of these taildraggers. Other taildraggers, for example, Cessna, Citabria, Champion, Scout, Aeronca, Taylorcraft, Stinson, Maule, Arctic Tern and others are popular and are regularly flown into the Alaskan Backcountry. Merrill Field has 900 individually owned airplanes (that's right, Merrill Field is not a commercial airport) with approximately 55 percent of these being taildraggers. Anchorage International and Lake Hood airports have similar numbers of privately owned taildraggers as Merrill Field. The large number of taildraggers found in Anchorage and elsewhere in the State form the basis for Alaska being at the pinnacle of taildragger and backcountry flying in the entire world.

Backcountry pilots in Alaska may be private or commercial pilots. The commercial pilots work as outfitters for big game and fishing guides and air taxi operators hauling passengers and cargo to every remote part of the state. Pilots flying to far reaching areas of the State should not be unexpected with the widely scattered villages without road connection to the state highway system and the large number of tourists, hunters, and fishermen coming to Alaska. What is truly remarkable and unexpected is the amazing number of private pilots in Alaska that take up backcountry flying more as an avocation (hobby) than as a vocation (professional career). They purchase a taildragger, routinely fly out to a local gravel bar and hone their skills, and join the ranks of the Alaskan backcountry pilots. This speaks volumes as to how attractive, challenging, and enjoyable off-airport flying is in Alaska. Another unexpected and revealing feature is that many Alaskans who do not own aircraft are our greatest allies; they are familiar with and share a keen interest in backcountry flying in Alaska.

The camaraderie of flying in Alaska is the best a pilot could possibly find anywhere. This is primarily due to the large number of highly skilled pilots to communicate with and to fly with you on backcountry missions. Flying with such a diversity of experienced pilots can be a very rewarding experience. There is nothing like it anywhere else.

Gary Lickle from Florida presents a noteworthy example of how influential it can be to observe taildragger landings in Alaska. Gary was a 28-year pilot with more than 3,000 hours in a twin-engine Cessna 310. Most of his flying was between the Bahamas and the southeastern United States. Gary came to Alaska in the mid-2000s for a fishing trip at Tikchik Lodge in Southwest

Alaska. While out on the river at one of the fishing camps, a Piper Super Cub came in and landed on a gravel bar next to Gary. Gary said *that landing awoke a new spirit of flying in me. That did it; I was hooked. Right there I decided to become a tailwheel pilot and experience backcountry flying adventures.* That says it all. Gary's long-standing flying career changed forever when he witnessed one Super Cub landing on a gravel bar in Alaska. Gary deserves a lot of credit, for he immediately understood that Alaskan backcountry flying far exceeds airport-to-airport flying. The latter is just flying through the air and very little else. Gary's first taildragger was a Cub Crafters Sport Cub S2 with 26-inch Alaskan Bushwheels. He flew the Sport Cub two years before upgrading to the Cub Crafters Carbon Cub SS. Gary flies the Carbon Cub on floats in the summer.

I take no delight in providing the many accolades for the amazing elite pilots of Alaska because it stirs up too much controversy. Nevertheless, these representations are necessary as the mission here is to present authentic material for a better understanding of what off-airport flying in Alaska is all about. With 40 years of flying airplanes in Alaska, I have the utmost confidence that my compliments provide not only a clear understanding but an accurate one to the reader.

Alaskan Style Training—Overview

Introduction

Most student pilots are taught by FAA's certificated instructors based on the agency's guidelines. After receiving the Private Pilot License (PPL), many pilots explore ways to advance their flying careers. Aviation articles in flying magazines recommend pilots obtain a tailwheel endorsement, instrument rating, seaplane rating, multiengine rating, commercial rating, aerobatic training, warbird and glider flying, and a few others. These ways to expand your flying career will be helpful; however, they will not provide the degree of advanced training a pilot will obtain from training like the elite pilots of Alaska. This type of training will take pilots to a much higher level than is possible with obtaining the above described ratings with FAA instructors. The reason for this is twofold. The first is that the Alaskan training combines both the FAA guidelines and the developed strategies and techniques from Alaska's elite pilots. Using both aviation domains makes an enormous beneficial difference when compared to pilots that use only the FAA approach. Pilots can pick and choose the best strategies and techniques from both aviation spheres that are in balance with their own personal traits. The second reason is the creative self-training style by the Alaskan pilot way. It is a powerful motivating force in elevating the training and pilot proficiency to the highest level possible. This type of advanced training fits perfectly with GA pilots that own an airplane and desire to be the best pilot they can be while flying it. This type of advance training will produce amazing results and pilots that learn the Alaskan way will be forever grateful in the remarkable pilot that they have become. Nothing else comes close to providing such an enormous amount of high level proficiency in flying an airplane.

The Alaskan pilot training is based on the *old-fashioned* style of flying. Flying by the *seat of your pants*—flying an airplane without the aid of instruments and using only instinct, visual observations, feel, and making practical judgments. Flying by the *seat of your pants* is a self-learned skill that becomes an art. It is not a calculated and standardized numbers game to follow. It requires the pilot's ability to create and execute a flying order that is simple, accurate, and safe to perform. It is the simplest of all flying procedures. No costs are needed to purchase expensive glass cockpits or other instruments such as sophisticated GPS devices. This type of flying is unorthodox (not standardized) and does not require memorization or check-lists for flying speeds and other parameters. Checklists with a multitude of items are not needed for low-speed and low flying aircraft. Experienced pilots already have the one or two important items that need to be carried out to safely fly their airplane. Keeping it simple is the key to stress-free and sustainable success in flying the backcountry. It is based solely on the pilot's ability to learn to decipher the airplane's situation by sight outside the cockpit, feel, and sound. This very accurate information from the airplane provides the basic knowledge for flying the airplane. Pilots must make reliable decisions based on practicable judgment. This training is based on Visual Flight Rules (VFR) which includes flying during daylight hours. It does not include night flying or Instrument Flight Rules (IFR) flights in marginal and severe weather.

All of the FAA learned strategies and techniques that are adequate are retained and utilized in routine flying operations by Alaska's elite pilots. However, the ones that are retained must be fine-tuned or redesigned to closely be in equilibrium with the pilot's own personal traits. Flying and training in your own airplane is necessary to carry out this task. The FAA techniques that are not adequate are abandoned and replaced with much improved ones. One primary example of an unacceptable flying technique is the FAA's landing approach which includes a stabilized airplane and a standardized landing pattern. This technique is much too complex and is highly problematic of producing routine precision land-ings. The elite Alaskan pilots have a *game changer* in their *Precision Landing Technique*. The improved strategies and techniques come mostly from Alaska's elite pilots flying repertoire. These unique strategies and techniques have been developed by Alaska's elite pilots over many years of flying and training in Alaska. The unique ones were developed because the conventional ones were simply not adequate to be useful in flying challenging Alaskan operations.

You will have to fully understand the FAA's *Aviation Guidelines* taught by certificated instructors and found in their flying manuals such as *Pilot's Handbook of Aeronautical Knowledge* and *Airplane Flying Handbook*. You will also have to take on the responsibility to learn the strategies and flying techniques from the elite Alaskan pilots. The latter have no manual and only a diminutive amount of written materials. Pilots will have to communicate with Alaska's elite pilots and learn their strategies and techniques. Reading and learning in both *Aviation Worlds* (FAA's and the elite pilots of Alaska) will provide the background for comparing and selecting the best from the *Two Aviation Worlds*.

After selecting the best strategies and techniques, pilots will have to incorporate them into their flying repertoire. This is accomplished by self-training in your airplane to integrate what you have learned into your flying program.

The task at hand for becoming your own exceptional self-reliant pilot involves five important steps that have to be carried out by the pilot. These are (1) An academic exercise in learning from both aviation spheres; (2) Comparing and selecting the best strategies and techniques; (3) Integrating the revised and newly selected strategies and techniques into your flying program by self-training in your airplane to accomplish the mission; (4) Flying by the *seat of your pants* to be able to perform precision landings; and (5) Transferring the pilot's learned skills into flying as an art.

Knowledge and Training to Be the Best Pilot

Many books have been written on backcountry flying, however, only a few provide instructions on advanced pilot training. Three books on backcountry flying that cover some of the broad aspects of pilot training are *Guide to Bush Flying* by F.E. Potts (1993), *Survival Flying* by Jay Baldwin (2010), and *Bush Flying* by Steven Levi and Jim O'Meara (1992). One other book that is quite helpful in taildragger flying and training techniques is *The Compleat Taildragger Pilot* by Harvey Plourde (1991). All four books mentioned above will provide an excellent beginning for a more in-depth understanding of the Alaskan elite pilot and the training techniques that these pilots use. These books discuss backcountry flying and training; however, they do not provide training instructions delivered in an orderly procession that clearly shows a pilot how training is accomplished. This book is essential in filling in the gaps left by the aforementioned books. First, a pilot will never get there without having a complete understanding of what Alaskan backcountry flying is all about. This background information is essential. Second, detailed, sequential training procedures about how to get started in learning to train the Alaskan way is also essential. Both of the latter are methodically presented in this book.

Not all pilots want to train the Alaskan way; that is a given. Nevertheless, the information on this subject is provided so pilots will have an understanding and the opportunity to train the Alaskan way if they choose to do so. You will never know if you want to train the Alaskan way if you are not well-informed on the subject. Even if you don't ever fly and engage in off-airport operations, the training journey is extraordinary and the learning experience will greatly increase pilot proficiency and a safer flying career. Being a better pilot is a reward in itself.

There are aviation businesses that specialize in teaching the fundamentals of off-airport training. Two in Alaska are Above Alaska Aviation, a limited liability company from Talkeetna, Alaska and Alaska's Cub Training Specialists, a limited liability company from Palmer, Alaska. One company in the Lower 48 states is Andover Flight Academy from Andover, New Jersey. These aircraft companies provide training operations that can provide a limited amount of knowledge that will be useful in beginning the journey for off-airport training. However, the lion's share of training the Alaskan way is substantially different from what these companies have to offer.

Alaska's elite pilots start out like all pilots with basic training from FAA-certified instructors. However, after receiving the PPL, that is when the adventure begins for the Alaskan or other pilot who is inspired to train like the legendary Alaskan pilot. To obtain the correct mind-set, the pilot has to understand that for the most part FAA instructors do not teach backcountry flying skills that off-airport pilots are seeking. Mort Mason, a long-time Alaskan pilot and a registered guide for 35 years (18,000 hours) of flying in Alaska's backcountry, said *in all that time, I never once came across an off-airport pilot flying course of any nature*. Mason retired from his Alaskan flying career in 1985.

The pilot has to take on full responsibility for *self-training* while flying in your airplane. Pilots have to understand the challenges ahead and it is mandatory that they place the responsibility for training on their own shoulders. The training is about you and your airplane. Once you understand the latter, you're on your way. It is really as simple as that. What has been stated above does not discount talking with FAA instructors and Alaska's elite pilots to gain knowledge on training strategies and techniques. A very important step to take is to fly with the most experienced Alaskan elite pilots you can find. It is more productive for each pilot to fly in their own airplane. You can fly as a pair of two airplanes. Flying with other skilled Alaskan pilots will be of enormous benefit in learning new skills at an accelerated pace.

Self-training while flying your airplane to become a skilled pilot takes on a leading role and a journey that most pilots would not expect. It takes a substantial amount of time; many hours of practice, drill, routine, and so forth. The pilot should plan on flying a minimum of 100 hours each year. Even with my full-time employment and working 50-hour weeks, I managed to fly well over 100 hours every year. It can be done. And don't expect to enter that hallowed ground with the highly capable Alaskan pilots until you have several years of learning under your belt. It also takes an open mind with the courage to explore and a willingness to make trials to learn all facets of flying the aircraft. Information or training techniques provided by an instructor or any other pilot has to be fully analyzed, understood, possibly modified, and only then incorporated into your flying skills. Copying instructors' or other pilots' flying techniques without analyzing and adjusting them to fit your own ability and natural traits is a wasted effort. It is not that important how you perform a certain technique in flying your airplane as long as you understand it and can consistently carry out the procedure in a safe and practical manner. The great elite pilots in Alaska apply their own true and tried techniques. These techniques vary from pilot to pilot.

The primary reason training the Alaskan pilot way is unparalleled is that the pilot is exclusively engaged in the most creative process for learning that is possible. How can pilots or others learning any subject be more resourceful than developing their own programs that fit their own person-alities and individual traits? This is the reason this type of training is so potent. Self-training caters to your own individual traits and makes learning less difficult. This is the beginning in learning to be your own pilot. With an open mind, it is incredible how much the brain can facilitate learning in this manner.

FAA instructors teach training techniques that have standardized proce-dures—*one shoe fits all pilots*. The pilots memorize or write down flight speeds for all types of maneuvers. You will be flying by the book and reading the speeds from the gauges. Pilots are not leading the training; they are following the instructor's training program. This type of teaching can be difficult to understand and learn and often is lacking in comprehensive coverage. Instructor training beyond the private pilot's license can dampen and often kills creativity in a pilot. Creativity is the stalwart of self-training, becoming your own pilot and categorically is the Alaskan way for training. Pilots seeking further training need to venture out on their own and learn to be creative and innovative. That's the key to becoming your own self-reliant pilot.

The elite pilots in Alaska discovered many years ago that they had a training strategy that really works. They have never wavered once about how they train because it has been exceedingly productive throughout the entire era all the way to contemporary time. There is also no way to deny the outstanding results from self-training the Alaskan way. This tells the complete story. It has always been controversial but it has always been the *gold standard* for Alaska's elite pilots. The Alaskan pilots would not have it any other way because the rewards are too great to pass up.

How the Alaskan pilots trained for all these years is now being brought to life by Sir Ken Robinson, an internationally recognized leader in the development of education. Dr. Robinson, Professor Emeritus of Education at the University of Warwick in the United Kingdom, is calling for a revolution in education. Dr. Robinson says that students need to be educated in an environment where they can confidently use their own independent thinking and preferences for learning. This leads to creativity and is the key to innovation. This should be the new paradigm for university education. Dr. Robinson stresses that the current conformity and standardization of education are features that are contrary to the kind of original thinking and confident imaginations that underpin real innovation. This type of training involves the students' taking control of their own educational program. This comes down to *self-training*, just like the training the Alaskan pilots have been engaged in all these years. What a revelation finding out that Alaskan pilots have been ahead of the pack training the best way possible for decades in remote Alaska. Alaskan pilot training will endure forevermore.

One additional affirmation for the value of self-training is eloquently covered in the book *Super Brain* by Deepak Chopra, M.D., the author of more than 65 books and Rudolph E. Tanzi, PhD, Harvard Medical school professor of neurology, one of the world's foremost experts on the causes of Alzheimer's. *Super Brain* is a user's manual that shows you how to effectively use your mind to cultivate and reshape the brain to best serve you. The professors sum up their book as follows: "In contrast to the baseline brain that fulfills the tasks of everyday life, Chopra and Tanzi propose that, through a person's increased self-awareness and conscious intention, the brain can be taught to reach far beyond its present limitations. Through a new relationship with the brain, you can transform the brain. In *Super Brain*, Chopra and Tanzi guide you on a fascinating journey that envisions a leap in human evolution." How is all of this mind–brain connection accomplished? It is accomplished by *self-training*. You must take command to guide and reshape your brain so that you can attain maximum benefit. *Self-training* is becoming paramount in the lives of all who expect to attain the most in life. You must *self-train* the mind to achieve your very own super brain, you must *self-train* yourself for the highest and most productive education possible, and you must *self-train* yourself to become an exceptional self-reliant pilot.

The FAA does not support Alaskan style pilot training. They say it is too dangerous to tell a pilot to go out and learn to fly by self-training; too many pilots will crash their airplanes. There are no confirmations that self-training is unsafe and leads to airplane accidents. If this was happening, self-training would have been abandoned long ago. The FAA says that we have our own training program with Certificated Instructors and after obtaining your private pilot's license, we do not restrain you from training as you desire. Alaskan pilots tell me that they are content that FAA is not involved in their pilot training because the government would degrade the program.

Alaskan Training Paradigm: Make Simple the Difficult Things

The elite pilots in Alaska have the most incredible way of learning and training to be greatly improved pilots. They take the traditional complex strategies and techniques taught by FAA certificated instructors and make them simpler. This is one of the primary ways of advancing their flying careers. In extreme situations when a technique is too flawed, it will be abandoned and replaced with a simpler and more useful one. These amazing pilots are aware of all the complexity of a specific technique. Nevertheless, for flying purposes, they reduce all the many features into only the dominant ones necessary for safely flying the airplane. Trying to concentrate on the broad aspects of an element in all of its complexity causes confusion, mis-understanding and distraction from multitasking failures. The complexity causes stressful environments for pilots flying an airplane. There are huge advantages of learning to fly an airplane with a more limited, simpler and sensible approach, fashion, method, and way.

FAA certificated instructors teach standardized training—*one-size-fits-all* solution. This may be sufficient for pilots when they first learn to fly; however, this is not the way that leads to a highly proficient self-reliant pilot. A pilot must be creative and learn by self-training to elevate pilot proficiency to its highest level. An excellent example of complexity in flight is the FAA's stabilized approach and standard landing operations. Alaska's elite pilots don't fly standardized patterns and they don't use stabilized approaches when landing an airplane. Both of these procedures are much too complex and are not dependable for providing accurate precision landings. The standardized and stabilized procedures cause too many difficult obstacles that prevent successful landings. The inconsistent landings result in too many go arounds many of which are highly problematic and are susceptible to accidents.

Alaska's distinctive pilots have abandoned these complex procedures long ago and have replaced them with simpler ones that provide consistent and flawless results. The simpler approach is a monumental step in a pilot's progression to a much-improved and safer flying career.

Simplified procedures for flying an airplane makes it exceptionally straightforward—the pilot can concentrate unimpeded on the most significant elements and carry them out in perfection. The pilot has a clear vision while flying in a stress-free environment. Pilots are not burdened with a checklist showing flying speeds and other parameters—they are not needed. Simplifying the flying operations not only facilitates carrying out the principal tasks but also provides the pilots with the preeminent way of flying an airplane. Pilots will never appreciate how advantageous this is until they change their way of flying and observe first-hand what it is like being an *Unconstrained Pilot*. A heavy burden has been lifted and the pilot is effortlessly enjoying the journey. This is one of the ultimate thresholds in the Joy of Flying. Leonardo de Vinci (1452-1519) says that *simplicity is the ultimate sophistication.*

Flying by the Seat of Your Pants

After learning to decipher initial stalls for the purpose of landing at the slowest speed the airplane can land, I began to venture out and think more about flying by the *seat of your pants*. In the end, what I have learned is that flying can be accomplished entirely by simply seeing, feeling, and hearing what your airplane is telling you. The airplane never lies and all variables such as wind speeds and directions, density altitude, and other factors are incorporated into what the airplane is experiencing. This will lead to a simpler way of flying that is much more precise than using instruments or modern glass cockpits. The airplane will tell you everything you need to know. Just pay attention and learn what the airplane is indicating by its signs. Early on, I really thought that there was no way this made any sense or that it could be productive. However, I never once doubted the Alaskan pilots' traditional training ways. The key here is to trust the training and to have an open mind, and slowly this simple and accurate way of flying will show up in your flying repertoire. One day after many training sessions, it will show up and you will recognize it. You will be so relieved that the Alaskan way of training is finally coming alive and you have succeeded on your own in learning it. What an accomplishment. You now have something that you are proud of and something to celebrate. This progression will show you that you can get the job accomplished. It will be a strong motivating force in continuing your training in all other areas that are needed. Building your confidence in this way is the beginning of becoming your own self-reliant pilot. Flying by the *seat of your pants* is based on the old-fashioned style of flying an airplane using only instinct, visual observations, and feel. All of these natural instincts are used in making practical judgments for flying the airplane. Creativity is the stalwart of flying an airplane by the *seat of your pants*. Check lists and written logs are not needed as well as glass cockpits and instruments—all of these provide less accurate data. *Seat of your pants* flying is a learned skill and art developed by the individual pilot. The learned art of flying by the *seat of your pants* is what makes this way of flying so potent. Once learned it is a simple and easy way to fly an airplane with the utmost in precision.

Situational Awareness

Situational awareness is one of the most important aspects of flying. It is especially important in remote flying with all the challenging events of flying at low levels that often happen in rapid succession. Pilots need to have a very active thinking mind to observe and to be aware of everything that is happening around them. When I am tired, sleepy, or don't feel well, I don't fly. Situational awareness helps tremendously when applied to discerning changes in weather. Situational awareness is needed not only in predicting weather but in all other conditions associated with flying. Examples of the lack of situational awareness is a pilot stating after an aircraft accident that the wind picked up my right wing and turned the aircraft over on the ground, or a strong gust of wind caught my airplane and forced it down hard on the runway breaking the landing gear. If you have situational awareness you'll be more alert and watching for these likely events when flying on windy days and you will have a better opportunity for quicker reaction and using the proper maneuvers to prevent accidents. Situational awareness provides the frame of mind and the focus on the critical events to counteract difficult flying challenges and to help in preventing accidents.

Alaskan Style Training—Methods

Precision Landings

I will never forget the quandary when I first wanted to begin training as an Alaskan pilot. I had a difficult time finding out very much on this subject even though I was talking with as many elite Alaskan pilots as I could find. Information was provided but it seemed so fragmented and incomplete that it was demanding to understand. The first idea that many pilots mentioned was that you must learn to fly by the *seat of your pants*. I had heard this before but had no idea what it meant. As I met new Alaskan pilots I asked for more details about flying by the *seat of your pants*. This subject was becoming so baffling that I decided to put it aside for the short term and pick it up later in my training program. I knew this was important but I'd make another attempt after I gained additional experience.

Other Alaskan pilots suggested that a good starting point is to concentrate on learning the technical skills for *Precision Landings*—precise spot landings in natural terrain. I was told not to train at airports or even on landing strips but to find a gravel bar that was sufficiently long to provide training for maneuvers in a safe manner. Many pilots told me that the best training ground was the Knik River gravel bars. This undeveloped area is southeast of Palmer, Alaska and is only 30 air miles northeast of Anchorage. The Knik River is a typical, much-braided, glacial river system with huge amounts of water in late summer due to massive melting glaciers. The river is less than a mile wide on the lower end near its mouth at Knik Arm but its width increases up river to over 3 miles in width near Wolf Point. The Knik River is about 30 miles in length from Knik Arm to the toe of Knik Glacier. This extensive area encompasses almost all natural sand and gravel bars that are mostly free from vegetative growth. After checking out the training opportunities on the Knik, I was very much impressed with such an appropriate place to train so close to Merrill Field. You can always select your own training area and never have to be bothered by other aircraft complicating your training, wasting your time, or distracting you.

Training for *Precision Landings* is more important than one might think. It is one of the most important techniques for controlling kinetic energy in a flying airplane. Properly managing kinetic energy in your airplane allows for consistent safe landings. Improper or erratic controlling kinetic energy in your airplane will cause many aircraft accidents. *Precision Landings* is the traditional entry step into the elite Alaskan pilot's flying world. The training time and the thoroughness of the training can never be overestimated. Even after you have learned and perfected this part of flying, you will still need to practice this type of training in perpetuity to maintain a high proficiency throughout your flying career. Don't ever underestimate the importance of this technique. It is one technique that you have to master to be able to safely land your airplane in natural terrain. There is no other landing alternative comparable to its necessity and its supremacy.

The first step is to fly to the Knik River or your selected training area and locate a gravel bar (sand bar is also acceptable) that is suitable to meet the pilot's need as a safe place for training. Remember; pick your own landing site with no visible airplane wheel tracks. You want the training experience to be on natural terrain because that is what you will be seeing over and over in the future for landing places. Make sure it is long enough so you won't have any problems in your routine practice maneuvers.

Once you have selected a gravel bar, land your airplane. Then mark off a 20 foot by 60 foot rectangular box with orange flagging material tied to rocks or stakes. You can also use 4 plastic orange-colored cones to mark the box. The long axis of the box is perpendicular to the landing direction of the airplane. This provides a box with 20 foot boundaries for placing the main wheels in the landing area. Make sure to leave plenty of space for a suitable landing if you touch down short of the box. This training box is for learning to land your airplane with the utmost precision. The goal here is learning to place your main wheels in this box at stall speed on every landing. The details of this mission are twofold—wheels have to touch down in this box and the wheels have to touch down at stall speed. Both of these two training operations have to come together as the wheels are touching down. They have to become routine and easily doable every time you land your airplane. Performing landings at stall speed is a precision technique that pilots have to learn. It is accomplished by flying your airplane by the *seat of your pants*.

After landing with the main wheels in the box, make sure to release your flaps immediately after the wheels touch down. This will place the airplane's weight on the wheels which will help to dissipate kinetic energy quicker and slow down the airplane on its ground roll. You'll want to practice the precision landings in variable weather conditions. Make certain you practice on days with every type of wind conditions; steady winds, gusty winds, headwinds, tailwinds, crosswinds, quartering winds, and so on. Also practice on calm days, hot days, and cool days. You'll want to experience all conditions. Later on you will be free from surprises which are a great advantage in flying your airplane.

It will be necessary to go out and train on the selected gravel bar in one-hour sessions twice weekly. This type of training should continue to be in your flying program for as long as it takes to achieve precise landings in the box on every landing attempt in all weather conditions. The reason this type of training is so important is that landings off-airport can cause challenging problems that often lead to aircraft accidents. These accidents are primarily caused by imprecise landings of coming in too high, too low, and too fast. Touching down faster than stall speed causes many accidents as airplanes can quickly get out of control. With the extra speed, the airplane is highly energized. This increase in kinetic energy with an airplane out of control provides the path to massive aircraft damage. Coming in too high will often lead to touching the wheels down a long ways past the landing target. This leads many pilots to make a *Go-Around* because they may not have sufficient distance to stop before running off the end of the landing area. *Go-Arounds* that are not well thought out can lead to aircraft accidents beyond the landing area. This happens because airplanes don't always have the power to advance to flying speeds in a high-angle climbing mode. The airplane usually responds by climbing in ground effect; however, it will slowly lose altitude and crash into the natural terrain as the forward speed does not build up fast enough to support flying speed. This is a common cause of off-airport accidents in Alaska and it happens over and over again. After you have become an expert in landing in the box, you will still need to practice this exercise intermittently for as long as you are a pilot to maintain the highest level of proficiency. This is one of the most important Cardinal Rules for becoming a self-reliant pilot.

Takeoff Operations

Takeoffs have always appeared to be straightforward and easy to perform. However, a few guidelines are in order. Taking off on short operational areas, for example gravel bars, pilots have to learn the distance they need for taking off. A reasonable percentage, i.e., 20%, should be added to the distance for safety considerations. Pilots have to get accustomed to not being able to have an operation area long enough to abort the takeoff at the halfway point if things do not appear to be suitable. There is no option for aborting takeoffs. If this had to be accommodated, off-airport operations would most likely be restricted to lengthy backcountry airstrips. This would just about completely negate the ability of backcountry pilots in Alaska to land on so many short natural terrain landing areas. That is why all the practicing is necessary—the pilot is becoming highly capable of making precise landings.

Another important item to consider on takeoffs is to use most of the operational area available for takeoffs. This means that it is not advisable to get airborne as quickly as possible because the airspeed is too close to stall speed at a high angle of attack. You don't want to stall the airplane and crash on a takeoff. This can happen with a quick lift off the ground when heavily loaded or in gusty wind conditions. A better and safer alternative is to use most of the takeoff area. When the airplane becomes airborne, it has a stronger climbing factor built in with the higher flying speed.

When taking off from a short landing area, it is advisable when the airplane lifts off to leave the high-angle takeoff configuration for a short time and then to lower the nose to level attitude or even slightly nose-down attitude so the aircraft can quickly build airspeed. Increasing flying speed is your friend on takeoffs, especially when the airplane is heavily loaded, in windy conditions, and on hot days. You are much less likely to stall your aircraft and crash in natural terrain beyond the landing area.

Short field takeoffs require lifting the tail off the ground as soon as possible. Having the airplane in a level attitude as it advances for takeoff without flaps will allow the aircraft to build forward speed faster than an airplane in a three-point attitude or with flaps set. Once the airplane is ready to fly, pull the flaps to the proper setting. This will provide the shortest distance needed for takeoffs. Setting the flaps on initial takeoff will shift partial weight from the tires to the wings. Shifting the weight to the wings greatly slows down the building up of forward airspeed. Soft field takeoffs require adding the flaps soon after opening the throttle so that a substantial amount of the airplane's weight can be shifted from the wheels to the wings. It is also important to keep the tail down to prevent the airplane from nosing over when soft ground is encountered. Soft field takeoffs require longer ground rolls.

One additional point that needs to be mentioned is that the propeller can be damaged from turning the airplane on the ground and from taking off from unimproved landing areas. A whirling propeller can suck up sand and gravel that can damage its leading edge. This will require filing the dents to smooth them out and prevent propeller blade breakage. Equal filing will be required on both propeller blades to keep them in balance. Pilots must learn how to operate on natural terrain to avoid propeller strikes. Propellers are expensive and need to be safeguarded.

When taxiing airplanes on natural terrain with exposed sand and gravel, the pilots avoid most propeller strikes by using taller landing gear and by using Alaskan Bushwheels (tundra tires). Both of these raise the aircraft higher off the ground and thus provide greater propeller clearance, which will help reduce the propeller's ability to suck up sand and gravel projectiles. Another important remedy to the propeller strikes is to learn to properly handle the aircraft on the ground. When you want to turn in these conditions, don't let the airplane slow down to a near stop, push the throttle in, and attempt to turn. This will require high power settings that will usually suck up sand and gravel. The proper way to taxi is with a brisk amount of speed, letting the momentum help turn the airplane. A small burst of power will be needed but the power won't be enough for the propeller to pick up sand and rock pieces. Raising the tail and using the rudder as the turn is being made is also beneficial. This helps to move the tail around with little engine power.

Landings Operations

When flying in for landing, remember that Alaska's elite pilots are known for being unorthodox pilots. They don't use standard landing patterns. This means that you need to practice all training operations in an unplanned manner. Come in and make your approach for landing different each time, for example, variable altitudes and speeds, straight in, turning maneuvers and so forth. Flying as unconventional pilots has substantial benefits. First, it is much easier not to have to write down and memorize standardized flying operations which you soon forget. Second, when you learn to be comfortable with your aircraft in variable positions in relation to your landing surface, you'll have become a much improved pilot. You will learn to observe your aircraft's position and to quickly change it to whatever you desire. All these training sessions are based on common sense, proper judgment, and routine practice. Once you obtain sufficient training time with this type of flying, you will be changed to a more complete pilot who has seen many challenges and has learned how to alter them as necessary. With all this unconventional training, what you are hoping to gain is not finding any new surprises. You have seen them all and you have learned how to handle them.

Learning to land your airplane at stall speed is really beginning to learn

39

to fly by the *seat of your pants*. You don't look at any instrument; you just watch the airplane. It tells you everything you need to know. This is really a simple maneuver and is easy to learn. Just go in for a landing on a long airstrip. To make it easy to learn, set up the proper pitch by pulling back on the elevator. Pull the throttle back until you have an appropriate descent rate. You don't need to flare your airplane—the steep pitch allows the airplane to land at a slow speed. As your airplane is flying its path towards the landing area, pull back on the throttle and let your airplane continue to slow down until you notice a pronounced vertical downward motion. The point where the airplane starts its downward motion shows the *initial stall*. This is as slow as your airplane can fly. So you don't fall out of the sky, add a small burst of power with the throttle and continue to gradually settle into a landing. This is touching down right at stall speed. It is important to get this correct. You don't want flying speed when you are landing; it is too fast. You don't want stall speed; your airplane falls out of the sky like a rock. What you want is initial stall speed. This is the speed that barely keeps your aircraft airborne as it settles to a landing in a gradual and slow deceleration. When flying in strong gusty winds, I still use full flaps and land at stall speed. However, I am watching like a hawk for wind tribulations. As soon as they appear, I make the necessary flight corrections—usually by lowering the airplane's nose and pushing in full power with the throttle. This will stabilize the airplane and prevent stalls or the airplane getting out of control. This will counteract rogue wind blasts, wind shear, wind changing directions and other wind difficulties.

Some pilots have a phobia about stalling an airplane. Think of it this way—what difference does it make if you stall your airplane at 1 or even 2 two feet above the ground? It really does not matter. No harm will be done. Of course you don't want to stall your airplane at 20 feet above the landing surface and let it fall to the ground. This should never happen—all you have to do to avoid this type of stalling is to lower the airplane's nose and add a burst of power with the throttle. Then pull back on the throttle. Your airplane will respond from its initial stall speed and gradual descent to flying speed and level flight. Use the throttle with a burst of power whenever it is needed to prevent a stall. Learning to use the throttle intermittently when coming in for a landing is essential for making precision landings.

There are two basic types of landing styles for taildraggers. These are the *three-point landing* and the *wheel landing*. The three-point landing requires the airplane to be flown parallel to the ground until it stalls and settles to the ground, touching down concurrently on all three landing wheels. The stick is pulled all the way back at the time of contact and held there throughout the landing roll. Stopping is boosted by moderate braking. The wheel landing is also performed by flying parallel to the ground but the landing is made on the two main wheels. The airplane has to be at initial stall speed or carry a small amount of speed above the stall speed to fly it in and land on the main wheels. As soon as the main wheels touch down, the application of forward elevator (stick forward) has to be made to reduce the angle of attack and keep the main wheels on the ground. The tail of the airplane will descend on its own with the stick in forward position. Once the tail is on the ground, apply full back elevator to keep the tailwheel on the ground. Use moderate braking to shorten the ground roll. Most Alaskan pilots have learned both of these landing procedures. They can perform both well. Under certain circumstances (low wind conditions) the three-point landing may be performed. However, under strong gusty winds (especially strong crosswinds) the wheel landing is necessary to properly control the airplane so it does not go into a ground loop. Wheel landings are preferred by most Alaskan pilots and many use them for all landings. Other advantages of wheel landings are that you have maximum controllability of the airplane through the touchdown point and excellent visibility during the landing approach. Wheel landings are also safer when landing in low light and when carrying heavy loads. Wheel landings reduce the likelihood of rocks kicked up from the main wheels damaging the fabric on the undersides of tail surfaces. When coming in for a wheel landing with minimum power, a small burst of power from the throttle may be necessary to maintain flying speed and aircraft stability prior to landing.

For wheel landings, Alaskan elite pilots learn two techniques. One is a steep approach to landing and the other is a shallow approach called *dragging it in*. The latter provides landings that are usually under or over the desired touchdown point. This may result in longer landing distances. The steep approach to final is far more accurate in spot landings and the steeper approach dissipates much more kinetic energy when the wheels touch down. For both of these reasons, the steeper approach to landing provides shorter landings. Therefore, it is traditionally the Alaskan pilot's method for landing.

Alaskan pilots learn to slip an airplane on final approach if they need to lose altitude fast because they are coming in too high. This is a cross-controlled maneuver accomplished by a left or right aileron and the opposite rudder. Check your Pilot Operating Handbook (POH); Cessnas may not recommend slips with the flaps down. If there is a crosswind, place the wing down into the wind. Immediately after touching the wheels on the ground, make sure to quickly release the flaps. This is important because all the energy in your aircraft has to be dissipated. Transferring the weight from the wings to the wheels will help facilitate the slowing down of the aircraft much sooner than if the wings are carrying a substantial part of the weight. This is also very important on windy days as the airplane could easily begin to fly again with the flaps extended.

Soft field landings should be made without the use of brakes although minimum braking may be acceptable under certain circumstances. Retract the flaps after the airplane comes to full stop. If the tail comes up, an application of throttle and full back stick may force it back down.

Sand and gravel bars along rivers provide the most numerous and highest-quality landing areas in Alaska's remote regions. These landing surfaces are firm and if obstacles are present they can be easily observed before landing. These landing areas most often do not have approach or takeoff obstacles such as trees or river banks that interfere with operations. Since most of the landing areas are level or only slightly sloping—landings and takeoffs can be made in both directions. Landing on gravel and sandy beaches on lakes and oceans are the second most important landing areas in natural terrain. These landings can be challenging, especially on steep-sloping ocean beaches. Landings in grass-covered and tundra are a distant third for landing areas in Alaska. Tall grass is highly problematic because it may cover up holes, logs, large boulders, and soft muddy ground terrain that could severely damage the airplane's landing gear or cause the airplane to be stuck. Tall grass that is dense and that is not covering up any obstacles may also be a big problem when landing. The resistance of the thick grass may quickly slow down the tires while the kinetic energy (momentum) of the airframe is much faster. This causes the same effect as the pilot stomping too hard on the brakes when landing. A nose over in tall grass is likely to occur even with little or no braking because of the high resistance of the grass to the landing wheels.

Landing on a sloping ocean beach will take lots of practicing to get comfortable with making these landings as they are atypical. When coming in for a landing, you will need to place one main wheel on the sand—that is the upslope wheel. Keep the airplane on a straight line down the beach with proper use of the aileron and rudder. The other wheel is high in the air above the beach. As the aircraft slows down on the landing roll, the wing will lose lift and the airborne wheel will gradually touch down at a slow speed. Landing on two main wheels will cause the airplane to veer left or right depending on which wheel encounters the most resistance or drag. Beaches are usually plenty long enough that brakes are not needed. If brakes are used, use them sparingly. The takeoff is made the same way as a landing. In the ground run, as soon as possible, shift the airplane to one main wheel; the wheel on the sand is again the one on the top side of the beach. This is an exercise in the coordination and proper use of aileron and rudder. Beaches with 20 percent or higher slope angles can safely and easily be landed on with this method. Practice one wheel takeoffs and landings at your home base airfield. You will need to perfect this maneuver before landing on sloping beaches.

When taxiing your aircraft on beaches, be careful to look for and stay clear of dead tree logs, large cobblestones, holes, seaweeds, and soft muddy areas. The areas on beaches to avoid like the plague are wet and muddy silt and clay soil. Your airplane is likely to get stuck if your wheels penetrate this type of substrate. It is always better to land on sand and gravel beaches. Dry sand and gravel is the safest as wet sand and gravel may contain sufficient amounts of silt and clay that could cause difficult landing conditions. Turning your aircraft on beaches especially sloping beaches may be made much easier by shutting down the engine, exiting the aircraft and turning it around by hand. Attempting to turn the aircraft around in loose sand and gravel, especially with a large increase in power, often results in picking up rock projectiles that can damage the propeller.

After extensive training for landing operations in the backcountry, a typical landing should look like the following. Fly into a prospective landing area and fly low-level approaches parallel but offset from the landing area at 50 mph (one notch of flaps). You'll be able to see much more detail at slow speeds compare to normal flying speeds. You are looking for how smooth or rough the landing surface is; for holes and swales in the landing area; logs or other woody debris lying along the landing area; the height of any vegetation (brush) that you may be landing in; the size of stones (gravel-sized rocks, cobbles, or stones). You will want to estimate the length of the landing area and determine if it is sufficient for landing under the weather conditions (primarily wind) that currently exist. Estimating the length of the landing area is a learned art that was derived from all the practicing from doing Precision Landings. There is no need to fly at a known speed and count the seconds of the landing area to obtain its length. My estimation of a 300-foot landing area from the air is very accurate and much easier to determine than attempting the flying method to determine its length. When all factors have been evaluated you should feel at ease and confident that this is a suitable landing area for your airplane on this given day. If I feel hesitant or apprehensive about landing after evaluation, I usually don't land. A difficult, unsuitable landing area always causes uneasiness in my gut. To be safe, I quickly depart the site and find a safer landing area.

After rigorous training twice weekly for a few months, you should by now have perfected your takeoffs and landings. To retain your proficiency, you'll need to continue practicing takeoffs and landings monthly. Every time you go flying land your airplane at least 3 or 4 times in natural terrain. At any time your takeoffs and landings fall short of your expectations or appear to be inconsistent, you'll need additional training to recover. Drill, drill, and drill until you reach a satisfactory conclusion. Remember that the training is simple; however, there are no shortcuts or escapes from spending the proper time to accomplish the mission. One additional reminder is to make sure you are landing precisely in the box at stall speed each time you go in for a landing. If there are any failures, you may need to refocus your training on precise landings until they are bulletproof.

Managing the Wind

Wind can be your greatest friend and also your greatest enemy. It will always be your greatest friend if you learn how to accurately determine wind speed and direction, understand how it affects your airplane and use common sense maneuvers in windy conditions. Pilots are still saying that before landing, you look at leaves on hardwood trees and bushes or water on a lake to determine wind direction. All pilots should know by now that one of the most important uses of the Global Positioning System (GPS) is that it is constantly reporting your aircraft's ground speed. This will allow you to determine wind speed and direction prior to landing. You already know your cruise speed when flying on a windless day; for example, 100 mph. All that is necessary is to fly both directions across the ground where you plan to land. Note the ground speed in both directions. If the wind is blowing, one will be lower than your normal cruise speed, for example, 90 mph. This indicates you are flying into a 10 mph headwind. The other direction will show 110 mph. This is a tailwind or the direction the wind is blowing. You'll need to land with the lower ground speed which is into the wind.

On windy days it is important when flying these ground speed detection flights to look for quartering winds or crosswinds when flying back and forth across your landing area. The strongest winds may be quartering winds or full crosswinds. Fly the crosswind routes and determine the ground speed your aircraft is flying. This will provide precise wind speeds of the quartering winds and crosswinds. If you find the strongest winds are quartering winds or full crosswinds blowing at 30 mph, you may consider landing somewhere else where your landing is more into the wind.

Your airspeed is one of the most important items to consider when making off-airport landings. When the wind is blowing, make certain that you take advantage of it. This means almost always landing into the wind. Headwinds of 10 to 15 mph greatly assist in landing your airplane. The headwinds lower the ground speed of your aircraft by that amount making landings slower and safer. Your airplane has much less kinetic energy and therefore the braking and landing roll is greatly reduced. Short landings are required for off-airport operations. The opposite is the case when you land your airplane with a tailwind. With an increase in ground speed from the tailwind, you have greatly energized your aircraft. This makes landings more problematic and difficult. The landings will be at a greater ground speed. This will result in a longer landing roll with heavier braking. It is much easier for your aircraft to get out of control and crash when landing at higher speeds with huge amounts of kinetic energy in your aircraft. It is wise to limit tailwind landings although sometimes they are necessary.

Don't forget when flying on windy days to look for an opportunity to land into the wind and avoid making difficult and problematic crosswind landings. Landing directly into the wind is the safest way to land an airplane when hard gusty winds are blowing. This should be your first consideration. Gusty winds are involved in and contribute to a large number of aircraft landing accidents in Alaska. What usually makes gusty wind landings such a difficult task is that many pilots are coming in for a landing with highly energized airplanes well above stall speed? (This combination of landing in gusty winds and excessive speed is very problematic and often results in aircraft accidents. This is one of the most perilous situations you could ever place your airplane in. The gusty winds are difficult enough to master without making it more difficult by increasing the kinetic energy in your airplane.) The landing accident rate under these conditions can be substantially reduced by landing at initial stall speed. When making landings at initial stall speed you must be cognizant of changes in wind conditions. When coming in for landing with the throttle at a low setting, strong gusty winds that are rapidly changing direction, causing a wind shear, or making a lull in the wind can take control of your airplane and wreck it. The first sign of shifting winds is a call for immediate action. The most important action to take is to lower the airplane's nose and open the throttle. This will allow a rapid increase in flight speed which will stabilize the airplane. A stabilized airplane will have positive controls for the pilot to safely fly the aircraft.

Crosswind Operations

Crosswind takeoffs require keeping the windward wing down with proper use of the aileron. A right crosswind will require full stick to the right before the throttle is opened for takeoff. The aileron will be raised on the right or windward wing. Opposite rudder is required in the takeoff run to keep the airplane tracking straight down the runway. The tail should be raised slightly higher than for normal takeoff so the airplane can accelerate to a higher speed before becoming airborne. After the airplane becomes airborne, relax the rudder and allow the airplane to weathervane into the Relative Wind. The crosswind takeoff will require a substantially greater distance on the ground roll when compared to the standard takeoff into the wind. Always prepare for this on a short field takeoff.

Alaska's elite pilots learn the wing-down and the crab method for performing crosswind landings. The wing-down method is traditionally used as it is more precise compared to the crab method. It is performed by keeping the windward wing down by use of full aileron into the wind and opposite rudder to keep the airplane aligned with the centerline of the runway. This is a cross-controlled maneuver. A wheel landing is made by touching down the main wheel which is into the wind. The other wheel comes down on its own after the airplane slows down and sufficient lift is lost.

When making crosswind landings, always be creative in your thinking. If you have arrived at your landing area, which has only two directions for landing, and find a sizable crosswind component, instead of trying to decide how you are going to perform this difficult landing, look for alternatives first; find a way to land your airplane into the wind. Landing into a stiff wind is always the best option. It is surprising how many times you can find a way to locate a place to land that is into the wind instead of the routine landing with a crosswind. An example of this was the landing in my Piper Cub many years ago at the Dillingham airport. Dillingham has a paved runway that is 6,400 feet long and 150 feet in width. The wind on the day I arrived was a direct crosswind blowing at 30 mph. The only creative way to make this landing less difficult was to land on the paved runway diagonally to reduce the angle of the direct crosswind. I still considered this too risky and decided that I should not attempt a landing on the main runway. I was low on fuel and needed to land at the airport for refueling. Maybe I could find a place to land on the Nushagak Bay beach or in the tundra near the village. Flying near the airport I noticed that a taxiway was aligned directly with the wind. Dillingham being such a remote and small village, I decided to call Dillingham airport and ask permission to land on the taxiway. I was very surprised when told that I could land on the taxiway but it would be at my own risk. I was also warned that hangars are on one end of the taxiway and to be careful not to crash into them. I was so relieved and although it is not normal to line up and land on a taxiway, I had no concerns because it was plenty long enough and the most important consideration was it was directly into the wind. This turned out to be a safe and stress-free landing. My takeoff was on the same taxiway. The main point to take away here is that creative ideas don't just happen; you have to use your incredibly creative mind to seek out alternatives that are useful and different from the ordinary or standard procedure.

Measuring Landing and Takeoff Distances

Now that you have a sufficient amount of basic training in takeoffs and landings and have learned to make precision landings, it is time to measure the distance required for takeoff and landing your airplane. It is essential to know these in accurate measurements. You can utilize the same landing area you have set up for precision landings. You can place your wheels in the training box for takeoffs and for landings. You'll need to mark each 100-foot section beyond the box for up to 600 feet. Use brightly colored 6-by-8-inch cones or flagging material tied on rocks or stakes to one side of the runway.

Remember to come in for landings at different speeds and heights. Don't use a standardized pattern approach like you use when landing at regular airports. If you are too high and need to lose altitude fast, learn to be a professional at slipping your aircraft. This is a cross-controlled maneuver; full left or right aileron and opposite rudder. If there is a crosswind, make sure you place the wing down into the wind. With a crosswind landing, touch down on the main wheel into the wind. The other main wheel will slowly fall to the ground as the forward speed slows down and the wing can no longer carry the load.

The first lesson is to measure your aircraft's takeoff and landing performance. Each time you take off note how many feet of runway are required to get airborne. Do the same for landings; write down the numbers for your landing roll. Use moderate braking pressure. This information is very important when selecting a short landing area in natural terrain. You never want to land your airplane if you don't have sufficient distance for a takeoff.

You also need to find out the difference in feet required for takeoffs and landings. Compare the two measurements and use this information when selecting a landing place in future flights. Of course, these measurements will change as you get more precise with your landings. After some time, you'll be more certain that the measurements are constant and you'll know that your aircraft can land shorter than it can takeoff, or it needs the same distance for takeoffs and landings, or the third option is that it requires a longer distance for landing than for taking off. Remember to practice this type of training in all sorts of weather, for example, cool days, hot days, calm days, headwinds, tailwinds, crosswinds, quartering winds, and others. Also vary your airplane cargo loads.

Selecting Landing Areas from Your Cockpit

Selecting landing areas from the cockpit of your airplane can be difficult or next to impossible if you don't learn how to properly do this. There has to be a way of verifying what you are seeing from your aircraft to what is the true situation on the ground. Routine training is necessary to fly over the potential landing area and look for key factors that have to be evaluated. First look at the length of the landing area and estimate its length in feet. Next look to see if the landing area is level or sloping. If sloping, estimate the percent of slope. Determine if the landing area can be used in both directions or is this landing area a one-way-in and one-way-out operation. Next, look for obstacles that can interfere with your landing or takeoff approaches; these are vegetation (bushes and trees); cut banks near a river, hills, and other impediments. Contemplate whether the landing area is long enough for landing and taking off given your airplane's loaded weight (cargo, fuel, passengers), the obstacles present, the slope and the weather conditions (especially the wind). Next, look for surface roughness of the landing area. Look for dips, holes, and swales and estimate their depth in inches. Next look at the rocks and stones and estimate their size (diameter in inches). Then look at the height of vegetation and trees that may interfere with your landing. Estimate the vegetation and tree height in feet. Estimate wing clearance from the vegetation. Also estimate propeller clearance for the brush that may be in the landing area.

Now, go in and land and park your airplane. Next, walk down the landing area and obtain measurements of the length of the runway (you can step this off in 3-foot strides if your steps are accurate), the height of the brush and the trees (may want to use a tape measure), measure the depth of the dips, holes, and swales with the tape and measure the size (get the diameter in inches) of stones and cobbles. The measurements you obtain on the ground have to be compared to what your estimates were from the airplane. When your estimates don't match, you'll have to adjust them so that they will be more accurate the next time. If you keep doing these estimates from the air and compare them with the actual measurements on the ground, you will find that you can estimate these variables very accurately. Determining the length of a landing area while airborne will become a learned skill and art that becomes subconscious with time and experience. When evaluating landing areas, it is important to add one notch of flaps and fly slower than cruise speed for much improved accuracy. The above training technique for evaluating a landing area from the air refers to a gravel bar.

River gravel bars (including sandbars) are the most frequently used off-airport landing areas in Alaska because they provide the best landing areas by a wide margin. Other landing areas frequently used is sand and gravel ocean and lake beaches. Gravel bars on rivers are firm, they are bare, and you can see exactly what is there. Vegetation on gravel bars is usually suppressed so it isn't a problem. Approaches to landing on river gravel bars are usually very good. Landing on grass-covered terrain is much more problematic. The grass can be slippery. It can be wet with standing water not detected from the air. The ground can be very soft and muddy. With only 12 inches in height, grass can completely hide a hole or a log. This can result in landing gear damage, or even worse, a nose-over with considerable damage to the airplane. Many accidents in Alaska are the result of landing in grassy terrain. These accidents often happen in remote areas far from repair services. Many of these accidents will require costly helicopters for the rescue.

When evaluating a landing area from the cockpit, make sure you know your airplane's performance capabilities. Does it require a longer distance for takeoffs than it requires for landings? Does it require the same distance for landings as it requires for takeoffs? Or does it require a longer distance for landings than it requires for a takeoffs? Your aircraft loads, density altitude, and wind conditions must also be used for making accurate evaluations to determine landing and takeoff distances required. Add a safety margin of 20%. Example: a required 300-foot landing area would be increased to 360 feet for safety considerations.

After learning and practicing this skill it will become an art and you will no longer need numbers written down to follow. The pilot can look at a gravel bar while airborne and immediately know its length by just viewing it. This makes the task simple and easy to perform.

Advanced Training

You would think that advanced training for General Aviation (GA) pilots after receiving their Private Pilot's License (PPL) would include first and foremost learning to be an improved pilot in the airplane that you are currently flying. You could review and improve your weak flying techniques. Abandon poor techniques and replace them with ones that are superior. This does not seem to be reality. *Advanced Training* by Marc C. Lee in the July 2014 issue of Plane & Pilot Magazine presented the conventional ways to expand your aviation horizon. It was astonishing to read that the recommended training involved not learning to be an improved pilot in the airplane you are flying but secondary options somewhat removed from the most important primary task. The magazine article recommended pilots should set up training in simulators like the Redbird, obtain a tailwheel endorsement, instrument rating, commercial license, seaplane rating, multi-engine rating, aerobatics training, and flying warbirds and gliders. These options for advanced training will certainly broaden your knowledge on the subject; however, they will not provide very much in the way of improving your primary mission of flying your airplane. Substantially improving proficiency and becoming a more capable pilot is the most cherished event in a pilot's flying career. How can a pilot find the most effective advanced training? Read on in the next paragraph.

Alaska's distinguished pilots focus their advanced training primarily on learning to be the best pilot in the airplane they are flying. A fledgling pilot in Alaska is always interested in finding out how can a pilot learn to be such an exceptional pilot like the elite Alaskan pilots. The correct answer to this question is not by the conventional training such as the ratings and licenses mentioned above but by academically learning from two aviation spheres—FAA's and the elite Alaskan pilots and selecting the best strategies and techniques from each and then incorporating them into your flying repertoire. There is nothing that comes close to providing such a boost in a pilot's proficiency as this form of advanced training.

The Alaskan approach for advanced training should be disseminated to pilots globally because of its fundamental importance. Think of what a difference this could make in providing highly proficient pilots that could reduce their aircraft accident rate by a substantial margin.

Preventing Aircraft Accidents caused by Ground Effect

There are accidents every year in Alaska caused by airplanes taking off and not being able to continue flying after coming out of ground effect. Most of these accidents could have been prevented with the proper knowledge on the subject. Fixed-wing aircraft, flying close to the ground (within an aircraft's wingspan) makes the wing more efficient by an increase in the lift to drag ratio. Ground effect causes problems both with aircraft landing and taking off. Airplanes coming in too high and too fast will float more when entering ground effect and will use up too much of the landing surface. This could result in not being able to slow down fast enough to avoid running off the landing area into rough terrain.

Most accidents caused by ground effect are ones related to takeoffs. Airplanes can take off in a shorter distance in ground effect due to more efficient wing performance. However, as the airplane rises out of ground effect, the wings begin generating less lift and producing greater induced drag that may result in marginal climb performance or even worse insufficient speed to continue flying. The airplane will initially lose elevation and speed until it accelerates to the proper flying speed necessary to continue flight. In extreme deteriorating lift conditions such as with a high gross weight and high density altitude the airplane may initially become airborne in ground effect with insufficient speed to continue flying when the airplane leaves ground effect. Under these conditions, the airplane will gradually settle back down into terrain beyond the landing surface and crash. This usually results in substantial aircraft damage and personal harm. Ground effect can also be a problem when an airplane is heavily loaded. If the pilot lifts the airplane off the ground after a short distance with slow forward speed, the airplane may not have sufficient flying speed for sustain flight after leaving ground effect.

Pilots that understand ground effect will use this knowledge to prevent accidents. Most accidents are caused by heavily loaded or overloaded aircraft taking off on short strips. Warm days above 70°F (we do have warm days occasionally in Alaska) and no wind degrades lift and may also contribute to ground effect accidents. Taking off with a tailwind may cause ground effect accidents. Under all conditions that degrade lift, the aircraft will become airborne in ground effect but the flying speed may be inadequate to continue flight after leaving ground effect. The airplane's acceleration will deteriorate and it will decelerate into natural terrain. How do you avoid this disaster? Reduce the cargo load in the aircraft. Don't take off with a heavily loaded airplane on short runways and under deteriorating conditions for lift. Divide the cargo load in half and make two lighter loads instead of one heavy load. Also, no matter how the airplane is loaded (light or heavy); use most of the runway surface before becoming airborne. The longer ground roll will provide increased airspeed after liftoff that is necessary when leaving ground effect for sustained flight. Not using most of the runway before liftoff causes a lot of accidents—many more than most would believe. One other important procedure is to lower the nose after taking off to near level position to allow the airplane to rapidly build-up airspeed. The sooner the airplane accelerates in airspeed after leaving ground effect the better and the safer you will be in avoiding accidents. The key to preventing accidents when leaving ground effect is to have the proper amount of airspeed needed for sustained flight.

Caution for Takeoffs in Heavily-Loaded Aircraft

Many aircraft accidents in Alaska are primarily or secondarily caused by heavily loaded or overloaded airplanes attempting a short field takeoff. Pilots must understand that heavily loaded aircraft must be flown with much greater precision than a lightly loaded aircraft. For a better understanding why a heavily loaded or overloaded aircraft has to be flown much different is the knowledge of all the degrading effects of overloaded aircraft. Below are listed the performance characteristics that will be adversely affected when an aircraft is heavily loaded or overloaded.

- Higher Takeoff Speed

- Longer Takeoff Run

- Reduced Rate and Angle of Climb

- Reduced Cruising Speed

- Reduced Maneuverability

- Higher Stalling Speed

- Higher Landing Speed

- Longer Landing Roll

- Greater Difficulty when Leaving Ground Effect

- Center of Gravity Shifts Degrade Takeoffs

When a pilot begins to understand these degrading flying outcomes with a heavily loaded airplane, it becomes clear that the airplane must be flown with comprehensive awareness, precision, and caution. When the odds are stacked against you, don't take off with a heavy load. These degrading conditions include short and rough runways, no wind or a tailwind, days with high temperatures and high humidity, high density altitude, cut banks or trees close to the end of the runway that have to be cleared on takeoff, and others. Wait for better conditions—the best option is to make two flights with a moderately-loaded aircraft instead of one heavy load. The latter will allow the cargo to be flown out at almost any time in a safe way. It may be difficult to determine if your heavily loaded airplane can gain sufficient speed on takeoff to climb out of ground effect and continue flying versus settling back down into the ground and crashing off the runway. If you don't fully understand exactly how the degrading factors will affect your takeoff, the smart option is to make two moderate loads instead of the one heavy load. Safety (avoiding wrecking your airplane) is the biggest concern with heavy.

Dangers of Landing in Low Light

There are a substantial number of accidents that are caused by pilots attempting to land airplanes in low light which is usually after sunset in twilight conditions. This happens because pilots believe they are seeing well enough to make safe landings. In reality, a pilot's visibility is hampered more often than they might realize by low light. They are not able to see important parts of the landing area well enough to prevent accidents. Since low light is a benign type of occurrence on a daily basis, some knowledge and strategy should be used on determining when it is safe to land an airplane under these conditions. This is especially important when landing on off-airport locations with no runway lights. It is also important with pilots that have reduced or poor vision in low light conditions.

The best visibility and light conditions for flying and landing your airplane is in normal daytime when the sun appears above the horizon. This is the time between sunrise and sunset. Sunrise is the instant at which the upper edge of the sun appears above the horizon in the morning. Sunset is the daily disappearance of the sun below the horizon in the evening. The time of sunset is at the moment when the trailing edge of the sun's disk disappears below the horizon. The time for sunrise and sunset vary on a daily basis. These precise times can often be found in daily newspapers such as the *Anchorage Dispatch News*. They are also available on GPS data base instruments.

Pilots that are extending landings into low light conditions after sunset are landing in twilight. Twilight is indirect illumination that is produced by the sun when it is below the horizon and is not directly visible. During twilight, the earth is neither completely lit nor is it completely dark. Twilight exists during a period in the morning before sunrise (dawn) and a period in the afternoon after sunset (dusk). Dawn and dusk intervals of twilight for Anchorage, Alaska may have duration of 40 minutes to over 1 hour.

There are three types of twilight designations that occur both at dawn in the early morning and at dusk in the late evening. They have a decreasing magnitude of illumination starting with civil twilight, then nautical twilight, and finally the darkest period astronomical twilight. Civil twilight begins in the morning when the geometric center of the sun is 6 degrees below the horizon and lasts until sunrise. Evening civil twilight begins at sunset and ends when the center of the sun reaches 6 degrees below the horizon. The duration of civil twilight at dawn and at dusk near Anchorage, Alaska is 25 to 30 minutes on average. Nautical twilight in the evening occurs when the center of the sun is from 6 to 12 degrees below the horizon. Astronomical twilight occurs when the center of the sun is 12 to 18 degrees below the horizon. Both nautical and astronomical twilight conditions have too little illumination and are far too dim to attempt to land airplanes on unlighted runways. Civil twilight intervals at dawn and dusk may offer sufficient light for landing an airplane but not always. Although civil twilight is described as sufficient light to discern terrestrial objects, on cloudy days light may be too dim for safely landing an airplane. Remember that civil twilight was developed for people on the ground and not for pilots flying airplanes. Motion (speed when flying an airplane) will exacerbate visibility by blurring objects in low light. Pilots that have reduced vision in low light will also be at peril in reduced light during the later stages of civil twilight. In conclusion, evening landings in civil twilight on airports, backcountry airstrips, or in natural terrain without runway lights can be problematic.

To avoid unsafe landings in the low light conditions of twilight, plan to take off after sunrise in the morning and land before sunset in the evening. If you come in for a landing five minutes after sunset there will usually not be a problem. However, coming in for a landing late in the civil twilight period can result in poor light conditions that will cause limited visibility on the worst days. This could result in an aircraft accident. Remember that low light is such a benign event that many times it is not easy to detect. Avoiding the low light conditions is a blessing in disguise. You will not wreck your airplane if you avoid these conditions. Not one but several accidents have happened with airplanes landing in low light conditions on the unlighted gravel strip at Merrill Field over the past 10 years. One airplane was completely demolished when it crashed into a concrete structure near the runway while attempting a landing in low light conditions.

Another low light condition that happens in Alaska is when airplanes are equipped with skis and land on snow-covered surfaces in the winter. These low light conditions in the winter on snow-covered surfaces are called whiteouts or flat light. Whiteouts can be defined as an optical phenomenon in which the snow-covered terrain blends into a uniformly dull sky reducing the visibility of shadows, clouds, the horizon, and so forth and one's sense of direction and distance. While in the air you will not be able to detect undulating terrain such as wavy snow created by strong surface winds, snow berms, depressions, and other variable features on the surface. This makes landings on severe whiteout days highly problematic, dangerous, and often will result in wrecking your airplane if an attempt to land is made.

Severe whiteouts are usually not a problem because pilots can decipher these and will avoid landing in them. The most difficult whiteouts that are dangerous for landing airplanes are the ones that are classified as mild whiteouts. Most pilots would not think so but in reality, these are the ones that cause the most accidents. These are the ones that will get you in trouble and over your head in attempting to land your airplane. The reason for this is because a mild whiteout is benign and pilots without mountaineering experience just do not have enough knowledge and familiarity with white-outs to fully understanding their dangerous side. When you look at a mild whiteout while flying over at low elevation it does not appear to be blotting out terrain features but it is in a very subtle way. Since it does not look like it is a problem, a pilot will attempt to land in these conditions. After the skis touch down then the pilot will see a larger than expected snow feature (snow berm) coming up right in front of the airplane. The pilot will have no way to prevent the airplane from crashing into the snow feature. This happens more times than most pilots would believe. An American Champion Scout (8 GCBC) landed on Eagle Glacier a few years ago on an overcast day in a mild whiteout. When the airplane touched down, the pilot then saw a huge snow berm which the airplane crashed into totally destroying the airplane. This is only one example but there are many others that have occurred in past years.

My only salvation from mild whiteouts is that I was a mountaineer prior to becoming a pilot. I have had lots of experience skiing on glaciers with the Alpine Cub of Alaska in the Alaska Range and with the Mountaineering Club of Alaska in the Chugach, Kenai, and Talkeetna Mountains. These mountaineering experiences were hugely helpful in understanding whiteouts and being able to know when it is safe to land my airplane on glaciers. I do not know what to say to pilots about landing their airplanes on glaciers without sufficient knowledge on whiteouts. Talk to experience pilots, fly with experience pilots and let them land first. Land in fresh tracks where another pilot has just landed or parallel to snowmachine tracks. If you can see ski tracks in the snow, whiteout conditions are not a problem. At least this narrative will provide a pilot with awareness and an understanding that whiteouts can be a very serious problem when landing your airplane. When in doubt, don't land.

Importance of an Engine Analyzer

The engine in my Arctic Tern was run out in 2006. The engine was removed and was being rebuilt in Alaska. Dan Hollingsworth who owns Dan' Aircraft Repair was preparing to repaint my airplane while it was down for the engine overhaul. During this time, Dan gave me a comprehensive discussion of the importance of having an engine analyzer installed in my airplane. Dan has had an engine analyzer installed in his Super Cub for a number of years so he has a pilot's perspective as well as an airplane maintenance perception of its use. I was so impressed with Dan's message that I told him I wanted an engine analyzer installed in my airplane. It is costly but seems to be a necessity to have an engine analyzer in your airplane. I have few instruments in my airplane as I fly by the *seat of your pants* and actually do not need them. Nevertheless, this instrument was not one that helps a pilot fly the airplane. It is installed primarily to monitor the cylinders to ensure proper temperatures are being maintained throughout flying time in the airplane. Excessive temperatures will eventually destroy cylinders.

Engine analyzers most important use is in proper leaning your airplane while in flight. There are endless articles about operating *lean-of-peak* or *rich-of peak* and what benefits each offer. There are also countless combinations of fuel flow and power that offer the best performance for a given trip. These techniques are useful; however, they do not show the temperatures of the cylinders. With any of these settings, you may not be flying your airplane with a healthy engine due to excessively high engine temperatures. That is why Dan does not recommend that a pilot lean an airplane engine in a taildragger when flying low level in Alaska. The reason for this is that without an engine analyzer you don't know what the cylinder temperatures are and they may be too high. Cylinders which are run at excessive temperatures will eventually result in cylinder failures. Running the airplane full rich will burn more fuel; however, the cylinders will be cooler and they will not be exposed to overheating and failure.

Another benefit from an engine analyzer is that cylinder head and exhaust gas temperatures may show hints of excessive temperatures of a cylinder well before it results in failure. After my new engine was installed, I made my first break-in flight for a little over an hour. The cylinder head temperatures were not too high; however, the exhaust gas temperatures were on the high side. The next day I took the Tern on its second engine break-in flight. In short time I noticed that the exhaust gas temperatures were excessive. I immediately went back to the airport and tied down the airplane. A call was made to the shop that rebuilt my aircraft engine. They were alarmed and told me not to fly the airplane until they found out what was the problem. The Lycoming O-320 aircraft engine was upgraded in horsepower when the engine was rebuilt. The carburetor was also rebuilt when the engine was overhauled. They suspected that the carburetor jet may not be the correct size for the upgraded engine. They changed out the jet to the one that was thought to be correct. I took the airplane on a flight to check out the cylinder temperatures with the new jet in the carburetor. The exhaust gas temperatures were excellent and were where they should have been all along. I was immediately gratified that I had installed an engine analyzer in my airplane. I saved my new engine from being overheated and certain engine failure. There is no way that I would have known that the temperatures were too high without the new engine analyzer. The engine analyzer has already provided me the means to prevent engine failure in my new overhauled engine. This experience showed me just how important an engine analyzer can be.

I use the engine analyzer on every flight to properly lean my aircraft engine. I wait until my engine temperatures have stabilized usually after 5-10 minutes of flight time. I lean my engine until I obtain healthy exhaust gas temperatures (under 1,400°F). My cylinder head temperatures at high lean mixtures are low in temperature (under 300°F) and I don't have a problem with them getting too hot when leaning. By leaning my airplane, I can go from a full-rich mixture burning 8.2 gallons of fuel per hour to 7.4 gallons per hour when fully leaned at proper exhaust gas temperatures. Leaning my airplane saves quite a bit of high-price fuel and I am assured that the leaning is not too hot for my cylinders. I am highly dependent on the engine analyzer so I can make the proper leaning for substantial fuel savings. Using an engine analyzer for the leaning is very easy to accomplish and is the safest way of flying an airplane. My airplane will always have an engine analyzer because it is such a highly valuable asset that is necessity in properly leaning an airplane and in ensuring healthy temperatures for an operating aircraft engine.

Emergency Equipment

You will need to carry in your airplane sufficient equipment and provisions that can sustain you and your passengers for at least one week. Freeze-dried or dehydrated meals are the lightest in weight and are recommended as essential items to be stored in your airplane for emergencies. In cold climates, you will need summer and winter paraphernalia that will need to be changed each season. If you have experience in trekking, backpacking, mountain climbing, hunting, and other outdoor activities you will already know what you need to pack away in your airplane for emergency layovers in the backcountry due to weather-related problems, aircraft failures, or aircraft accidents. The most important consideration is to keep the weight of your survival gear as light as possible by buying the lightest-weight items available and also to make sure you are not carrying unneeded items. In all my many days spent in the wild Alaskan outdoors in summer and winter, a tent is not only nice to have, it is a necessity. A light-weight and comfortable two-man tent can be found that weighs only five pounds. Every pilot needs to decide what to store away for emergencies. You know what you need to be comfortable. This will help tremendously in maintaining a positive attitude while grounded on forced layovers. It is important to schedule an excursion to stay overnight at a remote location and try out your equipment and food supplies. After the drill for an emergency layover, rearrange you survival kit and make it more efficient. A container should be used to pack small items so that they are not scattered throughout your cargo bin. Tie down the emergency container with straps so that it is not shifting and changing your airplane's center of gravity.

I highly recommend carrying a tool bag or kit in your airplane for use in making minor field repairs when necessary. This may keep you from being grounded far away from your home base where repairs can be easily made. My black zippered nylon tool bag (12" x 8" x 4" high) contains the following: spare spark plug and gas cap, screwdrivers, pliers (regular, long-nose, cutting), ratchet with 7/8 inch socket for removing spark plugs, crescent wrench, combination wrench set (1/4, 5/16, 3/8, 7/16, 1/2, 9/16, 5/8, and 3/4"), several types of tape, safety wire, safety wire twisters, nylon fastening straps, nylon string, sewing kit with dental floss cord for mending torn fabric, Scotch-Brite, a packet of screws, washers, and nuts of various sizes, spark plug kit with dental picks for cleaning lead fouling in the bottom of plugs. The tool kit is for removing the cowling, taking out and cleaning fouled spark plugs, adjusting the carburetor, patching torn fabric, and other temporary repairs in the back country.

If your airplane is equipped with skis in winter, you'll need an adequate-size snow shovel for digging your airplane out of the snow. The small backpacking shovels are too small and almost useless when you need to remove large amounts of snow. I use a lightweight full-size plastic snow shovel. Select your snowshoes carefully. Snowshoes with a small footprint are inefficient for packing down the snow for a takeoff or walking long distances across snow-covered terrain. Make sure the straps on your snowshoes are easy to put on and take off and designed to fasten properly so that they are not constantly slipping off your boots. In cold climates, a top quality warm sleeping bag is essential. Down sleeping bags are very warm and do well when the temperature is well below freezing. In warmer weather near or above freezing, synthetic insulation is a better choice as it will not absorb moisture and lose its insulating value. To increase warmth in your sleeping bag, carry a fleece liner (weighs two pounds). Place the fleece liner inside the sleeping bag, crawl in and zip it up around you—it is like a mini bag and provide a tremendous increase in warmth over just the sleeping bag.

Other important items to carry in your airplane are a first aid kit, compass, orange flagging material, and an ocean tide book. Extra-long nylon airplane tie down ropes are also essential to carry in your cargo bin. I carry a small shovel for summer use. This is a three-piece Lexan-bladed shovel with aluminum handles. It is a lightweight, extremely durable, and easy-to-assemble, practical, and useful shovel when needed to remove a hump or fill in holes on a backcountry landing area. Another important recommendation is to carry an efficient ax. Hatchets are built with short handles that are almost useless (horrendous shock and inefficient when cutting firewood). I have a Gerber ax that has a total length of 18 inches. This is the smallest size ax that it is efficient for cutting firewood. I also carry a folding cross-cut bladed saw for cutting brush on remote landing areas, fuel funnel, fuel tester, bicycle pump for inflating my Alaskan Bushwheels. The small light-weight bicycle pump works great as the tires only require about 6 to 8 psi of air.

Aircraft Tie-Downs in the Backcountry

Aircraft catalogs have numerous options for aircraft tie-downs. They offer corkscrews, triangular steel stakes, winding steel anchors and others. Corkscrews, 16 inches in length, are augured into the ground. Steel stakes,

14 inches in length, are driven into the ground with a maul. Driving stakes and anchors into gravel or stony substrate is next to impossible. In addition, on sand or gravel bars, these anchors would likely fail (pull out) in strong winds and provide no security for your airplane. I would not trust any of these toy tie-downs for my expensive airplane. I know of only one tie-down that is trustworthy—that is the duck bill. Once you drive a duck bill anchor into the ground, it is not coming out. The negative on duck bills is that once they are set in the ground, they can't be taken out again. If you're on a long backcountry trip, you'll run out of space, weight, and funding for carrying enough duck bills for each overnight tie-down. A heavy steel implement and a mallet are required to drive the duck bill into the ground. This requires lots of space and extra weight to haul around.

I pondered the tie-down encumbrance for a few years and came up with a solution that beats all of the traditional tie-down options by a wide margin. When you land in remote places, look around where your aircraft is parked. Almost every time, you will find something in the natural environment that you can (with a rope) tie your aircraft down. Trees, logs, boulders, and willow or alder bushes all work extremely well. (Tie a rope around the base at ground level of the entire clump of willows or alder bushes and not around a single stem.) You may have to taxi your airplane for correct placement for the tie-down. Before I land (if I am spending the night), I'll be looking for vegetation or logs where I can tie the airplane down. You'll need to bring ropes that are longer than normal for tie-downs. On a naked sandbar with no logs or willow bushes, I carry three heavy-duty plastic bags. These are not garbage bags, as they would be much too lightweight to hold a sack full of stones, cobbles, gravel, or sand. Use the plastic bags similar to the tough bags that cement comes in. You'll find these at hardware stores. Also, make sure the bags are large enough so that you can add sufficient weight to hold down your aircraft in a nasty windstorm. Fill the bags with natural materials with a shovel, dig a hole for each bag for the wing and tail tie-downs, and drop the bags in the holes and backfill material around the sacks. My tie-down strategy has never once failed in my many years of flying and camping in the backcountry in Alaska, and my airplane is not cluttered with heavy insecure anchors.

One other item on tie-downs is to make sure your knots are properly tied. The aviation knot is highly used and recommended for tying down your aircraft. Your rope should be of high quality nylon and highly pliable as knots are difficult to tie securely and may become untied with stiff rope. Make sure the diameter and the strength (fades with age) of the rope is adequate. Learn to tie knots with the hand massaging the knot so that it can be fastened properly and tight enough so that it will not untie in strong, gusty winds that push and pull on the tie-down ropes. After tying the aviation knot, place a half-hitch on top of and another one below the knot for added safety. This will ensure your aviation knot will not come loose. It is amazing how many aircraft are tied down with a fast and quick pull of the rope forming a loose looped aviation knot. The knot is not tight and is likely to become untied in windy conditions. There are substantially more instances reported than you would expect with improperly tied-down aircraft coming loose and being destroyed in windstorms in Anchorage.

Alaskan Bushwheels

Alaskan pilots have always known the utility of larger and softer tires for backcountry landing operations. Many versions of the so called *tundra tire* were developed and manufactured in Alaska during the past fifty years. The later development phase of the legendary Alaskan Bushwheels was originated in the 1990s by Guy Selman from Antique Tire and Rubber and later by Jim Pazsint of Alaska Tire and Rubber Company. In 2000, Bill Duncan bought the Alaskan Tire and Rubber Company and moved it to Joseph, Oregon. The name was changed to Alaskan Bushwheels Incorporated. The Oregon Company upgraded the tire-building technology, rubber formulas, and tire construction. They built tires that are of radial construction. Alaskan Bushwheels has FAA Supplemental Type Certificates (STCs) available for over 100 light aircraft. On January 1, 2014, Airframes Alaska purchased Alaskan Bushwheels Incorporated and moved the company back to Alaska. Manufacturing and office is currently at the Birchwood Airport in Chugiak, Alaska which is 18 air miles northeast of Anchorage.

No upgrade to an airplane used for backcountry operations will provide a greater benefit than Alaskan Bushwheels. This is so straightforward that little or no discussion is necessary. They are expensive but they are a must-have for your airplane. The Alaskan Bushwheels provide increased ground clearance both for your airplane and for your propeller. They also provide a substantial amount of shock absorption when touching the ground on the landing roll. Increased propeller clearance will help to reduce the amount of rock particles the propeller picks up. This reduces damage to the leading edge of the propeller and other damage to the airplane—holes knocked into the fabric on the undersides of the horizontal stabilizer and elevator. The Alaskan Bushwheels dissipate an enormous amount of kinetic energy when landing. This greatly reduces the shock on your landing gear and airframe. It also provides for a much shorter landing roll as a large amount of kinetic energy is absorbed by the Bushwheels when they touch down on landing. This leaves much less kinetic energy to be dispelled by braking.

I knew that Bushwheels for backcountry landings were important but when I made the conversion from the hard 8.50-6 conventional tires to the larger and softer Bushwheels, I was shocked at the difference. Hard tires absorb very little kinetic energy when landing. This means you are always landing and rolling on the ground at greater speeds. This means longer and rougher landings. Your airplane will bounce more. Your landing gear and airframe absorb a greater amount of shock and are much easier to damage. All these deficiencies are much improved when using Bushwheels. The Bushwheels will allow landing on shorter and rougher landing surfaces in the backcountry. You will be landing in marginal areas that you would not even consider if you were using hard tires. All landings will be much safer with the Bushwheels, and the landing options will have increased two- or threefold. Most pilots would not consider flying into and landing in the backcountry without Bushwheels.

Use of Flaps on Takeoff

Many pilots believe that there is no advantage for decreasing takeoff distance by waiting until the aircraft is moving at takeoff speed to employ the flaps. They think that the amount of additional drag generated by prepositioned flaps from the beginning of takeoff to the actual liftoff is negligible. They also believe that flaps have little or no effect on drag until the airplane is up to rotational speed. In the end, they believe that it is better to set flaps to takeoff position before power up than to add an additional procedure at the critical moment of rotation. Many pilots complain about the difficulty in reaching down with the head lowered to set the flaps when the airplane is near liftoff speed.

Setting flaps at rotational speed is not a difficult and unsafe procedure as many pilots believe. If a pilot has a positive attitude (open mind) and practices it with the intention of mastering the procedure, it will not be any problem at all. There are many pilots in Alaska that pull flaps at rotation speed and I have never heard one of them complain about it being difficult or unsafe. The pilots that say it is difficult are the ones that tried it a few times and gave up saying it was dangerous and distracting pulling flaps while you are on the takeoff roll. If they would have stuck with it and trained with a greater dedication of mastering the technique, they would have found it to be a very easy and safe maneuver to learn.

Alaskan pilots pull flaps at rotational speed because it provides for a shorter takeoff run. I have not seen test numbers that show this; however, with a full understanding of the consequences, it would surely seem that pulling flaps at rotational speed is more efficient.

Here are the consequences of setting flaps prior to powering up for takeoff. Flaps that are employed will cause wing loading (weight will be transferred to the wings) and this will rob power that would otherwise be used for horizontal speed acceleration. With the wings carrying part of the load, the tail will require more power and distance to lift to a horizontal position. The aircraft in horizontal position (with the tail raised) is the most effective for accelerating forward takeoff speed.

When the flaps are not set on takeoff, the tail comes up immediately with little power required so the aircraft can be placed in the horizontal position. All power at this time is pulling the aircraft forward (horizontal orientation) for the fastest acceleration on takeoff that is possible. There is no drag or power robbed by the wings directing vertical power for wing loading. With these noted differences of setting the flaps before powering up and setting the flaps at rotational speed; how can a pilot believe that there is no difference in efficiency between the two techniques? Alaskan pilots land their airplanes on the tiniest short field landing areas possible and using this technique will provide a shorter takeoff distance than setting flaps prior to powering up for takeoff.

Other Training Missions

Additional training will be needed besides what is covered in this book—that is a given. That should not be too difficult as what has been covered in the book is a primer providing a basic understanding on how to train. It is the pilot's responsibility to be aware of training that is needed and to go out and get it done. Since S*elf-training* is the Alaskan pilot way, the important consideration is to take responsibility, add the training to your flying program, talk to experienced pilots, read what is available, and then go out in your own airplane and integrate it into your flying repertoire. As you fly and train in your own aircraft, your confidence will build to the point that you will feel comfortable taking on new training challenges. You will also have utmost assurance that your self-training mission will improve your flying capabilities and make you a better pilot. There is nothing like knowing you are in control of your own destiny and that you have the confidence and diligence to get the job accomplished. Under these circumstances, you will excel in your flying capabilities—that will make you an extraordinary pilot.

Flying Difficulties Related to Weather

Alaska's Inadequate Weather Reporting System

The weather reporting stations in the Lower 48 States have adequate density required for making accurate weather forecasts across the Continental United States. Alaska's weather reporting stations are much less dense. There are only 133 automated weather reporting stations in the entire State of Alaska. Alaska would need to build 180 more weather stations (313 total weather stations) to have the same density as the Lower 48 States. Pilots use weather forecasts to predict flying conditions during flight. The limited numbers of weather observations covering immense areas in Alaska often results in pilots encountering inaccurate or no weather forecasts. Missing and poorly forecasted weather conditions may lead to controlled flight into terrain (CFIT) accidents. This is a huge problem in Alaska and pilots need to have a strategy and a plan for addressing the problem.

Learning to Read the Weather

One of the more challenging obstacles to flying in Alaska is weather. Ground fog, low ceilings, gusty winds, and turbulence are common weather problems that affect airplane performance and flying safety. Rapidly changing weather patterns and many areas in Alaska without comprehensive and accurate weather reports can also result in demanding flying conditions. In summer, long distance flights are often intercepted with areas with ground fog or low cloud ceilings. Pilots in Alaska learn to fly in 500 foot ceilings and 1 mile visibility. However, a more practical minimum is 1,000 foot ceilings and visibility of 3 miles. Although Southcentral Alaska does have thunderstorms occasionally, they are often not the highly dangerously ones that are found in the Lower 48 States. Alaskan pilots are also blessed with cool summers and minimum density altitude problems.

Weather dominated my first few years of flying in Alaska, especially on cross-country flights over remote and unpeopled lands. A flight from Merrill Field to Iliamna, which is 230 miles southwest of Anchorage, almost always presented very challenging weather-related problems. The flying route is along upper Cook Inlet, where fog can be a problem in summer. Then the route passes through the Alaska Range with valleys near sea level and mountains with glaciers to over 10,000 feet. The route passes through mountains on both sides for over 100 miles as you fly through Lake Clark Pass. Fog and strong gusty winds at Iliamna are notorious. It always seemed like you could never make that flight without finding challenging and difficult flying conditions somewhere along the route due to the weather. I was always briefed on the weather before beginning the flight. Since I am not a meteorologist, often I did not fully understand the weather conditions well enough to be prepared for the flight.

I tried the go-or-no-go strategy after obtaining a weather report but it provided little or no advantage. It was always very unnerving to me to find that somewhere along the way the weather report was incorrect and the flying became problematic, difficult, and stressful. Because the weather reported flyable weather conditions, I would keep flying when I should have turned back. More times than you would expect, current weather reports were unavailable for the areas you were flying in or you could not contact the radio frequency to obtain a weather report. All of this presented a chaotic condition when weather was brought into the flying equation.

To provide a more comfortable environment, I would obtain the weather report and begin the flight if weather conditions were not atrocious along the way to my destination. However, I was more concerned with the weather conditions where the flight was being launched. Merrill Field is only 137 feet above sea level but is built on a slight knoll. From Merrill Field, on a clear day, a pilot can see the snow dome of Mount McKinley, 130 air miles north-northwest. Pilots can also see Mount Susitna (4,396 feet), 40 miles northwest; the snow-covered Mount Spurr (11,070 feet), 80 miles west in the Alaska Range; the Talkeetna Mountains, 35 miles northeast; the Kenai Mountains 18 miles south; and the Chugach Mountains, 5 miles east. When I arrive at Merrill Field, I take a panoramic look at the above-described viewpoints and make an evaluation.

Do I want to fly in these conditions? If the answer is yes, I fly out of Merrill Field. If the answer is no, I hold off to a later time when the weather is more to my liking. The weather reports do little to change my own evaluation of the weather I'll be flying in when departing Merrill Field. A second and most important element I have incorporated into my flying repertoire related to weather is to be my own weather interpreter. As I fly toward my destination (Iliamna), I am constantly looking out, evaluating, and making an interpretation of how the weather will change in five minutes, fifteen minutes, half an hour, and one hour. I use my own weather analysis to provide real and accurate data essential for safe flying. This way of reading the weather has been the most innovative and successful way to manage this difficult and ever changing condition in Alaska. Being your own weather interpreter, you always have the information you need right out there in front of your airplane. My confidence and comfort are off the charts and far above inaccurate, difficult-to-understand, and missing weather reports. When conditions deteriorate, I immediately recognize them and determine if the trend is continuing in a downward spiral. Once this has been determined, I'm not concerned with flying in dangerous weather conditions to reach my destination—far from it. My goal is to find a place to land my airplane. All I need is a reasonably smooth gravel bar that is at least 300 feet in length. I have done this many times and it has always been the rational thing to do. Many times the weather will improve so that the flight can be continued in a few hours. Other times an overnight is required. This was never a problem as I have survival gear, tent, food, stove for cooking, and other essential camping gear.

The important question is: Can a novice really learn to be a reasonably accurate weather interpreter? I tried it and I do think I have mastered it. It has worked marvelously for many years without once leading me into a catastrophic weather problem. My take is that pilots do a majority of their flying within 100 miles of their home base. Learning to interpret the weather in a confined area in which many flights are made over time provides enormous learning opportunities. This is a trial-and-error way of learning. You make your weather prognostications based on current weather conditions. When time passes, remember the predictions that you made and compare it with current conditions. When you continually evaluate weather conditions over time, you will gain more confidence that you can do this. Flying in the same area most of the time, the weather has only so many tricks up its sleeve and over time you'll learn most of them.

Nothing I have done as a pilot has been more satisfying than learning to interpret the weather and becoming my own self-reliant weather predictor. After learning this, I have been able to fly in a stress-free atmosphere with complete confidence in all weather conditions. If I can't get current weather forecasts, I can easily fly without them. Weather reports during flight have a maximum value for obtaining information at your terminal landing site which may be many miles from your current flying location. For current weather information where you are flying—there is nothing more accurate and reliable than the weather right out in front of you airplane. What you are looking at is absolute reality; not a problematic weather forecast. All you have to do is learn to monitor and decipher it. The flying described above is for Visual Flight Rules (VFR) pilots, as I don't have training or instruments to fly Instrument Flight Rules (IFR).

Understanding VFR into IMC Accidents

I agree with many Alaskan pilots that weather is one of the most pervasive and prominent difficulties in flying an airplane. Flying VFR into IMC (Instrument Meteorological Conditions) is a major hazard that happens way too often and causes too many fatalities in general aviation. Weather is a vast and complex subject to understand. Meteorologists gather data to make a forecast that may or may not be accurate. Meteorologists are directing the pilot's decision when to continue flying or when to turn back. Many pilots depend entirely on the weather forecasting and weather reports to guide their flying in marginal weather conditions. There may be a safer way to handle this difficult task.

Pilots in Alaska are very creative and often go beyond the standard training procedures to increase proficiency and to be able to make better and safer decisions in flying. What I learned early on was that weather forecasts and reports are not the do all and end all in flying an airplane. There are numerous issues that need to be addressed and added to your flying program. The difficulty of a pilot with no formal training in weather forecasting fully understanding a complex report is the first hurtle. Next are inaccurate weather reports. These reports are forecasts not facts and are lacking in many incidences. Weather reports in rapidly changing conditions are highly problematic and are often not accurate. Weather forecasts provide a standard forecast of a huge area covered; however, weather is often variable especially in flying long distances. And finally, recent weather reports may not be available. What do you do as a pilot to counter all of these disrupting and stressful events?

You need an alternative plan to address and compensate for the inadequate and often unexpected weather trends. Continue to rely on and use weather forecasts and reports for providing a basic understanding of the current flying conditions. Decision making for determining the outcomes on whether to continue flying or to turn back can be made considerably more accurate by the pilot taking on this responsibility. The actual weather you are flying in is not necessarily what the forecast delivers but what is out in front of your airplane is total reality. Over time, pilots will learn precisely what safe flying weather is and what it is not. There will be no pressure to keep flying into IMC weather when forecasts are showing VFR conditions. It will be comforting to know that the decision is being made by the person who has the most reliable weather information. It is also encouraging that the pilot is in control and can be self-reliant on determining the highly important outcomes. Pilots perform their best when the responsibility is placed on their own shoulders.

Aircraft Accidents

Fatal Aircraft Accidents Down Sharply

General Aviation fatal aircraft accidents down sharply in the past 6 months of 2013 are good news. However, accurate data is not available on the number of hours that pilots have flown during this period. The FAA does have estimates on the number of hours flown, however, they may not be accurate. Lower numbers of hours flown by pilots could be the reason for the lower number of accidents and fatalities. FAA and NTSB have been working diligently for the past decade to lower the aircraft accident and fatality rate with little or no significant results. FAA is asking pilots to increase training. They have developed *Aeronautical Decision-Making Training* to improve pilot skills in risk factors associated with flight. NTSB keeps issuing Safety Alerts to warn pilots of the many hazards of flying in hopes for lowering the aircraft accident rate. They have issued 25 Safety Alerts for GA pilots since 2004. Five Safety Alerts were issued on December 27, 2013. All of this past effort to lower the aircraft accident rate has had little or no positive results. Convincingly, this indicates that training is important but it is not the dominant factor in the high accident and fatality rate. The most important factor is the flying strategies and techniques that pilots use. The aircraft accident rate is a direct reflection of these flying practices. Until the ineffective standardized flying methods are reworked or replaced with enhanced improvements, there will be no substantial and sustainable lowering of the aircraft accident rate for GA pilots. This is the logical conclusion based on NTSB accident reports and other available research data.

Alaska Aviation Safety Foundation Seminar

The Alaska Aviation Safety Foundation presented a seminar at the Alaska Aviation Technology facility at Merrill Field on November 23, 2013. There were large numbers of aircraft accidents in Alaska in 2013 with a huge number of deaths when compared to 2012 (Table 1). The total deaths in 2013 were over 3 times the number of deaths in 2012. The number of aircraft accidents in Alaska attributed to loss-of-control has increased from 12 in 2012 to 15 in 2013 (Table 2). The total deaths from the loss-of-control aircraft increased 10 times from 2 deaths in 2012 to 21 in 2013. What can we do to reduce the high number of loss-of-control accidents resulting in deaths? Pilots at the Seminar said to train, practice emergency procedures, do accurate weight and balance calculations; consider buying an angle-of-attack indicator.

TABLE 1. AIRCRAFT ACCIDENTS AND FATALITIES IN ALASKA

Year	Aircraft Accidents in Alaska	Accidents with Fatalities	Total Deaths
2012	109	9	11
2013	88	15	35

TABLE 2. LOSS-OF-CONTROL ACCIDENTS AND FATALITIES IN ALASKA

Year	Loss-of-Control Accidents	Accidents with Fatalities	Total Deaths
2012	12	2	2
2013	15	9	21

Be aware that the high number of aircraft accidents in Alaska and the large number of deaths from those accidents are closely associated with and are reflected in pilot training. Additional training may help a small amount in limiting accidents but without considerable changes in flying techniques it is not likely that they would make a significant difference in lowering the number of aircraft accidents in Alaska. Most of the pilots in Alaska have been trained by Federal Aviation Administration certificated instructors. That is a given and the pilots are only as capable as the training procedures allow them to be. Don't forget that Alaska has the legendary off-airport pilots and for a good reason. Their flying techniques are unique and were developed to increase pilot proficiency and to greatly reduce the aircraft accident rate. Alaska's elite pilots are celebrated as among the best pilots in the world. Once you learn to land your airplane like these Alaskan pilots your aircraft accident rate will be reduced to near zero because you will be a much improved pilot and your aircraft will be landing with all of the excess kinetic energy removed prior to landing. Pilots in Alaska and elsewhere have a great opportunity to train like these Alaskan pilots and learn to be a much improved and accident-free pilot. How to make the conversion to flying like the Alaskan pilots is hopefully contained in this book. Reaching out and learning to fly like Alaska's elite pilots is a renovation in the art of flying. It will make enormous improvements in your flying career.

Aircraft Accident Rate in Alaska

The Air Safety Foundation of Aircraft Owners and Pilots Association (AOPA) analyzed aviation data and found a rate of 13.59 accidents per 100,000 flight hours in Alaska between 2004 and 2008. The comparative rate for general aviation aircraft in the continental United States was 5.85 accidents per 100,000 flight hours in 2013. Alaska's aircraft accident rate was more than twice as high as the national average during these years. During this time frame, Alaska had 515 small airplane accidents making up 6 percent of the 8,010 accidents nationally in that period. By comparison, Alaska has 2 percent of the U S population. The NTSB records show 252 people lost their lives in aviation accidents in the last 10 years in Alaska. That is an average of 25 lives lost per year during the 2000s. The twelve-month period that ended on September 30, 2011 showed a total of 95 aircraft accidents and 19 fatalities in Alaska.

Why is the aircraft accident rate so high in Alaska? One leading motive for this is that there are many pilots in Alaska with low numbers of flying hours. Low-time pilots do not have sufficient training and the skills needed to avoid accidents. They also will not build up sufficient flying time over the years to be improved pilots. The third encumbrance is that for all practical purposes, they are not proficient pilots as they fly too few hours with large gaps between flights. Many of these pilots buy an airplane for one specific purpose such as hunting or flying to a recreational cabin. They use it solely for that purpose and almost never fly the remainder of the year. It sits parked at the airfield. When these pilots are out participating in their mission, they encounter challenging flying including weather-related conditions that require much greater flying skills than they possess.

Another major cause of high rates of aircraft accidents in Alaska includes the many pilots who own an airplane and decide they want to use it for off-airport operations. The FAA in Alaska reports that 80% of the accidents and fatalities in the State result from off-airport operations. Although we have the elite pilots up here, it is amazing how many pilots do not train the Alaskan pilot way. These pilots occasionally use an instructor that provides little of the skills needed for off-airport operations. When these pilots encounter a challenging situation, by fluke, they are exonerated or more often they crash their airplanes from the lack of required flying skills. Safely landing your airplane in challenging off-airport operations requires for pilots to learn better flying strategies and techniques than what the FAA offers. Selecting the best techniques from both the FAA and Alaskan pilots' aviation worlds will substantially improve pilot proficiency and reduce the aircraft accident rate by a wide margin.

Aircraft operations in Alaska that cause more accidents than any other are uncontrolled off-airport landing approaches that are too high and too fast. GA pilots in Alaska landing on airports and landing strips at accelerated airspeeds substantially above the stall speed of their aircraft are also subject to a high accident rate although not near as high as the pilots landing on off-airport locations. All of these aircraft operations with excessive amounts of kinetic energy in the landing airplane are even more dangerous and the accident rate substantially increases in gusty winds and turbulent flying weather. Additional flying speed in your aircraft that increases the kinetic energy in a moving airplane is the last thing you want when coming in for a landing. One half of the mass of your airplane times the velocity squared produces the kinetic energy in an airplane in motion. Remember that kinetic energy in your airplane increases with the velocity of the airplane's airspeed squared. The equation for Kinetic Energy ($E = \frac{1}{2} MV^2$) shows the enormous boost that an increase in aircraft speed can have in increasing the airplane's kinetic energy (energy in a moving airplane). All of this energy must be dissipated before the airplane can come to a complete stop. You must always keep kinetic energy in your airplane at the lowest level possible. That will save your airplane and often your life.

FAA instructors teach pilots to land an aircraft by maintaining a stabilized approach. The recommended landing speed is the FAA's approved 1.3 Vso with flaps employed plus or minus 6 miles per hour. This is the stall speed of the aircraft plus 30 percent added speed for safety considerations. A Super Cub with a gross weight of 1,700 pounds for this example has a stall speed Vso of 43 mph. Add the 30 percent safety factor and the flying speed is increased to 56 mph. A pilot flying in for a landing of 5 mph over the 1.3 Vso safety factor speed would be coming in for a landing at 61 mph. This is 18 mph over the true stall speed of the aircraft. When calculating the kinetic energy in a moving Super Cub with a speed of 43 mph and comparing that to 1.3 Vso plus 5 mph, (flying speed of 61 mph), notice that the kinetic energy generated has doubled. This doubling of kinetic energy happens because the velocity of the aircraft is squared in the energy equation. Landing at twice the amount of kinetic energy would quadruple the braking power needed to bring the aircraft to a complete stop. This could result in needing 75% more landing roll depending on how rough the landing surface is and how much the airplane bounces and floats as it lands. Alaskan pilots can't afford the longer stopping distance and do not want to energize the airplane with such a huge amount of unnecessary kinetic energy. This makes off-airport landings much longer, difficult, and problematic. In short field landing in Alaska, reducing the airspeed to the extreme minimum when landing is one of the most important procedures to master. Many aircraft accidents are caused by energized aircraft way beyond what is necessary for a safe landing. If you energize your airplane, it has the potential to easily get out of control and do horrendous damage. It is just the opposite when your airplane lands at low airspeeds. When landing at initial stall speed, the airplane does not have sufficient energy to get out of control and crash with a large amount of powerful force. The low landing speeds are a genuine blessing in disguise. They are one of the elite Alaskan pilot's most important *Cardinal Rule*.

Pilots who come in too high usually land a long ways down the landing area. This causes alarm and often go-arounds are attempted to abort the long landing because the remaining distance is too short to get the airplane stopped before running into rough areas. Pilots attempt way too many go-arounds in Alaska, many of which do not succeed. In various situations, go-arounds are not possible and no attempts should be made to do them. It appears that this problem is exacerbated by instructors training pilots to make a go-around anytime they don't like what they are experiencing in a landing. It is taught as a panacea that solves all landing problems. It is amazing how many retired ATPs that have wrecked their Super Cubs in the past ten years on remote landing strips in Alaska by attempting go-arounds. These accidents are all listed in the NTSB file.

Hazardous weather conditions in VFR flying are related to substantial numbers of aircraft accidents in Alaska. The conditions causing these problems are often low clouds and fog, powerful winds creating turbulence and wind shear, and intense rain and snowstorms. Inaccurate and missing weather reports can exacerbate the problem; however, it is the decision of the pilot that determines the outcome. The remote places in Alaska far from any civilization can also intensify the problem. In the end, there are too many pilots with inadequate experience flying difficult weather conditions and too many pilots making poor decisions for safe flying. This results in many accidents that are weather related.

Crosswind landings are another frequent cause of aircraft accidents in Alaska. It is amazing how many crosswind landing accidents happen on airports such at Merrill Field with towers and controllers. Accidents happen at crosswinds below 10 mph. They happen for two reasons. The airplane is coming in for a landing at excessive speed (loaded with kinetic energy) and the pilot is poorly trained for crosswind operations. Crosswind landings need to be practiced over and over again early in your flying career to prevent these easily avoidable crosswind accidents.

Carburetor icing causes aircraft accidents in Alaska, especially in summer on a cool day when there is high humidity in foggy weather. Pilots must know their airplanes; not all airplanes have problems with carb icing. My Piper Cub with the 0-200 Continental engine and the Arctic Tern with the 0-320 Lycoming engine do not have carb icing problems. I have detected no carb icing problems in the Piper Cub in 15 years of flying and perhaps only one time in 15 years in the Arctic Tern. Therefore, I do not pull carburetor heat on landings during the summer months. Being practical, I do only what is necessary. Pulling carb heat in winter when the temperature is below zero degrees Fahrenheit helps to improve fuel vaporization. Therefore, carb heat is recommended under these conditions when coming in for a landing. Because fuel vaporization is hampered in low temperatures, it is also highly recommended not to come in for a landing on final approach with a closed throttle. Keep the throttle opened as appropriate until touchdown. Engines do stop running due to vaporization problems in cold winter weather.

If you are only instructor trained about carb icing, you'll not have sufficient knowledge to properly understand and handle carb icing problems. I had the advantage of flying the Beechcraft C23 Sundowner. This was a real learning experience concerning carb icing because this aircraft flying on a cool and high-humidity day in summer would almost always succumb to carb icing somewhere along the way. With so many carb icing occurrences, I learned how to immediately recognize the problem and how to promptly correct it. Without this training, I would not have decided to refrain from pulling carb heat on landing for my two privately owned aircraft.

Other problems causing aircraft accidents in Alaska are fuel starvation, oil pressure problems, ignition problems, flight control problems, and others. Much of the emergency knowledge learned in many cases is not extremely helpful in these situations. The most important consideration is that you are here with this problem. You and your tremendous innovative mind will have to take charge and figure out what the problem is. You will also have to figure out how to counter the problem and continue to fly or if absolutely necessary to land the aircraft. Attempting to figure out the problem often will require trial-and-error techniques. This is no different from what Alaska's elite pilots go through on an extended self-training program. My experience reveals the amazing ability that the working mind has that can be of great help in solving these complex problems and also in relieving pilot stress.

The last incident that causes way too many aircraft accidents in Alaska is the lack of pilot training in extreme flying conditions. It is amazing the number of pilots that say I don't fly in extreme weather conditions; I don't fly in low clouds and fog, I don't fly in excessive wind conditions. This too often means that these pilots are avoiding training in all of these undesirable flying conditions. If any of these pilots that claim they don't fly in difficult flying conditions are caught unexpectedly in these conditions—they have no knowledge or understanding what to do. It is no surprise that these pilots make many simple and elementary mistakes that result in aircraft accidents when they are caught unexpectedly in extreme flying conditions. A small amount of knowledge and training could make a substantial difference to these pilots in reducing the aircraft accident rate to acceptable levels. It is incomprehensible to understand why pilots have this viewpoint. Maybe it is because they can't bear to face the *fear of the unknown*. I can say with experience that I never resented facing the unknown on my own terms. This way you can get familiar with the experience and be better prepared when it reoccurs unexpectedly.

Avoiding aircraft accidents is a very important consideration in making a decision to become a pilot. Individuals who want to be a pilot have to completely understand that being a reliable aviator takes a considerable amount of time and preparedness in fully engaging yourself in the undertaking. There are no short cuts in the flying and training time necessary in becoming a proficient and safe pilot. All the odds are against you as a pilot if you do not fly a sufficient number of hours every week, every month, every year, and so on. Sooner or later, a low time pilot that has large flying gaps in which the airplane is not flown will likely wind up in an accident that will wreck the airplane and possibly cause injury or death to the pilot and others. This is a major consideration that many pass over lightly and don't give proper attention. If you want to be a successful pilot, it is essential that you fly as often as possible and that you work diligently at learning each and every time you go flying. The lesson to learn is that trustworthy pilots must have consistent and ample flying and training time so that they can evolve into a more improved pilot as time goes forward. If you don't have the time to fly on a consistent basis or think that flying and training time is not that important, my recommendation is that you do not become a pilot—the risk level for accidents is too high. Airplane engines that are not flown on a regular basis are also subject to being damaged—corrosion.

This often leads to overhauling the engine hundreds of hours sooner than the estimated time before overhaul.

Pilot Error

A major effort in General Aviation is the continuation of innovation and training to reduce the high and unacceptable aircraft accident rate. Despite this tremendous effort, one factor remains the same—that is Pilot Error. Pilot Error is a major cause and contributing factor to aircraft accidents. It has been described as an action or decision made by the pilot that was the cause or a major contributing factor that led to the accident. It is estimated that 80% of all GA aircraft accidents are caused by pilot error (Pilot's Handbook of Aeronautical Knowledge by the Federal Aviation Administration; 2014). A study of fatal and serious accidents in Alaska by FAA during the years 2004 to 2009 say pilot error contributes to 90% of all aircraft accidents. The vast majority of these accidents occur during takeoff and landing operations. Chapter 17 in the Pilot's Handbook was written to emphasize this huge problem and to find ways to improve pilot's skills in risk factors associated with flight. The importance of good pilot judgment and decision-making is emphasized as critical to safe operation of aircraft and accident avoidance. Instructors currently are using FAA's training for improving the decision-making skills of pilots to reduce the aircraft accident rate.

Although this ongoing effort to reduce the aircraft accident rate by including aeronautical decision-making skills into the training has helped, the accident rate has not been lowered to an acceptable level. Pilot Error continues at a constant rate and is still way too high. Everyone agrees with this assessment. With all of the effort to reduce the accident rate—it is not being substantially reduced to a lower and more acceptable level. Further progression in reducing the aircraft accident rate to acceptable levels may need new strategies for accomplishing an acceptable goal.

FAA's data shows that over 50% of the GA aircraft accidents are occurring during takeoff and landing operations. Of all of these accidents, landing accidents are much more prevalent than takeoffs. That results in an enormous number of accidents that are consistent on an annual basis. What is the leading cause of this high accident rate? It is very likely that the prevailing cause of the high accident rate is the lack of attention to and the mismanagement of kinetic energy in the landing aircraft. Instructors teach all pilots the FAA approved 1.3 Vso plus or minus 6 miles per hour as the recommended landing speed for an airplane. That is coming in for a landing at 30% above the stall speed of the aircraft. In addition, extra speed is required when landing in gusty winds (add ½ the gust speed). This elevated speed in a landing aircraft greatly increases the kinetic energy in a moving airplane. The increase in airspeed is substantial and it causes a much longer ground roll requiring much heavier braking for the airplane to come to a complete stop. This could take a substantial longer runway length for landing. This amount of excess kinetic energy is lethal for causing aircraft accidents especially on windy days with strong wind gusts. It is difficult landing an airplane on a windy day into the wind and even more difficult landing in a crosswind. When the pilot adds excessive kinetic energy in the airplane prior to making these landings—it becomes very problematic in making consistent safe landings. It is just a matter of time when the airplane with all of that excess kinetic energy will quickly get out of control and the pilot will not be able to bring it back under control because the energy in the airplane and the wind is more powerful than the aircraft flight controls. Crashing an airplane that is out of control with all of that excess kinetic energy will be a very dangerous situation. It will often result in miserable pilot and passenger injuries and casualties.

FAA's reason for the 1.3 Vso Rule is to prevent stalling the aircraft when landing. The aircraft's airspeed indicator is not accurate in low speeds and at high angles of attack which is routine in landings. To counteract this problem FAA has developed the 1.3 Vso Rule. It is accurate to state that the extra speed in landing aircraft substantially lowers the numbers of aircraft stalls that lead to accidents when pilots adhere to this 1.3 Vso Rule. However, with no consideration for kinetic energy management—the 1.3 Vso Rule causes far more landing accidents on windy days than would occur from intentionally learning to stall your aircraft on landings. Stall landings are not a problem for a well-trained pilot that has learned and trained how to make safe stall landings. All of the increased training to reduce the aircraft accident rate will not solve the problem of highly energized aircraft coming in for a landing. The aircraft accident rate will always remain too high as long as the 1.3 Vso Rule is required. The high accident rate is a direct reflection of the training technique.

There must be a better way of landing so that airplanes getting out of control and crashing can be significantly reduced to an acceptable level. Existing strategies that can be used to substantially reduce the rate of aircraft accidents already exists. The extraordinary pilots in Alaska flying routine off-airport operations have solved this high kinetic energy landing problem a long time ago with their own true and tried techniques. *Precision Landings* is their modus operandi for making consistent and safe landings. This requires two landing techniques happening simultaneously—the main wheels touching down on every landing in a selected 20 foot by 60 foot symbolic box and the wheels touching down in the box at initial stall speed. With both of these operations happening simultaneously when landing, the airplane is safely contained for every single landing event. The airplane cannot get out of control with this low energy landing operation. In addition, the airplane will not use up too much of a short landing surface and run off the other end of the landing area and crash in rough terrain. This precision landing technique is accident proofing your landings by rigidly controlling your airplane on every landing. To make adequate stall landings pilots must learn to fly by the *seat of your pants*.

The elite pilots of Alaska all use *Precision Landings* as one of their most important *Cardinal Rules*. It is simply amazing how they can safely land their aircraft in the most difficult and challenging environments such as short and rough landing areas, horizontal landings on steep sloping beaches, vertical landings on steep sloping mountainous areas, curving and dogleg landing areas, and many others. These astonishing pilots make hundreds of difficult landings in summer and winter without ever wrecking their airplanes. GA pilots that learn to make *Precision Landings* could also benefit like the Alaskan pilots. The GA pilots would reduce landing accidents from highly energized airplanes by a substantial margin by making *Precision Landings*. GA accident reduction using *Precision Landings* would be an enormous improvement over the current 1.3 Vso Rule. It would make an overwhelming and substantial reduction in the GA aircraft accident rate.

Never Stall your Airplane

Unintentionally stalling your airplane is one event that you never want to happen. Stalling an airplane at low elevation often results in stall/spin accidents—the airplane falls out of the sky and crashes on the ground. The airplane's increased energy load from a combination of kinetic energy of an airplane in motion along with the downward pulling force of gravity causes dreadful crashes that often result in serious injury and fatalities. Pilots must have the necessary strategies to prevent unintentional stalls.

What you are attempting to avoid is exceeding the airplane's *critical angle of attack* which is what causes aerodynamic stalls. At the *critical angle of attack*, airflow separation from the top of the wing takes place and causes the stall—the wing can no longer provide adequate lift to support the airplane in flight. It is important to always be aware of situations that are subject to stalls—in takeoffs and landings and in turns. This is where the majority of stalls happen. *Situational Awareness* and applying the proper flying techniques are needed to ensure your angle of attack is never unintentionally exceeded.

General Aviation pilots are primarily trained by FAA certificated instructors. Typical training for stalls is to take an airplane to 1,500 feet or higher altitudes above the ground and to practice various stalls and their recovery. After pilots have attained the PPL, the stall training is often practiced once or twice a year with instructors or in some situations only once in a 2 year period when a biennial flight review is being conducted. This type of training is not sufficient for providing the knowledge and proficiency needed to reduce the stall accident rate to acceptable levels. The large number of seriously injured individuals and the large number of fatalities caused by stall/spin accidents validate the claim that the knowledge and training is lacking.

Charts are available that show stall speeds at different angles of blank that are close to the airplane's critical stall attitude. However, these flying speeds in the chart are not very reliable because airspeed indicators are not accurate at slow flight that is likely in turns. In addition, the airspeeds are not accurate due to variations in wind speed and direction and the gross weight of the airplane that changes with cargo loads. The airplane's weight is also constantly changing with the fuel load. A more accurate way to determine when your airplane is close to the critical stall attitude is to equipped your airplane with an *Angle of Attack (AOA) Indicator*. The *AOA Indicator* determines your airplane's attitude with reference to the critical stall attitude. It shows you the margin between your airplane's attitudes with the stall attitude. To avoid stalling your airplane, keep the *AOA Indicator* in the green. When the indicator shows red, your aircraft has reached the critical stall attitude and will go into a stall. Pilots report that the *AOA Indicator* is reliable; however, knowledgeable aviators say that the indicator may give faulty indications in uncoordinated flight. Be that as it may, the biggest problem is that very few GA airplanes are equipped with *AOA Indicators*. One reason for a lack of *AOA Indicators* in GA airplanes is because cost for an Alpha Systems *AOA indicator* is $1,995. In addition to purchasing the instrument, it will take a certified A&P mechanic 4 to 12 hours to install it in your airplane. After installing the *AOA Indicator*, it must be calibrated by flying the airplane and adjusting the *AOA Indicator* for accuracy. All of this is too much for many GA pilots. Even so, there is still another way besides the ineffective conventional instructor way and the high cost of installing an *AOA Indicator* that pilots can use to avoid unintentional stalls. This way only requires learning a new technique. Pilots will have to go out and perform the necessary self-training for developing the required proficiency. By taking on this challenge, pilots will be well-equipped to prevent unintentional stalls.

The strategy for improving stall knowledge and safety is learning to make *Precision Landings*. This is one of the most important *Cardinal Rules* developed by Alaska's elite pilots for landing airplanes off-airport in natural terrain. It requires two landing techniques happening simultaneously—the main wheels touching down on every landing in a selected 20 foot by 60 foot symbolic box and the wheels touching down at initial stall speed. The second procedure of making landings at initial stall speed is the one that can significantly increase a pilot's knowledge of aircraft stalls. When you perform every landing with the wheels touching down at initial stall speed, you become intimately involved and exceedingly knowledgeable about every aspect of stalls. You are no longer terrified of stalls since they are an everyday occurrence. Your understanding and familiarity with them are huge. Your situational awareness of stalls is extensive. All of these learned characteristics of stalls will provide a comprehensive understanding that will be exceptionally helpful in preventing your airplane from unintention-ally stalling. This is what is needed to ensure you will never unintentionally stall your airplane.

Other details to improve the odds against unintentional stalls are by consistently flying benign (gentle) maneuvers in conditions that are subject to stalls. This is smart strategy especially at low altitude near the ground. Always be aware of degrading conditions that increase the risk of stalls such as heavily-loaded aircraft, sudden or erratic flying maneuvers, steep bank turns, uncoordinated turns (skids), slow flight, and flying in gusty wind conditions. Maneuvers under these conditions have to be flown with utmost caution. Fly with the necessary precision in making smoother and less-steep turns, avoid turns with nose-high attitudes, lowering the nose after takeoffs to quickly build airspeed that is needed for sustained flight after leaving ground effect and using the entire runway before liftoff when carrying heavy loads on short runways. Using most of the length of the runway will provide a faster airspeed when becoming airborne. This extra airspeed is needed as the airplane rises out of ground effect where the wings are generating less lift and producing greater induced drag.

Myths about Stall Landings

Alaska's elite pilots have a multitude of techniques that go far beyond traditional FAA instructor training to make it possible for landing airplanes off-airport in difficult and challenging environments. These techniques were developed through necessity because traditional training is not adequate for the tasks at hand. There would be no need for small taildragger aircraft in Alaska if pilots had only traditional training. Pilots would be confined to airports and developed airstrips in the backcountry. There would be no Alaskan off-airport pilots landing airplanes in natural terrain—this would not exist.

One of the most important off-airport training techniques is making *Precision Landings* that involve targeting a spot for the wheels to touch down and landing at initial stall speed. Both of these techniques have to be practiced and have to come together near perfection for the pilot to be capable of performing their mission. Initial stall landings is the focus here and it is the more controversial of the two techniques. The modus operandi for certified instructors that teach FAA training policy for landing is the 1.3 Vso plus or minus 5 knots, with wind gust factor applied. This means your airplane must come in for a landing at a speed of 30% above stall speed with a plus or minus factor selected by the pilot. In addition, if gusty wind conditions prevail; the pilot must increase the aircraft's speed to accommodate the degrading wind factor. FAA's doctrine strongly indicates that landing an airplane close to its stall speed should not be attempted—it is forbidden, dangerous, and can be highly lethal. Airplanes are always to be landed at speeds well above the aircraft's stall speed for safety reasons.

The FAA's 1.3 Vso plus or minus 5 knots and adjusting the aircraft speed upward in gusty wind conditions presents a formidable barrier for Alaskan pilots landing aircraft in challenging natural terrain. FAA's instructions for landing speeds will, in all practical purposes, double the kinetic energy in your airplane when compared to the aircraft's energy at stall speed. Doubling the kinetic energy in the airplane will quadruple the amount of braking power for bringing the aircraft to a complete stop. This may require 75% longer landing distance than landing at stall speed. This does not present practical landing conditions for an airplane in natural terrain. Nevertheless, Alaska's elite pilots are relentless and if they are going to be capable of making challenging landings they will have to transform this difficult problem. These refined techniques come about by trial and error and this imposition is no different from any other. Pilots tried slower aircraft speeds than was recommended by FAA and found out the landings worked well. As time progressed the pilots explored the task of reducing aircraft landing speeds as low as possible. They finally progressed to the ultimate speed—landing an airplane at initial stall speed (taking out all of the excess kinetic energy from the airplane prior to touching the wheels down). What they found was a revolutionary change in making aircraft landings. This is one of the most important techniques that make off-airport landings practical. These landings at initial stall speed were easy to learn and to perform and the big shock was that they were safe—not likely to end up in an accident.

General Aviation pilots are still apprehensive about making stall landings. A common perception among them is that stall landings are dangerous and will ultimately cause aircraft accidents. I can't remember how many times I have heard—how do you keep from wrecking your airplane when a wind shear or a gust of wind comes up when you are landing? This is an annoying question to answer because of the enormous knowledge gap that exists between the two pilots. Where do you start? How many years of performing stall landings does it take to validate the effectiveness and safety of this technique? (Evidently, years of performing this technique are never good enough for others to accept it.) Alaskan pilots are worn out on this subject and they don't aspire to answer this question. They would rather just walk away and end the long discussion about one of the most important off-airport techniques.

To answer the persistent and misunderstood question about how to handle difficult wind conditions when coming in for a landing at initial stall speed—you have to have situational awareness and you have to act quickly when a changing or erratic wind event happens. Landing at initial stall speed or any other speed is all the same—you must be alert to what is happening and you must act within 1 second to correct a problem. Usually what is needed in wind trepidations is to briskly lower the airplane's nose by pushing the stick forward and applying full throttle. This will increase air flow over the wings to stabilize the aircraft and to counteract the destabilizing wind event. It will also ensure your airplane does not stall and fall out of the sky like a rock. If you make these changes in the appropriate time frame, you will not have problems landing your airplane in fluctuating and erratic wind conditions. This will not happen.

One other misconception that needs to be discussed is do you need an increase in aircraft speed when landing in hard gusty winds that are blowing 20 to 45 miles per hour? FAA's landing instructions recommends a wind gust factor be added (half the gust speed) when landing in windy conditions. What I have learned by trial and error many years ago is that no matter what the gusty wind speed is; I can always use full flaps and can always land (touch my wheels down) at initial stall speed. The one requirement for safe landings is that you must be alert and you must act within 1 second to counteract disruptive winds when they are detected. As a Pilot in Command, with over 30 years' experience landing at initial stall speed in all kinds of windy conditions—even landing one time in a microburst with a strong downdraft and a wind shear—not once have I experienced a major problem that could not be safely brought under control. With no major problems and no accidents in all of those years—this must be informing you that landing at initial stall speed is not a problem. Other Alaskan pilots will confirm similar observations in their experiences.

Alaska's elite pilots are flying their airplane by the *seat of your pants* and not by speed indicators that are inaccurate at low airspeeds. Varying conditions such as wind speed and direction, turbulence, and other factors make it difficult to understand safe landing airspeeds when flying by instruments. This is why FAA has installed the 1.3 Vso when landing an airplane. A faster approach and landing speed will counteract the imprecise airspeed and other factors so that landing will not result in stalling your airplane. This is standardizing your landing speeds which provide much higher speeds than by using precise landings. It may prevent stalling the airplane, however; it creates enormous problems with energizing your airplane that causes many accidents when landing in gusty wind and crosswind conditions. Alaska's off-airport pilots cannot land their airplanes with double the kinetic energy with the 1.3 Vso rule. They could not get their airplanes stopped on a short gravel bar and they would encounter too many wrecks landing in windy conditions. They don't have to because flying by the *seat of your pants* provides highly accurate airplane performance indicators that make it easy to land your airplane safely at initial stall speed. All variable factors such as wind, turbulence and others are incorporated into the aircraft. What you see, feel, and hear from your airplane is without a doubt extremely accurate. There will not be problems arising from using this flying technique for landing your aircraft. Alaskan pilots have proven the accuracy and the value of this technique over every landing for decades.

General Aviation pilots that read this message on stall landings will understand that this flying technique is in no way a highly problematic event as many in the group believe. This technique needs to be accepted and respected for what it is. It has been proven with the validation of hundreds of pilots using it. It will certainly continue to be used in the future because there is no other alternative. General Aviation pilots will better understand it by practicing it rather than discussing a technique that they know nothing about. Once they try it, they are likely to adopt it and add it to their flying program. It will make them an improved pilot and they will have a much more practical and safer landing technique.

Reduction in the Excessive GA Accident Rate

The FAA and the NTSB in frustration acknowledge the excessive aircraft accident rate for GA pilots. Their records show that 80% of aircraft accidents are caused by pilot error. Many of the accidents are repeat accidents (the same kind of accident) that happen over and over again. They are continually reminding pilots that this is a big problem and that the high accident rate is not acceptable. These two agencies spend an enormous amount of time and effort to reduce the high accident rate to an acceptable level especially during the past 10 years. They hold a large number of safety seminars and they issue many pilot safety advisories and alerts on a yearly basis. Nevertheless, there have been little or no improvements over all those years in their attempt to reduce the aircraft accident rate. Their assessment of this high accident rate is that it is due to lack of pilot training and for pilots not paying attention to FAA and NTSB advisories and safety alerts.

Most GA pilots are trained by FAA certificated instructors. Advanced training after receiving the Private Pilot License (PPL) to improve their flying skills is also provided by instructors. The training and the flying strategies including techniques that pilots use are involved in and are directly linked to the aircraft accident rate. Not been able to see any changes in the large number of aircraft accidents over many years of attempting to lower the aircraft accident rate strongly indicates that the accident rate is consistent with the contemporary training style and the flying strategies taught by FAA instructors. What FAA offers through certificated instructors is providing the large numbers of aircraft accidents. If you want significant changes to lower the aircraft accident rate to acceptable levels, you will have to offer changes to training style and to the flying strategies and techniques that are currently being used.

The elite Alaskan pilots offer the training style and flying strategies that are necessary for changes in lowering the aircraft accident rate to acceptable numbers. The reason for this is due to the training style and the selection of the best strategies and techniques that come from both aviation spheres—both the FAA's aviation world and the elite Alaskan pilot's world. Self-training and integrating the best strategies and techniques from both aviation worlds make an enormous difference in pilot proficiency and a significant reduction in aircraft accidents from a greatly improved pilot. This dramatic change in lowering the aircraft accident rate for all GA pilots is available by training like the elite Alaskan pilots.

Lower GA Aircraft Accident Rate

There is no shortage of aviation topics on improving GA safety and lowering the high aircraft accident rate. Federal Aviation Administrator Michael Huerta asserted FAA's and NTSB's growing frustration over the fact that the GA fatal accident rate has stayed the same over the past 5 years despite efforts to improve safety (*FAA's Plea to Pilots: Fly Safe this Summer, Flying Magazine, published May 29, 2013*). So far this year (January 1, 2013 to May 31, 2013), 149 fatal accidents have claimed the lives of 262 people. Huerta is asking pilots to be ready to fly; understand your strengths and limitations and make a personal checklist to follow. Huerta says this commitment will reduce fatal aircraft accidents. In December 2013 the NTBS added five new subjects to its growing list of Safety Alerts for GA pilots (*More Alerts for GA Pilots, Peter Katz, Plane&Pilot; May 2014*). In the last 10 years, NTBS has issued 25 Safety Alerts. Two scheduled discussions at The Great Alaska Aviation Gathering on May 3, 2014 are about improving aviation safety. One is NTSB efforts to improve GA safety by Dr. Earl F. Weener and the other is what to do about stall-spin accidents in Alaska by Dr. Dave Swartz.

The GA accident rate is way too high and all aviation groups recognize this problem. FAA is constantly holding aviation safety seminars to discuss the problem and NTSB keeps issuing Safety Alerts to warn pilots to pay attention to the elevated accident rate and to use their skills to reduce them. All of these efforts have not had a significant effect on reducing aircraft accidents to an acceptable level. Most of the training for GA pilots is from FAA certificated instructors. The standardized training program developed by the FAA is reflected in the aircraft accident rate. The high accident rate shows that the techniques and training strategy are not sufficient to reduce aircraft accident rates to a lower and more acceptable level. Major changes in the current flying techniques and training strategy are the only way to substantially lower the accident rate for GA pilots. There needs to be innovation to find new ways to change the current training program. This is what is needed to give the desired results.

There are ways to change the standard FAA approved training procedures and flying strategy that could provide superior results. The changes would increase pilot proficiency and substantially reduce the aircraft accident rate to acceptable levels. There are pilots that have already accomplished this mission. Why not use these pilots' outstanding results as a template for GA pilots. What I am referring to are Alaska's best trained pilots that have been called extraordinary, unorthodox, self-trained, and self-reliant pilots. They have a reputation of being some of the best pilots in the world. They were initially trained like all other GA pilots with FAA instructors. However, after receiving their PPL, they found out how Alaska's best pilots have been able to reach such amazing heights. By making the proper changes, the pilots have developed into safer and more reliable pilots that have substantially reduced their aircraft accident rate by a wide margin. They have developed into highly capable pilots far beyond the traditional GA pilots that were trained by FAA instructors.

The standard FAA flying techniques and strategy was not sufficient to allow these Alaskan pilots to land their airplanes off-airport in some of the most challenging short field operations in natural terrain in the world. It takes extraordinary proficiency and *edge-of-performance* flying skills to get the task accomplished. Alaska's top pilots are very creative and have changed or refined the techniques that were lacking to improve them to the highest and safest levels for aircraft operations. The modus operandi for learning these pilot techniques is by *self-training* in your own airplane. Pilots need to talk to Alaska's best pilots, read as much as possible, and then they have to go out in their airplane and learn on their own. The *self-training* is an enormous boost in becoming an extraordinary pilot. These Alaskan pilots have the highest proficiency and safety among all pilots flying fixed-wing aircraft.

FAA and GA pilots are dubious about *self-training*—that it is dangerous and pilots are likely to wreck their airplanes. There is nothing farther from the truth. Once you learn to take command and go out and get the job done, you will find out that it is easy to learn and as safe as or even safer than training with an instructor. Another misconception is that learning on your own is very difficult and many pilots will not be able to accomplish this mission. Initially it is difficult because for the first time you as a pilot are in charge of getting the entire job accomplished. It does take a while to get started and learn how to manage and learn on your own. However, after you go through the initial stages you will find that it is not difficult to add new techniques because you already have the basic foundation for learning. This is the most potent way anyone can learn any subject. You will be the best pilot by training this way. After a few successful missions accomplished, pilots will understand the importance and the huge gains by training on your own. It will become stress-free and exciting training that is the best way possible for any pilot to learn to improve their flying skills.

The FAA and GA pilots will have enormous gains to pick up by entering the Alaskan pilot's world and getting educated on their unique training and flying strategy. The Alaskan pilot techniques can be adopted and presented to GA pilots for learning and training to be improved pilots. Nevertheless, it will take more than biased government employees or inflexible GA pilots to look into the Alaskan pilot's world. It will require a team of authentic aviation scholars that are looking for the facts. The Alaskan pilots have already proven the value of their training techniques and strategy over many years of flying in Alaska. It is a foregone conclusion that academic scholars will be able to eliminate the illusions and make factual statements about how the highly beneficial Alaskan pilot techniques can be programmed into GA pilot training. This will be a transformative change in pilot development that will far exceed the typical GA pilot's skill level. This is necessary and more GA pilots should be requesting FAA to establish an academic committee or board to probe into the Alaskan pilot strategy and flying techniques. GA pilots could add the training strategy and techniques to their program after receiving the PPL. This could make a huge difference in the proficiency of GA pilots and it would reduce the aircraft accident rate to acceptable levels that would be substantially lower than the currently high rates encountered with FAA trained instructors. The final goal of the Advanced Aviation Academic Board would be to write a training manual with the Alaskan pilot techniques and strategy for GA pilots to follow after receiving the PPL.

An advanced training manual written for GA pilots after receiving their PPL would be a substantial gain for aviators in the Unites States and it would certainly spread around the entire world. GA pilot's flying skills will be taken to a higher level. The end result would be a worldwide accomplishment that would substantially advance pilot proficiency and flying safety. Nothing else could come close to achieving what this has to offer. There is no reason why this recommendation should not go forward. GA pilot's education on this subject will go a long way in convincing FAA that this needs to be accomplished. Implementing what is written here is giving the Aviation World a highly desirable *Gift* that is not likely to come again for many years in the future. To all GA pilots, aviation agencies including training schools and others—take advantage of this incredible *Gift*.

Cardinal Rules for Best Pilot

The Cardinal Rules for becoming the best pilot have evolved over the years by Alaska's elite pilots flying and training in Alaska. The rules have been fully demonstrated, tested, and proven to be highly effective by untold numbers of pilots. The techniques employed for following the rules are not difficult to learn and implement. The self-training required to follow these rules is not aircraft accident prone—it is certainly as safe as or even safer than the instructor-trained way. Following the Cardinal Rules will significantly enhance your flying skills and reduce your aircraft accident rate by a wide margin. Below are the Cardinal Rules that will make you the best self-reliant pilot you can be.

Cardinal Rule Number 1. Becoming a Scholarly Pilot
Use an academic approach by learning both FAA and Alaska's elite pilot's aviation worlds. Select the best flying strategies and techniques from the two aviation spheres and incorporate them into your flying program. There is no advanced training available today that will even come close to topping this effort for becoming the best pilot you can be.

Cardinal Rule Number 2. Mastering the Art of Flying
This is a creative skill that is learned by the pilot. Pilots must focus on this way of flying on every flight. It will take a substantial amount of flying time to learn how to incorporate this type of flying into your everyday routine. It is the simplest way to fly an airplane that will provide the safest and most accurate results.

Cardinal Rule Number 3. Flying on a Regular Basis
This is important in maintaining proficiency and at the same time to increase your total number of flying hours to continue your progression as an improving and competent pilot. If you cannot fly on a regular basis; it is important to consider whether it is sensible to continue being a pilot

and flying airplanes. There are many other endeavors in life that will not end in a tragic aircraft accident. It comes down to how much risk you want to take.

Cardinal Rule Number 4. Self-Training

Set-up your training program for your own airplane. Schedule the training necessary to integrate the revised and newly selected strategies and techniques into your flying program. The training is a self-taught skill conducted by the pilot. An open-minded pilot with innovative and creative skills is essential and is the hallmark for being able to carry out this mission. Your goal is to train yourself in your airplane to become your own self-reliant pilot.

Cardinal Rule Number 5. Flying by the Seat of Your Pants

As a pilot, you must have the feel for flying your airplane. This is a creative self-learned skill and art. This will allow pilots to fly airplanes and make safe takeoff and landing operations with the utmost precision. It is simple—you will not need a manual or have to memorize numbers to fly by the *seat of your pants*. Seeing, feeling, and hearing what your airplane is telling you are easy to comprehend. All variables such as wind speed and direction has already been incorporated into your airplane. What you see, feel, and hear is absolutely accurate and it provides the most useful information while flying your airplane. Flying by the *seat of your pants* is absolutely necessary in making *Precision Landings*—landing at initial stall speed. *Precision Landings* and flying by the *seat of your pants* are the elite Alaskan pilot's most important Cardinal Rules.

Cardinal Rule Number 6. Learning Precision Landings

This landing technique is one of the most important assets for pilots landing in off-airport operations in Alaska. Likewise, it is also of paramount importance as a high-quality and very safe landing technique for GA pilots landing at airports and on fixed airstrips. *Precision Landings* are essential for all landing aircraft and every landing must be made with the utmost precision for the highest safety considerations. It must be on target and at the same time the wheels must touch down at initial stall speed. It is not acceptable to land your aircraft in a highly energized condition—this causes too many aircraft accidents. Always select a landing target where the wheels need to touch down. Place the main wheels every time in a

20 foot by 60 foot symbolic rectangular box. The long axis of the box is perpendicular to the landing direction of the aircraft. This is the *Cardinal Rule* that has helped the most in limiting the author to zero accidents in 35 years of landing taildraggers in Alaska's wild backcountry. All pilots will be able to substantially reduce their landing accident rate to near zero by applying this *Cardinal Rule*. As a fledgling pilot, you may want to review this *Cardinal Rule* a second time—it is almost too good to be true. You can now start a new flying career without the fear of wrecking your airplane on landing operations. It will rarely if ever happen if you apply this *Cardinal Rule*. *Precision Landing* operations offers pilots a huge double bonus. First you can abandon FAA's highly accident-prone 1.3 Vso landing speed by opting to land your airplane at initial stall speed—removing all excess kinetic energy from the airplane prior to touching the wheels down. The second bonus in using *Precision Landings* is that you are becoming exceedingly familiar with making landings at stall speed. This will provide all the training necessary to ensure you will never unintentionally stall your airplane. By reducing your aircraft accident rate on landings to near zero and by preventing stall/spin accidents—pilots have now done away with the ineffective techniques that have caused the two highest accident rates and fatalities for FAA instructor trained GA pilots.

Cardinal Rule Number 7. Focusing on Situational Awareness

Always be attentive when flying your airplane. Notice what is going on around you at all times and think how changes will affect your flying capabilities. Make the changes that are necessary in a timely and orderly manner. Being situational aware will help you avoid many aircraft accidents. The way it works is that you first have to be aware and then you can act as appropriate to keep your flying safe. You cannot improve your condition without first being aware.

Cardinal Rule Number 8. Mastering the Weather

Every pilot needs to understand the weather so that it does not become a major distracting and intimidating force. My way is to be your own weather predictor as you fly your airplane. Other aviators will choose other ways to work through this highly difficult task. All pilots must have a workable plan that is useful and stress-free for flying in marginal and difficult weather conditions.

Cardinal Rule Number 9. Cross and Gusty Wind Landings

Sufficient training is needed to master crosswind landings. Practice until you are knowledgeable and confident that you can perform acceptable crosswind landings. Don't forget when flying on windy days, by being creative, you can often find a way to land into the wind and avoid making difficult crosswind landings. Gusty winds are involved in and contribute to a large number of aircraft landing accidents in Alaska. Prevent these accidents by learning to make precision landings. These landings will reduce landing accidents by a wide margin and also reduce the ground roll and stopping distance.

Cardinal Rule Number 10. Evaluating Off-Airport Landing Areas

Pilots must practice this airborne examination until they become highly proficient at selecting suitable landing areas from the airplane's cockpit. This examination starts out with routine measurements but soon becomes a learned art with no numbers required for accurate results. This will provide reassurance for a safe landing experience in off-airport operations.

Cardinal Rule Number 11. Smart Braking for Off-Airport Landings

Many aircraft accidents in Alaska are caused by improper braking when landing in off-airport operations. An accident that happens over and over in Alaska is an airplane coming in for landing highly energized because the airspeed is way above stall speed. When the wheels touch down, the distressed pilot stomps hard on the brakes to slow down the runaway aircraft. This often results in the wheels of the airplane digging into soft terrain and flipping the airplane over upside down. When you learn how to make precision landings and touch down at initial stall speed, you will not need heavy braking to stop your airplane. Any heavy braking needed should always be applied gradually. Never stomp on the brakes. The first sign of wheels digging in or the tail coming up requires the pilot to immediately release the brakes and reset them at a lower level. The throttle may also need to be applied under these conditions.

Cardinal Rule Number 12. Limiting the Number of Go Arounds

NTSB reports during the past 10 years clearly show that *go arounds* are causing unacceptable numbers of aircraft accidents in Alaska. The concept of a *go around* is important as it provides an alternative option when landing your aircraft. This is useful; however, too many pilots use go arounds as a panacea or a way out for every flawed landing operation.

More times than you may think, successful go arounds are highly doubtful because they depend on problematical circumstances that are often not feasible. Learning to make *precision landings* at initial stall speed is the way to limit the number of go arounds that are necessary. Once you learn to make *precision landings* with all of the excess kinetic energy taken out of your aircraft, rarely is there a need to make a *go around*. Touching your wheels on the ground to assess conditions of a landing place and then opening the throttle for lift off should be continued. This is a planned test landing operation—not a haphazard go around that occurs spontaneously after a botched landing procedure. Rolling aircraft wheels over your landing area or dragging skis over snow-covered surfaces and becoming airborne has little or no danger of wrecking your airplane. Make certain that dragging a place for a test landing is always accomplished downhill on sloping terrain.

Winter Flying Operations

You would think that pilots in Alaska who fly in winter would all have hangars of some sort to shield their aircraft from the harsh low temperatures and snow from October to late April. This has never been the reality as Alaskan pilots have always kept their airplanes right out in the cold environment and have developed techniques to deal with them. Only recently in the past five to ten years hangars have been built at many airports in Alaska. I think that the cost of building hangars was too high in the past and they were not considered because of it. At the present time, that doesn't seem to be a point of contention as all hangars seems to be purchased as soon as they are built. Still, many pilots cannot afford to purchase a hangar because of the enormous price.

Keeping your airplane tied down out in the open in winter requires well-tailored nylon covers to keep horizontal surfaces free of snow and ice; for example, wing covers, tail covers for horizontal surfaces, windshield cover with extended area to cover the top of fuselage, propeller cover, nose cone cover and a well-insulated cowling cover. There is so much more than just purchasing these covers and placing them on the aircraft. First, it is important to find a sewing specialist who has been doing this type of work for many years. It is also necessary to have the cover makers come out and measure your airplane surfaces so that the covers fit snugly. You don't want sagging covers that blow around and rip and become torn in strong winds. Waterproof nylon works well, especially when melting snow and ice conditions exists. This will keep water from accumulating on the surfaces underneath the covers that later turn to ice when the temperatures drop below freezing. Black color for the covers is necessary. This is simple physics; a *black body* absorbs and reradiates the most sunlight into long-wave heat rays that will melt the greatest amount of snow or ice on the covers. This helps to keep the covers free of snow and ice so that you don't have to manually remove it. This saves lots of time. It has always amazed me to see the *black body* efficiency in vaporizing water or melting snow and ice on the covers in the middle of winter when low temperatures would appear to not allow this.

The above information on covers for your aircraft is my own recommendation after many years of learning. Certainly, other pilots have different ideas and their own way of selecting the covers they desire. You will have to talk to them to obtain this information. I always advise that a pilot should review information and in the end be creative and learn to select the choices that fit your own needs best. You are the only person who can make this decision because you are an individual with your own personal traits. This is like all aspects of being a pilot—learn to make decisions on your own. You can always change if you see something better. The learning experience will also be helpful. The important point here is to be creative and to learn to be comfortable with your own decision.

The next item on winter operations for an airplane tied down outside in the natural weather elements is the heating necessary to prevent damage from starting a cold-soaked engine. Multiviscosity oils (Shell 15W-50, Phillips 20W-50, Chevron 20W-50) are used in cold climates. These oils flow well even at zero degrees Fahrenheit. Warming the oil pan with an electric heat pad (100 watts) will keep the oil thin for better engine and cylinder lubrication and less of a problem for the battery in turning over the engine when starting. Nevertheless, heating the oil alone will not be sufficient to avoid damage to an engine in a cold start. The engine must be preheated inside the cowling when outside air temperatures are 20 to 30 degrees Fahrenheit and below. This will warm up the crankcase and the cylinders to operating temperatures that are safe for starting the engine. Cold starts can seriously damage an engine and must be avoided. The following paragraphs provide information on several methods to preheat a cold-soaked engine.

Tanis provides a multipoint electric preheating system for small airplanes. It consists of six 50-watt electric heating elements connected by a wiring harness. These units are permanently installed on the aircraft engine. The heating elements are screwed into the threaded CHT-probe bosses in each cylinder head. Another heating element (flat silicone rubber heating pad) is glued to the crankcase with high-temperature RTV. One additional heating pad is glued to the bottom of the oil pan. The wiring harness has an AC plug that can be connected to an electric cord.

Reiff also provides a preheat system designed for small airplanes. It uses 50-watt heating elements mounted on large stainless steel clamps that mount on the non-finned portion of each cylinder barrel. It also has an oil pan heating pad but not a crankcase heating pad. It depends on sufficient heat to the crankcase by conduction from the oil pan and cylinder heating elements.

Both the Tanis and Reiff preheating systems work well. However, they are costly to purchase and install. Pilots have developed other successful methods. If your airplane is being flown once or twice weekly, it is an advantage to keep it from getting cold-soaked. Keep the well-insulated engine cover over the cowling. Use an oil pan heating pad (100 watts) and one 100-watt electric bulb placed inside the cowling. These two heating elements are plugged in to an electric cord and left on at all times. Two hours prior to engine start-up, a third heater will need to be placed inside the cowling. This is usually a small (7"x 5 ½"x 1 ¾") automotive heater (1,000 to 1,500 watts) with a circulating fan. The oil heating pad and the 100-watt light bulb will keep the cylinders warm and the seat heater running for two hours will provide sufficient heat to warm up the engine case. Check the cylinders and the crankcase to make sure they are warm to the touch prior to start-up. You can also look at the cylinder head temperatures if you have an engine analyzer installed. Other pilots use forced-air preheating units such as Herman-Nelson and Red Devil. Smaller forced-air heaters are fired by propane, kerosene, or gasoline.

Pilots will also need to carry in the airplane a preheating element that can be used in the backcountry where there is no electricity. A *heat box* of some sort is required to prevent hot air from a heater from being lost due to convection on windy days. Sheet metal shops can easily build a heat box that works well. It will need a hinged door in which a small camp stove or at least the stove burner can be placed inside. A 4-inch-diameter stovepipe or flexible aluminum tubing 4 to 6 feet long can be used to connect the heat box which is placed on the ground to the gap in the underside of the cowling that leads to the engine. Sporting goods stores have a multitude of camp stoves to choose from. The MSR multifuel stove has an advantage in that it can use aviation fuel from the aircraft.

Fuel contamination is very important to avoid. Water is the most likely contaminant. Standard recommendations are to keep the fuel tanks full when the aircraft is idle; this will help prevent condensation and water developing in the tanks. Pilots need to intensively know their aircraft. Neither of my aircraft, the Piper Cub (15 years) and the Arctic Tern (15 years) have a water condensation problem. I leave my tanks near empty until I'm ready for a flight. It is very important not to overload your aircraft with fuel you don't need. I put in the tanks only the fuel that is needed with a small reserve for safety considerations for the day's flight. If your tanks have water condensation problems and you fill your tanks to the brim, then you'll have to drain fuel so that you are carrying only the amount that is necessary for the mission you are on. Water and contamination are so important that all fuel that goes in my aircraft is filtered with a fine mesh Mr. Funnel filter to retain water and other contaminating debris (sand, rust, bits of rubber and plastic particles) from entering the fuel tanks. In over thirty-five years of flying in Alaska not once have I had a fuel contamination problem.

Ski Flying Operations

Ski flying can be included as the most unique and rewarding flying in Alaska; nevertheless, it is the most misunderstood and the most underappreciated way of flying in Alaska. With all the taildraggers in Alaska, only a small number are operated on skis in winter. One Alaskan pilot even asked "Why would you land on a glacier?" This caught me by surprise. I answered that the vista was beautiful up there and said no more. Many pilots in Alaska fly only when there is a mission to complete. Traditional missions are using the airplane for hunting, fishing, trapping, flying to your remote cabin, and many other activities related to hauling cargo or people to remote areas. In my evaluation, many pilots don't include the most important reason to own an airplane in Alaska; that is flying for the aesthetic value and inspiration. That is my primary mission and the airplane makes it all possible. You can fly to any place in Alaska and usually you can always find a summer and winter landing area in complete wilderness.

Alaska has some of the most stunning landscapes on earth. Why not include this in your flying repertoire? What I mean by this is to contemplate getting airborne on a good-weather day only for the purpose of flying into the mountains, glaciers, and fjords and finding scenic landing places where you can take short hikes. Many of my flights are dedicated exclusively to this purpose. The inspiration is sensational and the life enhancement is off the charts. An airplane equipped with skis in winter opens up an entirely new paradise that rivals flying destinations with wheels and floats in summer.

Ski flying in winter is unique because most landing areas are on natural terrain and not on prepared landing strips. Ski operations are carried out without the use of brakes. The landing areas selected are usually quite long and brakes are rarely needed. Frozen lakes covered with winter snow are excellent places for ski landings. Mountainous terrain above tree line in places such as benches and ridges and mountain slopes are great landing places in winter. The vast marshes and wetland areas of Alaska that is impossible for wheel landings in summer provide excellent landing areas for ski-equipped aircraft in winter. For all the flying in Alaska, ski-equipped aircraft provide by far the most landing places. Ski-equipped aircraft are also necessary as a safety factor for winter flying in Alaska. Forced landings with wheels on snow-covered terrain result in virtually all airplanes nosing over and damaging the airplane when the wheels dig into the snow. For all the above reasons, ski flying in Alaska in winter is very rewarding, necessary, and should be part of a pilot's flying operations in the Northland.

Glacier landings are very special. They offer the only surface access into this stunning setting of flowing ice surrounded by awe-inspiring mountains and provide the most distinguished of all flying in Alaska. Excellent landing conditions throughout the winter are provided as the glacial ice aids in keeping the snow on the glacier's surface consistent. Glaciers are only 30 minutes away from Merrill Field in the Chugach Mountains. There are hundreds of glaciers available for landings within one hour's flying time from Anchorage. Pilots land on glaciers in the Chugach Mountains from 2,000 feet above sea level to over 7,000 feet. Super Cub pilots land on a glacier at 10,000 feet near the summit of Mount Spurr, which is eighty miles west of Anchorage. The spectacular Harding and Sargent ice fields on the Kenai Peninsula are 80 miles south and southeast of Anchorage. Mount McKinley's mammoth glaciers of ice in the Alaska Range are slightly over 100 air miles from Anchorage.

Pilots can fly over glaciers on wheels in summer and skis in winter. These flights at low level provide enchanting vistas of glaciers and mountainous landscapes. However, there is nothing quite comparable to landing and walking on a glacier on snowshoes or skis. This is truly an out-of-life event that cannot be experienced without being on the glacier in person. This great opportunity with ski-equipped airplanes should not be squandered.

Snow conditions in Alaska are misunderstood. For the most part snow provides the magical surface for many types of winter activities, for example, cross-country on snowmachine, skis, and snowshoes. Nevertheless, there are times and conditions when snow causes challenging and difficult ski landings. Snow conditions are highly variable and this variability can greatly degrade ski landings. Powder snow blown into waves by windstorms can cause enormous landing problems when snow later melts and then refreezes. The waves become hard, almost comparable to concrete. You often can't land in such places without breaking your landing gear. Pilots flying on skis have to learn to drag the snow before each landing and determine whether the snow surface is suitable for landing.

One of the rewards of ski flying is that most landing places are quite long and rarely is there a problem with taking off with such distance available.

Making use of your aircraft landing tracks for taking off makes the departure on snow packs easier. Landing at high elevations in the mountains and glaciers usually is not a density altitude issue because the cold in winter counteracts this problem. Taking off on sloping terrain has a profound built-in efficiency. The distance required for takeoff on a 20 percent slope is one half the distances compared to level ground. Sloping terrain can be found on many landing places and especially on glaciers.

Many pilots are apprehensive about falling into a crevasse when landing on glaciers. There is a real possibility of this happening. Nevertheless, it does not happen very often. I can't recall the last time this happened; possibly more than a decade ago. I have long-term experience traversing glaciers on skis when I was an active member of the Alpine Cub of Alaska in Fairbanks and the Mountaineering Club of Alaska in Anchorage. We were always roped up. I would not land an airplane on glaciers if I thought it had a high risk factor for falling into a crevasse. Many pilots don't realize that their winter boot heel print (20 pounds per square inch) has over 12 times more pounds per square inch than skis on their airplane (1.6 pounds per square inch). This means that a pilot walking on a glacier has a much greater chance of breaking through a snow bridge and falling into a crevasse than the airplane does. Always put on your snowshoes (2.2 pounds per square inch) or skis (2.3 pounds per square inch) before moving away from your airplane. This may lower the foot pounds pressure sufficiently to prevent collapsing a snow bridge and falling into a crevasse. This one important step could save your life. Pulling someone out of a crevasse is not a routine event; it is much more difficult and dangerous than most could imagine. If a pilot fell into a crevasse and had to be pulled out, it is highly doubtful he or she would be capable of flying his or her aircraft back home. This can cause much anxiety. In winter I usually carry the necessary equipment to extract a person from a crevasse—strap harness with leg loops, climbing rope, aluminum stakes, pulley, climbing ax, and Jumar ascenders.

The safest place to land an airplane on glaciers obviously is an area free of crevasses. Nevertheless, crevasses are not always easy to discern, especially after massive snowstorms have dumped large amounts of snow over the glacial surface. A pilot with experience of traveling many miles on glaciers on skis can detect the areas where crevasses are most likely to be found with a flyover. However, landing in areas where crevasses are present often is not a problem after the large snowstorms in early winter dump massive amounts of snow on the glaciers. The snow fills in crevasses and the snow bridges become stable when winter temperatures drop in the teens and below in November and December. The glacier's snowpack remains stable throughout the coldest part of the winter; January through March. In May and June, because of warm sunny days, the snow bridges become weak and the greatest danger of falling into crevasses can happen. By this time most ski flying operations have ceased.

Air taxi operators from Talkeetna can land on glaciers near Mount McKinley later than in most other places. The pilots use several landing sites they know are safe for landings late in the spring and into the summer. Climbers on Mount McKinley are flown into the Kahiltna Glacier at 7,200 feet in April, May, and early June. Sightseers are flown into the Ruth Glacier near the Sheldon Mountain House at 5,800 feet all summer and into August.

September is the best time to fly above glaciers and to observe the exposed glacial ice free of snow cover. This will reveal the vast areas on the glaciers where crevasses are found. You'll need to take pictures of these areas or at least remember where they are so you don't attempt to land there in winter when snow covers them up. You can also fly over your favorite winter landing places and verify that there are no crevasses in the locality. My greatest concern is falling into crevasses while moving across a glacier. It is always reassuring to know that there are no crevasses in the vicinity of the glacier that you are moving across.

Several types of wheel skis are used for winter operations in Alaska. Wheel skis are typically used by pilots who have an airport home base where the runways are plowed and free from snow. Hydraulic skis are rigged to raise and lower the wheels as needed at the airport and in the off-airport setting. Wheel-penetration skis provide fixed wheels that protrude below the ski for landing on snowplowed runways. When landing in the snow, the wheel penetrates down below the ski and results in increased drag on landings and takeoffs. Tail skis are usually the wheel-penetration type with the fixed wheel protruding below the ski.

The other type of ski used in winter in Alaska is the wheel-replacement or straight ski. The main wheels are removed from the aircraft and the simple straight skis are placed on the wheel axles. This type of ski should not land on snowplowed runways. Merrill Field has two main paved runways (16–34 and 7–25) where the snow is plowed in winter. The third runway at Merrill Field is a 2,000-foot gravel strip (runway 5–23) that is left unplowed in winter. This is where all aircraft with straight skis park. Aircraft with straight skis at International Airport use the ice of Lake Spenard for landings, takeoffs, and parking.

There are three choices for the tail ski. You can use the tailwheel without any alterations. It will sink into the snow and cause drag that slows forward speed on takeoff. It will also sink into the snow on landings and shorten them, similar to light braking. The next option is to use a wheel penetration tail ski. This landing apparatus will slow down the aircraft on landings and on takeoffs but not as much as the tailwheel without any alterations. The third option for a tail ski is the wheel-replacement or straight tail ski. The tail wheel is removed and the straight tail ski is installed for winter operations. My favorite option is the wheel-replacement or straight ski. It will keep the rear of the airplane from descending deep into the snowpack and slowing down aircraft acceleration on takeoff. It also makes turning the airplane in deep powder snow much easier.

For small taildraggers (Taylorcraft, J-3 and PA-11 Cubs, Champion) and medium sized taildraggers (Super Cub, Piper PA-12, Citabria, Maule, Scout, and Arctic Tern), straight main skis and the tail ski with the tail wheel removed is by far the way to go. All types of wheel skis are very expensive, excessively heavy, create excessive aerodynamic drag, and are much less efficient when operating on snow surfaces than are straight skis. Straight skis have all the advantages with the exception that they cannot be used on airport runways that are plowed in winter and kept free of snow. If you have ever gotten your aircraft stuck in the snow and had to dig your way out and use snowshoes to pack down the snow to get off, you'll understand the nuisance of operating aircraft in winter with wheel skis. So that you don't get stuck, you'll have to greatly limit where you can land an aircraft on wheel skis. These places are lakes with bare ice or thin snowpack, old landing tracks than have been packed down and have refrozen and other snow-packed runways. The straight skis, you can go just about anywhere and land on the fresh snowpack and not get stuck. There are a few exceptions such as wet, sticky snow, loose snow that may have hollow sections that will collapse on the weight of one ski, and a few others.

When selecting a straight ski for your small or medium-sized taildragger, make certain that the skis have sufficient surface area (measured in square inches) for your type of aircraft. You'll regret having a smaller surface area on your skis than is required when you have difficulty taxiing and turning in deep powder snow and making takeoffs. This will limit where you can land, not as much as with wheel skis but still to a degree that is annoying. If your skis are just a bit undersized, you can improve performance of the skis by extending the plastic bottoms on both sides of the ski. If this is insufficient, you can buy a ski the next size larger than the one on your aircraft.

Skis for the heavier taildraggers such as the Cessna 180s and 185s, Beavers, and Otters are more problematic because of the larger weight of the aircraft. Most Cessna 180 and 185 pilots do not use skis on their aircraft in winter because of the high risk of getting the airplane stuck in the snow and the laborious task and time required digging it out. The pilots that do fly skis on these heavier aircraft are very selective where they land. They will need to be carrying a full crew if any snowpack manhandling of the aircraft is required. A one man operation in a C185 will provide zero manhandling help.

Take the Young Flying

When someone asks or whenever you get a chance, take a young person flying. This is a rare event for an individual at five to ten years old. The flight most likely is the first opportunity for them to climb into a small airplane, get airborne, and fly away. Over the years, I have taken my share flying in the Piper Cub and in the Arctic Tern. I remember taking one tiny boy who was only five years old. He needed two pads in the back seat to sit on so that he could see out the window. My fights are into the nearby Chugach Mountains six miles east of Merrill Field, across the glaciers, and showing them Alaska's magnificent wildlife along the way. I usually make several landings on short gravel bars in Lake George basin and along the Knik River so they can experience the taildragger's unique advantage of being capable of landing in miniscule places in the backcountry. Most of the ones I have flown were very quiet; however, they were highly excited and to a certain degree, stunned at this very unusual and first-time airborne experience. They don't talk very much at such an early age; however, the flight often makes a lasting impression for the lucky ones that get the chance to go on the flight.

I ran into a friend recently that I worked with in the 1980s and 1990s on the joint military bases. I had not seen him in about 10 years. What he told me about his son was amazing and it surprised me. I had taken his son flying when he was about eight years old. He told me that his son graduated from the University of Alaska with a degree in aviation technology. He also has his pilot's license and now is working on an instrument rating. After that he wants to obtain a commercial rating. Eventually, he may decide on becoming an ATP but is not certain that he can obtain employment after paying for the high cost of all the ratings that are necessary. I mentioned that this is the *golden age* for ATPs. There is an airline shortage that is now worldwide. (*Airline pilots: Coming up Short, by Marc C. Lee, Plane&Pilot, October 2012*). I also included a critique providing useful information on how to finance the expensive training *(Financing the Flying Dream by Marc C. Lee, Plane&Pilot, July 2012)*.

This shows how one flight early on in a person's life can have a profound influence in guiding a person toward a professional career. I am overjoyed for making that flight and being a part of helping others find their way. Most of the youngsters you take flying will not become pilots; however, they will have a first-hand experience with flying in Alaska and will likely be life-time aviation advocates.

Flying Wildlife Surveys in Alaska

First Wildlife Surveys

I began flying aerial moose surveys in Alaska during the early 1970s on the Fort Richardson and Elmendorf military bases (seven miles northeast of downtown Anchorage) and upper Ship Creek in the Chugach Mountains. Army Huey helicopters were used to fly the first surveys. The area on the coastal plain and in the Chugach Mountains encompassed 90,000 acres. The surveys would be flown after snowstorms provided a complete snow cover. This was usually in November or early December. The daylight time interval became too short to complete the surveys after mid-December. The goal was to fly a complete coverage of the military reservations and upper Ship Creek, and cover all areas where moose are likely to be present. The survey required a composition count consisting of all moose (cows, calves, yearlings, and bulls). This provided useful data for determining the number of moose to harvest in the fall and winter hunts on the military reservations and in Ship Creek. For accuracy in the composition counts, we had to circle each moose found to pick up calves and other moose bedded down nearby. Without circling each moose observed, other moose would have been missed.

Accurate surveys demanded that a high percentage (above 80 percent) of the moose be found. In those days, our total number of observed moose for the 90,000 acres was about 450 to 480. This information was provided to the Alaska Department of Fish and Game (ADF&G). The bases worked with the ADF&G to determine the yearly moose-hunting quotas for these lands. Approximately 125 hunting permits were issued by ADF&G each year. In the mid to late 1970s, ADF&G required Super Cubs for flying the surveys. The Super Cub was the long-established wildlife survey airplane for ADF&G in Alaska. The Super Cub made much less noise than a helicopter. This greatly reduced the disturbance factor to wildlife. The Super Cub cost less to operate and could also make tighter circles around a moose than the Huey helicopter. ADF&G provided the Super Cubs and pilots to conduct the surveys. I continued as a biologist flying in the backseat of the Super Cubs recording the moose data. My tenure on conducting annual moose surveys continued on the military reservations and upper Ship Creek for more than 20 consecutive years. In the early 1980s, I found that there was a need to fly additional surveys on the military reservations.

The military bases had both migratory and nonmigratory moose. The migratory moose would spend the late winter and early spring months on the coastal plain on the military bases and move to the Chugach Mountain slopes and into the upper Ship Creek watershed for the summer and early winter months. The nonmigratory moose were mostly found on the coastal plain but also on the mountain slopes and upper Ship Creek. They stayed the entire year on the coastal plain or in Ship Creek. I realized that we needed to fly surveys to determine the timing of the migration and the number of migrating moose. There was no funding for additional moose surveys. The surveys had no chance of ever being conducted. I decided that I would like to volunteer my services for this task.

This would be an excellent opportunity for me to begin learning how to fly wildlife surveys. I had already purchased a Piper Cub in 1979. This would be a new and challenging flying adventure. The surveys would have to be flown in my own aircraft and on my own time. The federal government would not likely approve the surveys as an official government-sponsored project so I never asked for permission. I would accomplish this mission on my own dime.

The traditional way of flying wildlife surveys in Alaska is having a pilot flying the airplane and a biologist recording the data. I don't think flying wildlife surveys for me would ever have gotten off the ground if I had tried this approach. I decided that what was more realistic for me was to be a one-person operation. I would be the pilot and also the biologist recording the wildlife data. This is something that I could take responsibility for and a task that I could accomplish.

My initial moose surveys were made on the Chugach mountain slopes and upper Ship Creek in midwinter to determine the numbers of moose in their winter habitat. The flying time could be substantially reduced since these surveys were needed to determine the total moose present and not compositional data. This meant that it was not necessary to circle every moose.

From the very first survey, I really enjoyed the flying and using my airplane not for drilling holes in the sky but for performing a practical purpose. Flying the surveys was not difficult because it was pure pleasure; I enjoyed it so much. From conducting official moose surveys with ADF&G, I had learned all the nuances of flying the surveys. Being my own pilot with lots of time for contemplation, I also learned a lot as I continued to fly the moose surveys. The survey data collected were very useful and have been used for many years in managing the military reservations' moose herd.

Moose Surveys in the Piper Cub and the Arctic Tern

From these initial background surveys on the military bases, I progressively began conducting moose surveys in my Piper Cub and later (after 1997) in the Arctic Tern. I would complete several surveys every year from February through March to provide additional data on the military reservations' moose herd. After a few years, I started to venture out and began conducting moose surveys of wintering moose in other areas in Southcentral Alaska.

ADF&G conducts most of their surveys in November and December after the ground has a complete snow cover to obtain compositional data for managing moose herds in Alaska. Very few surveys are flown during midwinter when moose are on their wintering grounds. Not all moose in Alaska migrate to wintering grounds. Some moose migrate only when food availability is lacking and when the snowpack becomes deep enough to impede movement. Nevertheless, there are many traditional wintering grounds for moose in Alaska and I've always thought that these areas should be monitored. Since no one was conducting these surveys, I decided to fly them in my Piper Cub.

The first moose wintering area I was interested in surveying was the MacKenzie Dairy Farms 14 miles northwest of downtown Anchorage. The boreal forest in this area was never an important moose wintering area. However, the establishment of dairy farms in 1982 changed the environment. Thirty-one farms were established and 12,736 acres of boreal forest (spruce and hardwood trees) were cleared and planted in forage crops. After five years, many of the dairy farms became unprofitable and were abandoned. By the year 2000, approximately 55 percent or 7,075 acres of the farms had reverted back to early-successional deciduous vegetation because of the lack of cultivation. The early-succession birch, cottonwood, aspen, and willow saplings have become exceptional moose habitat. Moose from as far away as 30 to 40 miles migrate here to take advantage of this bountiful food supply. The deeper the snowpack in Southcentral Alaska, the more moose migrate here for the winter.

It is surprising to find such large numbers of moose migrating to the MacKenzie Farms. A survey on February 26, 2000 showed an estimated population of 638 moose. Other surveys showed these results: 728 moose on February 18, 2001; 585 moose on February 2, 2002; 544 moose on December 31, 2004; and 644 moose on December 19, 2008. Three surveys conducted in one winter showed these results: 249 moose on November 15, 2008; 644 moose on December 19, 2008; and 493 moose on March 14, 2009. Approximately 20 aerial moose surveys (average of two surveys each winter) have been conducted at MacKenzie Farms during the years 2000 to 2010. Each survey covers the 7,075 acres of moose habitat and requires approximately 1.5 hours of flying time to complete.

There is a great lesson to be learned from MacKenzie about moose habitat management in Alaska. The large numbers of moose that migrate here annually are doing so through happenstance. There was never any intention of developing this area for wintering moose. It happened due to the failure of the original plan of developing a dairy farming area. The lesson to take away from this is that Alaska needs additional wintering areas similar to MacKenzie Farms. These areas are needed to boost moose populations depleted by hunter overharvesting of moose in Alaska. The primary limiting factor with increasing moose populations in Alaska is the lack of winter habitat. The State (ADF&G) could develop additional winter habitat areas for moose by vegetation manipulation (removing mature forest) that could duplicate the changes that were made at MacKenzie. If the State made this a primary goal; they should be more capable of making this happen than the chance happening at MacKenzie. That would be a revelation for Alaska. Maybe the State could then ease off on blaming wolves for depleted moose populations and killing so many of them.

Another moose wintering area that has been surveyed for the past 10 to 12 years is Big Lake. Big Lake is located 22 air miles north of downtown Anchorage. The surveys conducted here are in the area that burned in the Miller Reach fire in 1996 on the north and east sides of Big Lake. Hardwoods including birch, aspen, and willow have flourished since the fire and have produced an outstanding food source for wintering moose. The biomass of these hardwood saplings have been increasing for the past 10 years. The survey area is divided into three segments, which are: (1) North and northeast of Big Lake comprising 14,720 acres; (2) Lucille Creek drainage with 7,040 acres; and (3) East and southeast of Big Lake with 10,240 acres. The three segments comprise 32,000 acres (50 square mile Sections). Surveys in the Big Lake area were flown one time each winter during the past 10 years beginning in 2001. Survey results showing the larger numbers of wintering moose include a population of 306 on February 23, 2002; 501 on November 7, 2003; 471 on February 8, 2008; and 533 on February 17,

2011. An all-time high number of moose were observed at Big Lake in 2013. The survey conducted on February 25, 2013 showed an estimated population of 956 moose.

The *Miller Reach* fire burned sufficiently hot in many of the areas near Big Lake to destroy part or all of the organic and duff layers which lie above the surface of the mineral soil. The exposed bare mineral soil provides excellent substrate for germination of hardwood seeds naturally broadcast by the wind. Five years after the burn, native early successional hardwood saplings were flourishing and producing excellent winter moose habitat. This was a human-induced fire and would never have been allowed to burn in this area because of the many scattered homes and recreational cabins. Nevertheless, this area was similar to MacKenzie in that it was not a prime wintering area for moose prior to the fire. Prescribed fires are another way to provide new winter habitat for moose. Prescribed burns on selective sites would also be a way to increase the moose populations in Alaska.

The third moose wintering area surveyed is the Palmer Hay Flats which is 7 miles southwest of Palmer, Alaska. This area has only marginal winter moose habitat; however, the area usually has the shallowest snowpack in Southcentral Alaska because of the strong southeast winds that frequently blow in winter from the Knik River. The wind sublimates the snow; the snow goes from a solid state to a gaseous state (water vapor). Winters with large snowstorms and deep snowpack will trigger moose to migrate here to avoid wasting so much energy moving in deep snow. Surveys were conducted here only in a few winters. Survey results include a population of 302 moose on February 21, 2000 and a population of 101 on February 9, 2002.

Trumpeter Swan Surveys

The Knik River was visited many times and used as my primary airplane off-airport training area beginning in summer 1979. I began noticing resident trumpeter swans that nested here, other trumpeters that summer in the area, and migrating trumpeters that passed through the area. I often wondered how the swans were able to bear the high disturbance levels from individuals using recreational all-terrain cycles, trucks, jeeps, and power boats (air boats and motor boats). I already knew that trumpeter swans, when they are on the ground, are more alarmed at the proximity of man than any other living creature. The Knik River is the recreational playground for riders of motorized vehicles not only from the Matanuska-Susitna Valley (Palmer and Wasilla) but also from Anchorage. The Knik River region accommo-dates the largest gathering of off-road vehicle riders in the State of Alaska.

The hub for the recreational area is Butte, Alaska on the lower Knik River. Highway vehicles (many with trailers) park here in several large parking lots. Recreational vehicles are off-loaded and riders travel up and down the river valley from below the Knik River Bridge on the Old Glenn Highway to the terminus of Knik Glacier, a linear distance of over 25 miles.

I asked several waterfowl biologists working for USF&WS and ADF&G about the swans. I wanted to know if they were flying surveys to find out how the swans were surviving in the heavily used motorized environments. USF&WS told me they conducted complete censuses of trumpeter swan summer populations in Alaska beginning in 1968 and continuing in 1975. From 1975, the censuses were conducted on a five-year interval all the way to 2010. The swan population has shown a State wide increase in number in every survey since the first one in 1968. I asked about additional swan surveys in the Knik River and the Palmer Hay Flats to monitor this specific population of swans. I mentioned surveys for monitoring nesting swans and their broods of cygnets and the large number of migrating swans stopping in the Palmer, Alaska region during the spring and autumn periods. They said since the Alaska State trumpeter swan population is increasing, they did not perceive any need to fly additional surveys. They had more important wildlife obligations elsewhere in Alaska. ADF&G's reply about monitoring the swans was the same.

I could never agree that swan surveys in the Palmer region are not needed. They need to be flown to obtain a better understanding of the interaction of human recreational activities with the nesting and staging swans in the region. There needs to be a balance between recreational use and the wildlife that resides here. The surveys will help to provide answers to these concerns. I decided that if the responsible agencies would not fly the surveys that I would fly them in my own airplane and on my own time. My federal government work was taking up fifty hours per week and provided little time to devote to flying swan surveys as often as they were needed. However, I would accept a slow process of gradually, over many years, collecting useful information on the swans.

The surveys were also a great learning adventure as I went along. I learned what data were important to collect and how to conduct the surveys. I retired from my federal government employment in 2004 and in the years after retirement I had more time to spend on the surveys. Surveys on the trumpeter swans were flown for over 20 years; however, the highest-quality data were collected during the period from 2008 through 2012 when the surveys were flown in a more comprehensive manner.

Swan data for each flight were recorded in a notebook during the surveys. These data for each survey was later used in the preparation of written memoranda on my home computer. The memoranda were used as base documentation to write four swan papers for publication. Two of my swan papers were presented at the Twenty-Second Conference of the Trumpeter Swan Society held in Polson, Montana on October 13, 2011. These two papers will later be published in *North American Swans, Special Edition, the Proceedings and Papers of the Twenty-Second Swan Society Conference.* This is a bulletin of the Trumpeter Swan Society, Plymouth, Minnesota. A copy of my third swan paper was provided to John Cornely, executive director of the Trumpeter Swan Society. He will review the paper and decide whether to publish it in the proceedings. The fourth paper was presented at the 5th International Swan Symposium on February 6, 2014 in Easton, Maryland.

The four swan papers comprise 37 pages including 13 tables. The focus of the four papers is as follows. The first three papers are on the status, staging strategies, and disturbance levels of the swans in the Palmer, Alaska Region. The fourth paper is on the density and productivity comparisons between two populations of Trumpeter Swans in Southcentral Alaska. The two swan areas used in the comparison are the Palmer, Alaska Region and the Susitna Flats 20 miles northwest of Anchorage, Alaska. These four swan papers are being disseminated to State and Federal agencies and other interested organizations and individuals in Alaska. My goal now, through public outreach, is to enlighten Alaskans on the aerial swan surveys, the swan papers, and the need for reducing the high swan disturbance level in the Palmer, Alaska region. A balance between public motorized recreation and wildlife use in the region is being sought out. This requires managing swan disturbance by regulating human activities that are negatively affecting the swans. This can be accomplished by amending the Knik River Public Use Area Management Plan and revising the Palmer Hay Flats State Game Refuge Management Plan with policies to mitigate swan disturbance. After policies have been enacted in the management plans to reduce the impacts on the swans, it will also be necessary to educate the hunting and recreational users concerning swan disturbance. Recreational operators of motorized vehicles are entitled to use public lands but must be educated about wildlife behavior and the need to respect wildlife.

Beginning in the summer of 2009 and continuing through 2012, I have conducted aerial trumpeter swan surveys in the Susitna Flats west of Anchorage, Alaska. The survey area includes the Cook Inlet coastal marsh (1 to 2 miles inland from salt water) from Point MacKenzie west to the

Susitna River and southwest to the Beluga River and including the Susitna River delta north to Flat Horn Lake and Susitna Station. The survey area is entirely within the borders of the *Susitna Flats State Game Refuge* and the coverage encompasses the important swan nesting areas in the 301,947 acre refuge. The swans nesting and summering in the Susitna coastal marshlands provide a useful comparison to the swans in the Palmer, Alaska region as the Susitna coastal swans inhabit remote lands with negligible infrastructure and with little to no human disturbance during the summer months. There are no roads and limited motorized human disturbances. Airplanes and occasional motorboats are the only intrusions into these lands and disturbance levels are light to nonexistent. The nesting swans in the Palmer, Alaska region average ten pairs per year and the nesting pairs in the Susitna coastal region average fifteen pairs. A paper was written in 2014 to compare these two populations of Trumpeter Swans. The paper was presented at the *5th International Swan Symposium* on February 6, 2014 in Easton, Maryland.

Dall Sheep and Mountain Goat Surveys

Dall sheep are Alaska's mountain monarchs that are found only in Northwest Canada and Alaska. Flying surveys to obtain population evaluations of these marvelous white sheep means flying into some of the most scenic alpine terrain in Alaska. Sheep surveys were conducted throughout the 1980s and 1990s. Areas surveyed were in the Chugach Mountains east and northeast of Anchorage including the Lake George Basin and the following watersheds: Knik River, Eklutna River, Peters Creek, Eagle River, Ship Creek, and Turnagain Arm of Cook Inlet.

A Dall sheep survey was conducted on September 7, 1998, in the mountainous portion of Ship Creek, 10 miles east of downtown Anchorage. The number of Dall sheep observed was 184. This survey was not flown to capture composition data which would include tallying the number of rams, ewes, and lambs. It was an efficient survey to capture the total population of sheep in the Ship Creek drainage. A Dall sheep survey in the early 1980s found slightly over 300 sheep in Ship Creek. This is a large number of sheep for a creek with a short drainage of 25 miles. A few years later the sheep population in Ship Creek was greatly reduced due to starvation—thick snowpacks covering winter food resources. In recent years the sheep population still has not recovered to the 1980s level.

A Dall sheep survey on October 28, 2005 found 225 sheep on the south-facing slopes of the Chugach Mountain range north of the Knik River drainage. The area covered was on the west side of the Jim Creek Basin

Lakes on the lower Knik River and proceeded east along the mountains to Grasshopper Valley north of the Knik Glacier. Mountain goats were found in two areas on the east side of Metal Creek. Eleven goats were found west of Grasshopper Valley and three goats were found in the Glacier Fork Canyon east of Metal Creek.

A wildlife survey into the Eklutna River drainage on May 22, 2008 showed 95 Dall sheep, 72 mountain goats, 12 black bears and 1 brown bear. This was a very special day in which a variety of Alaska's most magnificent wildlife was found on a single flight into the Eklutna River Valley. This river valley is in Chugach State Park and is only 25 miles northeast of Merrill Field in downtown Anchorage.

Mountain goat surveys were conducted in the 1980s and 1990s in the Lake and Glacier Forks of the Knik River, Lake George Basin at the head of the Knik River, Eklutna River, Eagle River, and Bird Creek. Mountain goats often have escape cover nearby with the steepest and most rugged rock faces imaginable. Mountain goats have summer and winter habitats. The goats seek a cool environment in summers high in the mountains near the top of the glaciers and winter on steep south-facing slopes with the least amount of snow cover.

Bald Eagle Surveys

Bald Eagle surveys on the military bases northeast of Anchorage were completed in 1998, 2000, 2004, 2005, 2011, and 2012 to locate nesting pairs. Protection and management of bald eagles are mandated by the *Eagle Protection Act of 1940* and the *Migratory Bird Treaty Act of 1918*. Surveys consistently found 6 to 8 pairs of nesting eagles each year. Bald eagles nest in cottonwood trees.

Brown Bear Surveys

Bears inhabit primarily the northern hemisphere. Alaska is one of the prime destinations in the world if you are interested in bears. Alaska has all three species of bears found in North America—brown, black, and polar bears. The number of bears in Alaska is exceedingly high for such enormous size predators. The polar bear found in the Chukchi and Beaufort Seas off coastal northwestern and northern Alaska are among the largest terrestrial carnivores in the world, rivaled only by the coastal brown bears in southern Alaska. The Alaskan coastal brown bears that gorge on salmon in summer are the largest of all brown bears living on earth. Alaska also has the smaller brown bear found in central and northern Alaska, often referred to as the

117

grizzly bear. One important reason Alaska is so attractive to many people is that this is the *Land of the Bears*—magnificent animals found throughout the State in stunning landscapes.

State and federal agencies in Alaska do not conduct aerial surveys to capture compositional data on bears. The reason for this is that survey data cannot demonstrate a measure of statistical reliability. In other words, it will not be possible to numerically duplicate the results that you have obtained. I can understand this reasoning as it certainly is the best way to obtain field data. However, if you cannot obtain data that can be duplicated, there must be a way to obtain data that is less reliable than desired, but data that has a value. It always seems to me that most wildlife data collected have value. This is what I tried to accomplish by conducting my own improvised black and brown bear surveys.

My initial brown bear surveys conducted in the 1980s and early 1990s had limited value as there was no method or guide for determining composition data, and ultimately the density or total population of bears in the area surveyed. Individual bears were not classified as to age and sex. Repeat surveys in the same area could not distinguish between bears on one survey versus bears on successive surveys. All this has changed with the excellent video presentation prepared by biologists from the ADF&G and the Yukon Territory in Canada. The video tape *Bear ID, Take a Closer Look* was produced by *Yukon Renewable Resources* in 1990. From reviewing the tape several times and applying the lessons learned when locating brown bears on aerial flights, the author has learned to identify individual brown bears with a high level of precision. With this new skill, bear composition data can be collected on multiple flights on different calendar dates into the same area. The data can be useful in determining the total population of brown bears in a defined area.

My first attempt to try this technique of identifying each brown bear sighted was in the coastal areas of Trading and Redoubt Bays along the west side of Cook Inlet 75 miles southwest of Anchorage. Bears show up here in large numbers in late June and remain here until mid-July when they retreat to the mountains. A bear biologist from ADF&G told me that the bears came to the coastal areas in these bays to pick up salmon. My surveys clearly showed the bears were not feeding on salmon but were feasting on the tender sedges that grow here. The spatial distribution of bears on the western side of Cook Inlet on July 1, 2000 showed that predominantly sows with cubs were using the coastal habitat in Trading Bay (12,000 acres surveyed). All bears observed here were sows with cubs with the exception of one adult found south of McArthur River. The bears observed in Redoubt

Bay (20,000 acres surveyed) showed a more uniform composition. Their numbers were doubled the number of bears found in Trading Bay. A total of 46 brown bears were found in these two bays—15 bear in Trading Bay and 31 bears in Redoubt Bay. One conclusion that should be drawn from this survey is that there are a sufficiently large number of bears using this habitat to establish it as a *Keystone Habitat* for the brown bears of Trading and Redoubt Bays. Active management to protect the habitat and the bears while they are present should be a goal of the land manager.

Inventorying brown bears in most habitats is difficult or impractical because brush or forest cover prevents the detection of a sufficient number of bears to provide accurate data. The coastal wetlands of Trading and Redoubt Bays provide an exceptional opportunity to gather composition data on a large number of bears in midsummer because of excellent survey conditions. Surveys under these conditions result in observing a large percentage of the bears. The aerial surveys can be very efficient and one survey covering the 32,000 acres can be flown in about two hours' flying time. The surveys could provide the most comprehensive data for brown bears inhabiting these two areas and could possibly provide reliable trend data—multiple surveys over several years. This would be representative of a large number of the brown bear population between the coastal areas and the mountains. This data could be used to properly manage the coastal brown bears in this region.

Identifying each brown bear on this survey by sex and age and using physical characteristics to distinguish between adults, sub adults, and sows with cubs was much easier than expected because the bears were in the open on sedge-covered terrain where they could be easily evaluated. My next effort to try this technique for estimating the total population of brown bears was in upper Ship Creek which is 10 to 12 miles east of downtown Anchorage. I have made many flights into Ship Creek in the 1980s and 1990s to search for brown bears. Although Ship Creek appears to have a high density of brown bears, you are not likely to find very many on any one survey. Multiple surveys are needed in a summer to collect sufficient data to accurately estimate the bears that inhabit Ship Creek.

In the summer of 2000 I conducted more than a dozen aerial surveys into Ship Creek to locate brown bears. Sex and age and their physical characteristics were identified so individual bears throughout the summer could be used to estimate the total population of brown bears in the Ship Creek drainage. The total number of individual brown bears observed in Ship Creek in the summer of 2000 was 13. A conservative estimate of the number of brown bears in Ship Creek based on observing 13 individual bears in the summer of 2000 would be a total of 15 to 20 bears. The high density of brown bears in this watershed would indicate that this is prime habitat with excellent food resources for the bears. ADF&G reviewed my results but did not support the data collected because it did not have statistical reliability. Nevertheless, the survey results did inspire ADF&G to begin a radio-collar study of brown bears in Ship Creek. This was the first attempt by ADF&G to monitor the brown bears in the Ship Creek watershed.

Black Bear Surveys

The military bases have a large population of black bears often observed on aerial flights in summer. I have always aspired to conduct aerial surveys in an attempt to accurately estimate the total population. After learning how to identify individual brown bears, I thought this technique could be duplicated on black bears. In 2003, I tried this method of identifying black bears on Fort Richardson.

Twenty-two aerial surveys were conducted primarily on Fort Richardson. A total of 35 black bears were observed on Fort Richardson and in adjacent Ship Creek. Of the 35 black bears observed, 28 were on Fort Richardson, six were in Ship Creek and one was observed on Elmendorf AFB. From identifying all individual black bears, it was astonishing how few repeat sightings were made in 2003. The minimum number of black bears observed on Fort Richardson in 2003 was 25. The projected or estimated population for Fort Richardson black bears was calculated by using a conservative correction factor (CF) of 30 percent added to the survey results of 25 bears. Calculations show the projected or estimated population on Fort Richardson to be 33 black bears in 2003. Dave Bostick attempted to estimate the black bear population for the two military bases in 1997 and came out with a total population of 38 to 50 bears. The latter represents a close comparison to my numbers on Fort Richardson, considering that mine are for Fort Richardson only. Neither of these two studies have statistical reliability. Nevertheless, they do show reliability when making a comparison between the numbers that have been reported. I do think both of these studies provide very useful information. Prior to these black bear surveys and estimations, no data was available.

Other Wildlife Surveys

A few other types of wildlife surveys have been flown in Alaska beside the principal ones discussed above. Many waterfowl surveys were conducted to obtain approximate numbers of geese, ducks, and swans (trumpeter and tundra swans) using the Eagle River Flats on Fort Richardson as a staging area in the autumn. A few attempts were made to fly aerial surveys in the Palmer Hay Flats and the farmers' fields south of Palmer, Alaska to determine the spring numbers of migrating waterfowl in this region. Waterfowl peak numbers in the spring can be in the thousands of geese and ducks. I remember observing a large number of snow geese on April 25, 2012 with several large clusters within a two-square-mile area near Duck Lake in the Palmer Hay Flats. The estimated number was 6,000 to 8,000. With this many waterfowl, you would have to count the geese in groups of 50 or even 100; like 100, 200, 300, 400, and so forth. You might think that this type of counting waterfowl is wildly inaccurate. It turns out to be a lot more accurate than anyone would expect. To check on your accuracy, count the same cluster of geese several times and observe the numbers each time. You can also compare the total geese counted with aerial images. The images will give you great accuracy. The image can be printed on your computer. With a pencil, you can draw a circle around 15 to 20 geese. Continue with the circles until the whole cluster is included in the small circles. Then count and write the correct number of geese in each circle. Use a calculator to sum up the entire population of geese in the cluster. This will provide close to 100 percent accuracy if you don't make mistakes counting the number of geese in each circle and with summing up the totals. Recount each cluster several times until you obtain the same number.

Surveys that were inordinately difficult were several Beluga whale surveys that I attempted in Turnagain Arm (south of Fire Island), Knik Arm (mouth of Eagle River), and upper Cook Inlet near the mouths of the Beluga, Little Susitna, and Susitna Rivers. Beluga whales always seem to be traveling in large pods and in a certain direction. As they move along they continually swim underwater most of the time. However, they appear to have a routine sequence of surfacing after covering a set distance. I don't know the distance or if each whale has a different sequence for surfacing. All that I know is that you can't see the whales when they are swimming underwater. The only time they can be observed is when they surface and that is only for ten seconds or less. It appears that about one third of the whales in a pod are surfacing at any one time. This makes attempting to accomplish complete counts of the whales close to impossible. After a few surveys, I gave up on the Beluga whales.

Aerial Wolf Observations

Wolves are one of North America's most iconic native wildlife species. They are *keystone predators* that have an enormous capacity to create and maintain a well-balanced ecosystem. Wolves were reintroduced into Yellowstone National Park in 1995 and 1996. Recent studies in Yellowstone have found the effect of wolves cascades down throughout the park's ecosystems. Grizzly bears, black bears, wolverine, coyotes, foxes, martens, bald eagles, golden eagles, magpies, and jays benefit because they feed on carcasses of animals killed by wolves. These scavengers depend on the wolf for their primary food supply. The coyote population declines as wolves chase down and kill them in their territory. This increases the small rodent population in the park, which helps to increase the declining food supply for birds of prey and other small mammals that depend on rodents for their primary food source. Elk changed their behavior by staying out of the streambed habitats for most of the time to avoid wolf predation. This allowed willow, aspen, and cotton-wood regrowth in streambed habitats where it had been almost wiped out. This, in turn, has provided abundant food that was lacking for beavers and nesting habitat for songbirds. Without the wolf acting as top predator, the ecosystem becomes unhealthy and out of balance with all species of plants and animals suffering from extreme conditions. The wolf has been eliminated from most of its native habitat throughout the continental United States by federally mandated poisoning programs. The wolf in Alaska, although it is continually being reduced in number by State predator control programs to increase prey populations, still runs wild in most areas in remote Alaska. The wolf is the largest member of the canine family and Alaska's gray wolf is the largest of its species found throughout the world. North American gray wolves weigh from 40 to over 140 pounds with females weighing slightly less than males. Wolves in northwestern Canada and Alaska tend to be larger with males reaching 140 or more pounds. The heaviest wolf on record weighed 175 pounds and was killed in the Fortymile Region of Alaska in 1939. Wolves are not monitored and population censuses are not conducted by aerial surveys in Alaska because of the difficulty of locating wolf packs. ADF&G does place radio collars on wolves to monitor a few packs.

I have not conducted wolf surveys as such in Alaska; nevertheless, I have often taken advantage of monitoring wolves when observed in flying other missions. This is especially the situation when I find wolves participating in rare and interesting activities. One noteworthy occurrence took place in the 1980s when I was flying over the Davis Range on the south part of Fort Richardson. This was in early summer, late in the evening with low twilight. I saw a lone adult wolf chasing a moose calf. The cow moose responded by racing toward the wolf and chasing it away momentarily. I decided that I would circle these animals at a sufficient elevation that they would not detect the airplane and see what was going to happen. This was a cat-and-mouse game as the wolf hung around the cow moose and calf looking for an opportunity to run in and separate the calf from its protective mother and chase after it. I circled for a long time, perhaps fifteen minutes, and saw several encounters where the wolf chased the calf away from its mother; however, each time the cow moose would come barreling down the wolf's rear end and chase it away. Now, I was watching the cow moose chasing after the wolf one more time. By this time the cow moose was tired of this predatory action by the wolf and wanted to end the harassment. She looked awfully angry and determined to stop the wolf threats on her calf. What the cow moose did next was astonishing. This time she did not end the chase but kept coming full steam ahead. I wondered what the wolf would do now that it was in serious trouble. Finally, the wolf decided it had to find a safe haven to prevent a disaster. The wolf dove into a large alder bush with a dense array of many closely spaced branches that were perhaps 4 inches in diameter. It crawled and maneuvered its way into the center of the alder bush, which was about 12 feet from the outside branches. The wolf laid down there. I thought it was all over and that the cow moose would retreat and go home. The cow moose did not blink or turn around but pushed her way between the large and strong branches of the alder until she had reached the center where the wolf lay. As soon as she reached the wolf, she reared up on her hind legs and began stomping on the wolf with her front legs similar to a boxer punching his opponent. It was incredible to observe how hard and in what a rapid succession she was stomping on the wolf. The stomping went on for a long time, maybe sixty seconds. Finally, the cow moose stopped the brutal attack and went back to her calf. The wolf appeared to be seriously injured with many broken bones and would die there in the alder bush.

The wolf lay still in the center of the alder bush for almost five minutes. Then surprisingly, it struggled to stand and slowly worked its way out of the alder bush. It walked very slowly and was limping and swaying from side to side as it walked. It was severely injured and it likely would not survive the encounter with the moose. The most amazing action noted was the moose pushing the strong alder branches apart to move into the center of the bush where the wolf lay. I did not think this was possible (the wolf also thought it had a safe haven) but the cow moose proved both of us wrong. This was a lucky day for the moose calf and a horrible day for the wolf. It was a rare event and I was fortunate to be able to watch it play out.

Another incredible event with wolves took place in the late summer and fall of 1997. One of the most interesting events with wolves is finding a den site. I can't believe how lucky I was to find a wolf den this year. I found it while flying over the Davis Range on Fort Richardson only two miles east of Muldoon (east Anchorage) late one day on September 8, 1997. This was certainly a rare finding and I knew that I might not have the opportunity to monitor another wolf den site in the future, so I would take full advantage of this one. Although this den site could have easily been located (by walking to the site) and the wolves observed from the ground, I decided that I would probably disturb the pack and they would move on. I did not want this to happen. Monitoring the den site and the wolf pack from the air in my airplane would be the best possible approach of observing the wolves while not disturbing them from their daily activities.

At 7:05 PM, while flying between Bunker Hill and the Chugach Mountain slopes, I spotted a large adult wolf lying on the grass with outstretched legs. The big wolf was in the bottom of a glacier kettle that had steep sides rising to about 120 feet in a circular pattern. I made several more passes and all were sufficiently high so as not to disturb the wolf. It appeared that the wolf might be dead. However, the next pass revealed that the wolf's legs had shifted from pointing east to now pointing west. I became really excited. This wolf was exquisitely colored with bright silver on its belly and lower legs, dark gray mottling color on its side, and very dark gray streaks on its back. Its midsection on the top of its back had a smattering of silver guard hairs. The wolf was very large and probably weighed over 110 pounds. It was particularly long. Its tail was a very large dark gray plume pulled out from its body and lying on the grass.

At 7:10 PM I noticed several small black objects in the grass in the bottom of a second kettle 200 yards to the north of the one where the adult wolf lay sleeping. The black objects appeared to be black bears from a distance but on closer inspection, they could clearly be identified as four wolf pups playing in the grass. The adult wolf identified was most likely the alpha male sleeping in peace a short distance from his playful pups. On another pass over the north kettle, I located the alpha female wolf, solid black in color, lying down and resting in the bottom of the kettle about 50 feet from the pups. I monitored the wolves in both kettles for another ten minutes and always at elevations sufficiently high and horizontally away from the kettles so as not to alert them and alter their behavior. The alpha male wolf never got up while I was circling the kettles. The frisky pups continued to play, chasing one another. They were clearly visible as their solid black bodies contrasted strikingly with the straw-colored grass background. The alpha female changed positions several times while I was flying over north kettle; however, she did not get up and move toward the pups.

Observing the comfort level of the wolves with their four black pups playing in the bottom of a kettle gave me assurance that the den site was nearby. The next few flights provided wolf sightings that helped to pinpoint the den site. It appeared to be on a ridge to the west of the north kettle. This same ridge top was where the wolves rendezvoused each evening at twilight. From my initial finding of the wolves, it appeared that my best opportunity of finding them on each future flight was to fly at twilight. This worked exceedingly well. I made 15 flights over the den site from September 8 through November 30 and found wolves on 12 of the 15 flights. I did not always find all of the pack on each flight although some of the pack was present. I did not fly directly over the pack but around them so as not to disturb them. Each flight terminated when it got too dark to see the wolves. At that time, I would return to Merrill Field which was 6 miles away (four minutes' flying time).

A good look at the alpha female wolf in bright light showed that she had a dark black coat of hair with sparkling tiny silver speckles over her back. The most striking colors you could ever imagine. It was magical to be able to follow this wolf pack even though I was working full time. I would attempt to fly as often as I could after work as this was an once-in-a-lifetime event. Weather conditions with low clouds and fog or turbulent winds prevented flying on some days. It would be difficult to describe how interesting and satisfying it was to find the wolf pack so many times and to observe the wolf family interacting with each other, sitting down like sentinels as they were preparing for the night patrol, or lying stretched out in a deep slumber. I looked for these wolves in subsequent years but they were not to be found near the two glacial kettles.

One last wolf event in Alaska is the notable wolf chasing prey animals by using a relay tactic. As much as people talk about this happening, you would think that a pilot flying a lot would have seen this chase technique several times in a long flying career. However, I have witnessed wolves chasing moose in a relay scheme only once in my long flying career in Alaska. This happened in the wintertime in the early 1990s in the Chugach Mountains 7 miles southeast of Merrill Field. It was twilight near sunset in late February when the tundra mountaintop covered with winter snow appeared on my left as I was flying back to Merrill Field in my Piper Cub. I could see an adult moose running upslope in a westward direction towards the top of the mountain which was at an elevation of 3,000 feet. I quickly turned my airplane in a benign circle to find out why the moose was running. The moose continued at a steady running speed as it reached the top of the flattop mountain. The light coming from the west cast a stronger illumination on the top of the mountain and I could clearly see a grey wolf chasing the moose from perhaps 60 yards behind it. I watched closely as the moose continued at a steady running speed—the wolf did not seem to be gaining any ground on the moose. This moose and wolf spectacle continued until I saw the wolf that was chasing the moose slow down, turn to the right, take a few steps and then stop. It was just standing there in the deep snow. Immediately up ahead I witnessed a second wolf coming out of nowhere and streaking up close behind the moose. Second wolf must have been lying down in the snow because it was not seen until it jumped up and began chasing the moose. Second wolf gained only a meager distance on the moose as it continued its life struggle to stay ahead of the wolf. It was getting very exciting now as the moose was heading downslope toward the coniferous forest below. The moose had the advantage on the down slope as it widened the distance between the wolf and the moose. As the moose entered the forest, Second wolf slowed down and gave up the chase. This wolf/prey struggle was over. Neither of the two wolves showed a great desire to push harder to get closer to the moose. It seemed as if they realized that this moose had lots of strength and stamina and showed no weakness of any kind. Even if they caught up with the moose, their chance of killing it was slim to none and the wolves could be in for serious damage in the struggle. These two wolves were hungry for a meal and were testing the moose to evaluate its strength. Since the wolves did not find a weakness, they did not work too hard in a losing confrontation. They will need plenty of energy for the next encounter hopefully with a promising moose that has much weaker strengths.

We are fortunate to have magnificent wild animals in our presence close to a large urban population for so many to enjoy. We certainly are blessed. We don't have to encounter the wolves but only knowing that they are there so close by is a great feeling of richness and well-being. This is a uniquely Alaskan experience and we have an obligation to do our best to help these animals remain free from strife. The wolves already have a tough life and don't need human-induced calamity. This will greatly impede the wolf's arduous task of providing food for all the scavengers it feeds and balancing the animal and plant ecosystem in which they live their fascinating lives. Let the wolves be wolves.

Part II: Compendium of Alaskan Images

Author's Images of Alaska's Exquisite Flying Environs

The author's Arctic Tern on a Knik River gravel bar 15 miles southeast of Palmer, Alaska. The Knik Glacier and the Chugach Mountains are in the background. (July 13, 2008)

Bull Moose strolling through Anchorage, Alaska.
(October 15, 2010)

One of Alaska's renowned Brown Bears from the Susitna River Basin northwest of Anchorage, Alaska. (June 18, 2010)

Cal on the left and guide with a robust king salmon caught in the Kenai River. (July 13, 2003)

A Piper Super Cub near the terminus of Lake George Glacier. A self-trained pilot can increase learning and proficiency to safely make this type of landing and takeoff. The landing area is a soft sand bar only 175 feet in length. Precise landing and takeoff is required—no room for error. (October 3, 2012)

Mammoth glaciers and snow-covered mountain peaks are found in the Chugach Mountains 50 miles east of Anchorage, Alaska. Mount Gannett at 10,005 feet ASL is the completely snow covered mountain in the center background. (July 10, 2012)

Airplanes that arrived at Pioneer Field for the May Day Fly-In and Airshow in Valdez, Alaska. (May 8, 2011)

The Thomas Training Center is the black-colored building shown at the top of Eagle Glacier at 5,800 feet ASL. Alaska Pacific University's Nordic Ski Center trains America's top skiers on Eagle Glacier during the summer months of July and August. (March 18, 2013)

Chugach Mountain Range creates a formidable barrier over 7,000 feet separating western Prince William Sound from the Knik River. Glaciers calving into Harriman Fjord from the left- Cascade, Barry, and Coxe. (September 22, 2007)

Piper Super Cub landing on a short sand bar on the Knik River. Notice the wheel marks in the sand—heavy breaking to slow down the airplane in limited space. (July 11, 2008)

Nylon covers on the Arctic Tern at my home base on Merrill Field. Note the sculptured wing and fuselage covers. This prevents the wind from bellowing the covers. The cover for the cowling has to be well-insulated. Insulated covers are also needed for the propeller and the nose cone. (February 23, 2013)

Shown here is a winter engine heating system with a sheet metal firebox. A 4" diameter stainless steel stovepipe fits on top of the firebox and connects to the inside of the engine cowling. The heating system is carried in my airplane in winter and used where electricity is not available. (January 5, 2010)

The author's Tern on the Upper Cook Inlet beach 50 miles west of Merrill Field. Beaches and river bars provide Alaskan pilots with thousands of places to land airplanes in natural terrain. (June 23, 2006)

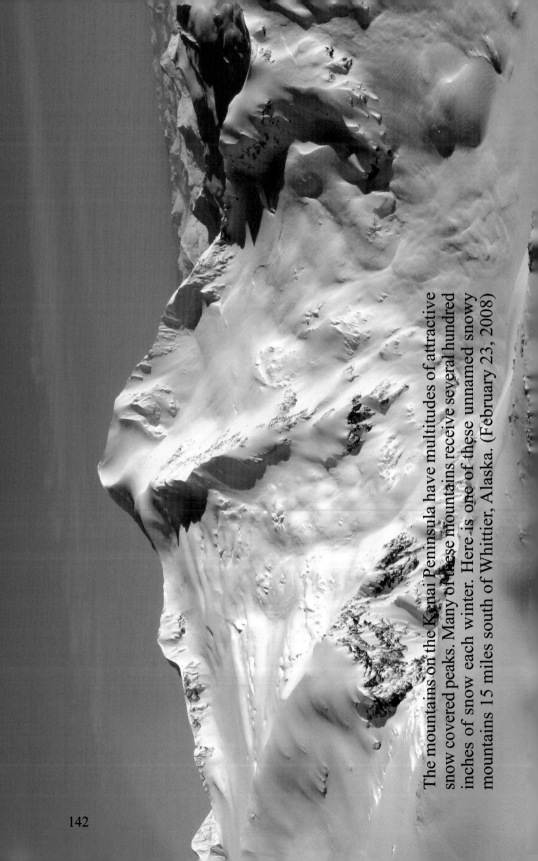

The mountains on the Kenai Peninsula have multitudes of attractive snow covered peaks. Many of these mountains receive several hundred inches of snow each winter. Here is one of these unnamed snowy mountains 15 miles south of Whittier, Alaska. (February 23, 2008)

Pilots cross-country skiing near the terminus of Spencer Glacier. (March 13, 2011)

143

Ski landing on the top of Little Susitna Mountain 45 miles northwest of Merrill Field. The elevation is 3,100 feet ASL. The ambient temperature is 8° F. Big Susitna Mountain is in the background. (February 18, 2007)

Ski landing on the massive Harding Ice Field 80 miles south of Merrill Field on the Kenai Peninsula. Elevation is 5,600 feet ASL. Ambient temperature is 26° F. View is northeast. (January 23, 2010)

Willow Highlands 50 miles north of Merrill Field. Elevation is 3,200 feet ASL. Talkeetna Mountains are in the background. The highlands receive twice the amount of snow as Anchorage and have deep powder snow all winter. This is a great choice for cross-country skiing and is only half an hour by flight from Merrill Field. (February 6, 2007)

Dee Deoudes, one of Alaska's elite backcountry pilots walking in his Piper 12 ski tracks on the top of Lake George Glacier. Elevation is 4,600 feet ASL. The glacier is 40 miles east of Merrill Field and 6 miles west of Harriman Fjord in Prince William Sound. (March 11, 2007)

The Iditarod Trail Sled Dog Race begins in Anchorage, Alaska the first Saturday in March each year. I fly 40 miles northwest from Merrill Field on Sunday and land on the frozen Yentna River to watch the dog mushers as they pass through on their restart from Willow, Alaska. This image shows Lance Mackey from Fairbanks, Alaska with his 2013 team of 16 hard-working dogs. Lance came in first in the Iditarod Race in 2007, 2008, 2009, and 2010. (March 3, 2013)

Preparing for cross-country skiing on the Willow Highlands at 3,200 feet ASL. Ambient temperature is 24° F. (March 28, 2007)

Ski-landing on Spencer Glacier 50 miles southeast of Merrill Field. From left—Piper Cub, Piper 12 and the author's Arctic Tern. Carpathian Peak rises to 6,000 feet above the Piper 12. Landing elevation on glacier is 4,600 feet. Temperature is 10°F. (March 3, 2007)

Author's airplane in the Ruth Gorge at 5,000 feet ASL. The Great Gorge is 1 mile wide and the ice is 3,800 feet deep. The granite rock pillar on the right is the Gargoyle and it rises 2,000 feet above the Ruth Glacier. Ambient temperature is 6° F. (March 15, 2013)

151

Landing approach to the Root Canal Glacier. The flying approach elevation is 9,000 feet. The glacier landing requires flying over the snow covered granite pillar in center and between the giant granite walls left and right. The landing is near the bottom of the mountain headwall in the background. The Moose's Tooth (10,335 feet) is the granite wall on the upper left. (April 2, 2013)

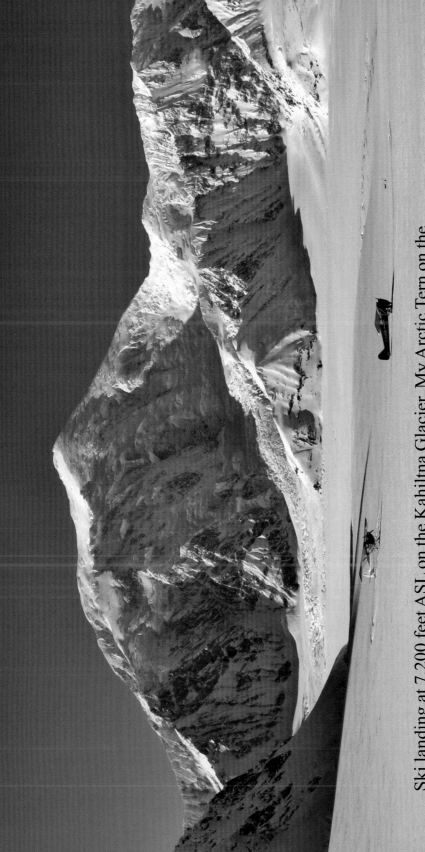

Ski landing at 7,200 feet ASL on the Kahiltna Glacier. My Arctic Tern on the left and Sean's blue Piper 11 on the right. This is Mount McKinley's traditional Base Camp for climbing the mountain. Mount Foraker (17,400 feet) is shown in the background. Ambient temperature is 12° F. (March 21, 2010)

Hand-turning the Arctic Tern in deep powder snow at McKinley's Kahiltna Glacier Base Camp. Ambient temperature is 15° F. Mount Hunter rises to 14,580 feet on the upper right. (April 12, 2011)

154

This shows the snow-covered mountain ridges in the Ruth Amphitheater where the Sheldon Mountain House is located. The Mountain House is on the higher elevation ridge in the rear. The Mountain House is on the left—toilet structure is on the right. Three cross-country skiers can be seen on the trail to the right of the ridge. Airplanes with skis land on the Ruth Glacier to the left side of the ridge. (April 3, 2012)

The legendary hexagon-shaped Sheldon Mountain House in the Ruth Amphitheater. Elevation is 6,100 feet ASL. Temperature is 12 degrees F. (March 7, 2014)

The Great Gorge of the Ruth Glacier is lined on both sides with gigantic granite mountain peaks. This image shows the peaks on the west side when departing Ruth Amphitheater. The name of the peaks from the left is Mount Church, Grosvenor, Johnson, Wake and Bradley. (April 3, 2012)

Ski landing on the Root Canal Glacier. My Tern on the left and Sean's Piper 14 on the right. Elevation is 7,800 feet ASL. Ambient temperature is 14° F. (April 26, 2013)

When pilots learn to be extraordinary pilots they will perform routine landings where most pilots would not dare to go. Here is one of those Alaskan pilots practicing landing and taking off on a small sand bar surrounded by water in the Knik River near Palmer, Alaska. The airplane has already landed (notice the wheel marks on the sand bar) and now is set for the takeoff. From the position of the aircraft, the pilot has 250 feet of sand bar forward for takeoff. This takes the utmost—not only in pilot skills and proficiency but in self-confidence. (September 11, 2005)

Pilot Sean Sylvester (left) and the author standing on the ridge where the Sheldon Mountain House is built. The Ruth Amphitheater is in the background. Our airplanes are on the Ruth Glacier at 5,800 feet. (March 21, 2010)

Part III: Memoranda

Short Titles for Memoranda

MEMORANDUM 1
SUBJECT: Flying in Alaska

December 30, 2014

1. Alaska had the lowest population of any state in the U.S. from 1960 until the 1990 Census when it surpassed Wyoming. Alaska's population has continued to grow and now has a higher population than Vermont. A recent census in late 2014 recorded 736,732 people living in Alaska. More than half of Alaska's residents live in and around Anchorage and the Matanuska-Susitna Valley (Palmer and Wasilla). Alaska Department of Transportation and Public Facilities reported 4,857 miles of paved roads in Alaska in 2009. Many of the remote communities in Alaska are not connected to the road system. Due to the scarcity of highway infrastructure and the vast distances across Alaska, aviation serves as a major transportation link. There are 700 airports and more than 3,000 airstrips in Alaska primarily for commercial use. Alaska's elite pilots access remote areas in Alaska without airports and landing strips, by landing in natural terrain.

2. The best flying environment is right here in Alaska. There is no place where the terrain, which includes mountains, glaciers, and fjords, is more spectacular. See *Prophetic Pronouncement of Coastal Alaska* by Henry Gannett, written in 1904. The glacier-covered Chugach Mountains and Prince William Sound are located east of Anchorage. Lying to the north of Anchorage is the arcing 450-mile-long Alaska Range with Mount McKinley, its centerpiece, at 20,320 feet above sea level, 130 air miles to the north–northwest. To the south of Anchorage across Turnagain Arm of Cook Inlet is the awe-inspiring Kenai Peninsula with its spectacular glaciers, snow-clad mountains, salt water fjords, the massive Harding and Sargent ice fields, the world-famous salmon runs in the Kenai River and the halibut capital of the world in Homer, Alaska. All this magnificent and incomparable wild country is accessible by small aircraft from Anchorage. Alaskan pilots traditionally fly into this wild country without infrastructure and land their taildraggers in natural terrain.

3. Alaska has some of the best flying weather with long daylight hours (20 hours or more) in the summer months. Although the mountains in Alaska reach high elevations, the valleys are usually low in elevation. The days are cool in summer, and cold in winter. This makes for excellent flying weather with great lift in summer when the day temperatures are in the 50s and 60s

Fahrenheit. This contrasts with the high temperatures (from 80 to over 100 degrees Fahrenheit) and miserable flying conditions (greatly reduced lift) in the Lower 48 states in the summer months. Alaska can have extreme windstorms (Chinooks, Williwaws, and others), clouds forming low ceilings, fog banks, huge snowstorms, extremely low temperatures in winter (minus 20 to minus 40 degrees Fahrenheit in winter), and other serious weather problems that can be real challenging when flying. However, there are ample good weather and satisfactory flying conditions for many days in Alaska in both the summer and winter months.

4. The snowpack in Alaska in winter provides first-rate conditions for ski-flying operations. Pilots change out their landing gear from wheels to skis after the first snowstorms establish a stable snowpack suitable for landing ski-equipped airplanes. Ski flying with sufficient snowpack runs from December to the first part of April—over 4 months. Ski flying in winter provides by far the most landing places compared with wheels or floats in summer. The summer landing places on wheels are suitable for winter landings on skis. Frozen lakes that are snow-covered in winter provide excellent landing places for ski-equipped airplanes. Glaciers covered with a deep snowpack also provide excellent landing areas on skis. Many places in the mountains where wheel landings are not suitable in summer offer excellent conditions for landing in winter on skis. Examples are benches, saddles, valley bottoms, and plateaus above tree line. Airplanes equipped with skis in a forced landing are much safer than wheel-equipped airplanes, as they can be safely landed almost anywhere on the snowpack. Wheeled-equipped airplanes in forced landings will almost certainly flip over when landing on the snowpack.

5. Many pilots use airplanes for access to their privately owned cabins located in remote areas within 100 miles of Anchorage. These cabins are used primarily for recreation, hunting, and fishing. Most of these cabins are not road accessible and the airplane provides the primary conveyance. These cabins are scattered in every direction from Anchorage. Large numbers of cabins are found in the Susitna River basin that lies north–northwest of Anchorage. It is a mammoth-sized boreal forest (spruce and hardwoods) that is mostly uninhabited with the exception of the Parks Highway, which bisects it in a north–south orientation. The Susitna River basin has hundreds of lakes that are accessible with floatplanes in summer and ski-equipped airplanes in winter on the ice-covered lakes. The basin is 125 miles north–south and 75 miles wide at its widest part—over 3 million acres. There are

many cabins on the northwestern part of the Kenai Peninsula, which has over 4,000 lakes. Many other cabins are found in Redoubt and Trading Bays, which are located on the northwestern side of upper Cook Inlet.

6. Flying wildlife surveys in Alaska is another very rewarding experience with the scenic landscapes and the magnificent wildlife. Surveys are traditionally flown to obtain population and composition data for moose, caribou, Dall sheep, mountain goats, and waterfowl. Alaska Department of Fish and Game hires many pilots throughout Alaska to complete the surveys.

7. Many other pilots in Alaska with commercial licenses fly passengers and cargo to remote villages and other places in Alaska. There are many air taxi positions in Alaska to fulfill this need. Other commercial opportunities in Alaska are flying charter flights for sightseeing tours and dropping off passengers in remote areas for fishing, hunting, bear viewing, rafting, kayaking, backpacking, and other outdoor adventures.

8. The camaraderie of flying in Alaska is the best a pilot could possibly find anywhere. This is because of the large number of skilled pilots to learn from and talk to about flying in new and exciting places. Flying to places already traveled will offer exciting new experiences as the weather and the wildlife sighted are never the same as the previous fly-in. Flying with experienced pilots can be a rewarding and safe experience for all that participate.

MEMORANDUM 2
SUBJECT: Location of Anchorage in Relationship to the Mountains, Glaciers, and Fjords

January 14, 2013

1. Anchorage lies on a coastal plain near sea level on upper Cook Inlet at the western end of the Chugach Mountain Range. The Chugach Mountains extends eastward from Anchorage for 250 miles along the north side of Prince William Sound. The mountain range stretches inland from salt water for 50 miles or more. It is magnificent mountain, glacier, and fjord country with no human infrastructure with the exception of the Richardson Highway, which bisects the Chugach Range from Valdez north through Thompson Pass. Apart from the Richardson Highway, the remaining portion of the Chugach Range is pristine wilderness with mountains, mammoth glaciers, and immense sized ice fields.

2. South of Anchorage across Turnagain Arm of Cook Inlet is the Kenai Peninsula (6,424,320 acres) with the massive Harding and Sargent ice fields. The glacier-clad Kenai Mountains on the eastern and southern two-thirds of the Kenai Peninsula have a large number of glaciers facing the Gulf of Alaska. These mountains receive several hundred inches of snow annually. The snow feeds the glaciers and ice fields. Kenai Fjords National Park (669,000 acres) is along the southern coastline of the Kenai Peninsula southwest of Seward, Alaska. The Kenai National Wildlife Refuge includes almost 2 million acres along the western portion of the Kenai Peninsula while the Chugach National Forest on the eastern portion of the peninsula includes slightly over 1 million acres.

3. Fifty miles northeast of Anchorage are the Talkeetna Mountains. This is a range of mountains with small glaciers near the highest mountain peaks, which are about 8,000 feet. Eighty miles west of Anchorage is the southern end of the 450-mile long Alaska Range. Mount Gerdine (12,600 feet) and Mount Spurr (11,070 feet) are the highest mountains in this part of the Alaska Range. Massive glaciers surround these mountain peaks. Mount Spurr is an active volcano, 80 miles west of Anchorage, which last erupted in August 1992. The first eruption struck at 2 PM. The light passed from daylight to twilight (almost dark) in one hour. A thick cloud of ash completely covered Anchorage with one to two inches of the volcanic material. I collected an ash sample and placed it in a jar for safekeeping. The ash color is dark grey. Mount Redoubt is another volcano 60 miles south of Mount Spurr in the Alaska Range. Mount Redoubt had massive eruptions in 1989–1990 and again in March 2009. Its ash color is distinctive from Mount Spurr—tan or light brown.

4. Mount McKinley at 20,320 feet above sea level is the only mountain in North America that is over 20,000 feet. It is located in the central part of the Alaska Mountain Range 130 air miles north, northwest of Anchorage. Massive glaciers flow off this mammoth mountain. The largest glaciers are the Kahiltna (45 miles in length); Ruth (38 miles); Eldridge (29 miles); Yentna (28 miles); Muldrow (27 miles); Dall (22 miles); Lacuna (22 miles); and the Tokositna (21 miles). The widest of these glaciers (rivers of ice) range from 1.8 to 3.6 miles; the ice thickness can be several thousand feet. The elevation of the terminus of the Kahiltna Glacier is less than 1,000 feet above sea level. The top of the Kahiltna Glacier is 10,000 feet at Kahiltna Pass—an elevation gain over 9,000 feet. Private aircraft are allowed to land in Denali National Park on wheels, floats, and skis. Ski-equipped aircraft

can land on all popular glacier landing sites including the Mount McKinley mountain climbing base camp on Kahiltna Glacier at 7,200 feet and the Sheldon Mountain House in Ruth Amphitheater at 5,800 feet.

MEMORANDUM 3
SUBJECT: Gannett's Prophetic Pronouncement of Coastal Alaska

January 12, 2013

Anchorage is located in Southcentral Alaska along the upper part of Cook Inlet. The city lies directly below the western slopes of the Chugach Mountain Range. The coastal mountain ranges in Alaska, including the Chugach, were chronicled by Henry Gannett, an early pioneer of geography and topography in the United States. He became Chief Geographer of the US Geological Survey in 1882, three years after its creation. A stunning mountain in the Chugach Range with a permanent snow cone was named after him. Mount Gannett is 58 miles east of Anchorage near the lower part of Knik Glacier. The peak's elevation is 10,005 feet and its base on the north side is 1,400 feet, giving it a topographic prominence of 8,600 feet. Henry Gannett's *Prophetic Pronouncement of Coastal Alaska* was brilliantly written in 1904. His vision into the future is amazing. Gannett's pronouncement follows.

There are glaciers, mountains, fjords elsewhere, but nowhere else on earth is there such abundance and magnificence of mountain, fjord, and glacier country. For a thousand miles the coast is a continuous panorama. For the one Yosemite of California, Alaska has hundreds. The mountains and glaciers of the Cascade Range are duplicated and a thousand fold exceeded in Alaska. The Alaska coast is to become the showplace of the entire world, and pilgrims, not only from America, but from far beyond the seas, will throng in endless procession to see it. Its grandeur is more valuable than gold or fish or timber, for it will never be exhausted. This value measured by direct returns in money from tourists will be enormous; measured in health and pleasure it will be incalculable.

MEMORANDUM 4
SUBJECT: Alaska's Calling Card

January 10, 2013

1. Alaska has extraordinary pilots and at the same time it has so much more to attract people to the Great Land. Alaska is the *Land of the Giants*.

With a mammoth size of 663,267 square miles, Alaska is larger than many countries in the world—larger than Norway, Sweden, Germany, France, Spain, Iran, Pakistan, Egypt, Kenya, Tanzania, Venezuela, Peru, Bolivia, and Chile. Alaska is one-sixth the size of the Lower 48 and has in access of 49,000 miles of coastline, more than all of the contiguous United States combined. It is estimated that there are approximately 100,000 glaciers in Alaska with more than 600 that are named. The Bering Glacier and its adjoining Bagley Icefield is the largest and longest glacier (114 miles in length) in continental North America and is the largest temperate glacier system in the world. The Hubbard Glacier is the largest tidewater glacier in North America reaching 76 miles in length. The Malaspina Glacier in Alaska is the world's largest Piedmont glacier. It is 40 miles wide and 28 miles long with an area of 1,500 square miles (the size of Rhode Island).

2. Mount McKinley at 20,320 feet is the highest mountain in North America. It is part of the 450-mile Alaska Range, one of the 39 mountain ranges in Alaska. McKinley is not the only big mountain in Alaska. The Wrangell–St. Elias Mountain National Park and Preserve has 9 of the 16 highest mountain peaks in the country. Mount St. Elias at 18,008 is the nation's second-tallest mountain. Other mountains are Mount Bona (16,421 feet); Mount Blackburn (16,390 feet) and Mount Stanford (16,237 feet). Mount Hunter, between Mount McKinley and Mount Foraker (17,400 feet), is higher in elevation at 14,573 feet than Mount Whitney (14,495 feet), the highest mountain in the Lower 48 states.

3. Moose are the world's largest member of the deer family and the Alaskan moose (*Alces alces gigas*) is the largest of all moose (bull moose in Alaska weigh from 1,000 to 1,600 pounds). Moose inhabit northern forests in North America, Europe, and Asia (Russia). In Europe, they are called elk. Alaska's coastal brown bears also grow larger here than in any other area in the world. Mature males in Alaska average 1,058 to 1,175 pounds over the course of the year with the largest bears weighing up to 1,600 pounds after gorging on salmon during the summer months. When standing upright on its hind legs, a large male will reach a height of over 10 feet. These bears share the title with the polar bears as the largest land-based predator in the world. Alaska's polar bears are off the northwest and northern coasts (Chukchi and Beaufort Seas). They live on the ice and feed on seals. The largest polar bears weigh up to an astounding 1,700 pounds, slightly heavier than the brown bear.

4. Alaska has over 49,000 miles of coastline, over 3,000 rivers, and more than 3 million natural lakes (lakes that are over 20 acres in size). This provides for the most prolific salmon habitat in the world. Every summer, millions of adult salmon that feed in the Gulf of Alaska and the Bering Sea return to Alaska's rivers for spawning and rearing their young. Alaska's giant king salmon is the state's fish. The largest king salmon ever caught weighed 126 pounds. It was caught in a fish wheel near Petersburg, Alaska in 1949. The largest sport-caught king salmon was 97 pounds and 4 ounces. It was caught by Les Anderson in the world-famous Kenai River in 1985. The largest red salmon also comes from the fabled Kenai River. The red salmon world record was 15 pounds and 3 ounces and was caught by angler Stan Roach on August 9, 1987. The world's most abundant source of wild native rainbow trout and steelhead are found in Southeast Alaska westward along the Gulf of Alaska to Bristol Bay in Southwest Alaska. These wilderness fisheries are as unique as they are prolific. The Alaska Department of Fish and Game gives trophy certificates for anglers taking rainbows that meet the minimum weight standard, which is over 15 pounds. The largest rainbows in Alaska exceed 20 pounds in weight.

5. Alaska's diverse and magnificent wildlife not only includes the largest moose, brown bear, polar bear, gray wolf, king, and red salmon, but also has the largest gathering of bald eagles (several thousand) north of Haines, Alaska and more than half of the world's population of humpback whales. Bowhead and beluga whales summer in the Bering, Chukchi, and Beaufort Seas. A small population of beluga whales (284) is found in Cook Inlet and frequently can be observed from aircraft flying over Turnagain and Knik Arms of upper Cook Inlet near Anchorage, Alaska. Blue, finback, sperm, killer, and other whales are found in the Bering Sea and the Gulf of Alaska. Walrus and many seal species are found in the Bering, Chukchi, and Beaufort Seas. Other large land mammals found in Alaska include the bison, black bear, mountain goat, Dall sheep and caribou. The caribou are distributed in 32 herds totaling approximately 950,000 animals. The western Arctic caribou herd is the largest with an estimated 348,000 animals in 2009. Smaller mammals in Alaska include the wolverine, gray wolf, coyote, lynx, Arctic fox, red fox, beaver, fisher, marten, mink, red squirrel, northern-flying squirrel, ermine, least weasel, and small rodents.

6. The birdlife in Alaska is also a top attraction. The list of known avian taxa in Alaska in 2012 includes 493 naturally occurring species in 64 families

and 20 orders. This checklist includes birds common to Alaska as well as species that are rare (occurring annually), casual (not annually but at irregular intervals), and accidental (one or two Alaska records). Alaska is a haven for waterfowl as half of its land is wetlands. Alaska's waterfowl include 2 species of swans, 5 species of geese and 27 species of ducks. The annual migration of waterfowl flying to Alaska in the spring and departing in the autumn includes 120,000 swans, 1 million geese, and 10 to 12 million ducks.

7. The trumpeter swan is the most magnificent of the northern swans and the largest of all waterfowl (weighing 20 to 38 pounds). It summers in Alaska and raises its brood of cygnets here. Izembek Lagoon (30 miles long and 5 miles wide) located 600 miles southwest of Anchorage along the southern tip of the Alaska Peninsula contains one of the largest eelgrass beds in North America. It is considered one of the most important wetlands in the world and in 1986 became the first wetland in the United States to receive global recognition by being named to the list of Wetlands of International Importance. The pristine environment and the abundant food source attract large numbers of Canada geese, virtually all of the world's population of Pacific black brant (130,000), puddle and sea ducks for a two-month period beginning in late August and ending in early November. The Pacific black brant is the smallest and fastest of the geese. They leave Izembek with a brisk tailwind and fly southeast across the Pacific Ocean nonstop 4,420 miles to their primary wintering grounds in Baja California in just two and a half days.

MEMORANDUM 5
SUBJECT: May Day Fly-In and Air Show held in Valdez, Alaska

May 25, 2010

1. The May Day Fly-In was held on May 7, 8, and 9, 2010. This was the fourth consecutive year that I had flown the Arctic Tern to Valdez to attend three days of aviation activities. The Fly-In kept getting better each year—better organized and managed. It is always interesting to meet pilots (some already known and some new pilots) and others that attend the aviation events in Valdez. The weather always seems to create difficulty flying from Anchorage to Valdez and back home. I found Thompson Pass closed twice because of low clouds and fog and had to go around it by flying down the Copper River. The strong winds blowing up the Copper River were whistling by at 45 miles per hour. I had to fly 3,000 feet above the river to escape the dust clouds coming up from the river sand and gravel bars. Flying across Prince William Sound

is a shorter distance to Valdez but I don't like flying an hour over open water with almost no place to land if an engine failure happened. Most beaches in Prince William Sound are too narrow and rocky even at low tide to land on in case of emergency. The weather this year was sunny with light winds for three consecutive days during the Fly-In. More than 200 pilots arrived by airplane for the Fly-In. Most pilots were from the Kenai Peninsula, Anchorage, the Matanuska-Susitna Valley, and Fairbanks. There were also several pilots that flew their airplanes from the Lower 48 states to Valdez.

2. The annual May Day Fly-In and Air Show brings together some of the best pilots in the world. They test their skills in the Short Field Take-Off and Landing (STOL) competition which is the major flying event. Airplanes are divided into the following classes: Light Touring (Cessna 150, 170, 172, 175, 177; Stinson 108); Heavy Touring (Cessna 180, 185, 182, 206, 210; Maule M-7, M-9); Experimental Bush Class and Bush Class (Piper 12, 14, 18, 22; Stinson 105; Citabria, Arctic Tern; Scout; Maule M-4, M-5). Can you imagine a Super Cub taking off from a starting line in 68 feet and landing in 63 feet past the line? Those were Paul Claus' numbers when he won the Bush Class competition. He has over 25,000 hours of flying in Alaska and is one of our best pilots. Paul also won the Heavy Touring competition in a four-place Cessna 185 with a takeoff distance of 180 feet and landing in 250 feet. Paul won the Experimental Class in a Carbon Cub with about the same performance as the Super Cub. Paul won again in the Bush Challenge in a Super Cub loaded with 300 pounds of cargo with a takeoff distance of 96 feet.

3. Other scheduled events include pilot sessions (discussions on bush flying and maintenance tips), airplane rides, aerobatic demonstrations (flown in a Super Cub by Marc Paine), remote-control airplane demonstrations, Flour Bombing (pilots throw sacks of flour out of airplanes to a target on the ground), and the Poker Run .

4. The Poker Run is for pilots who arrive in Valdez for the Fly-In and desire to make an organized group flight into Prince William Sound. It was scheduled for Saturday afternoon beginning at 3:30 PM. The Poker Run is a 204-mile counterclockwise circuit through the eastern portion of Prince William Sound. It starts at Valdez and you fly west on Port Valdez, then south on Valdez Arm to Tatitlek. Next is a landing at the gravel strip near the Native village of Tatitlek. From here you continue the flight across 40

miles of open water on Prince William Sound to Hook Point on the southeast coast of Hinchinbrook Island. Here on the sandy beach facing the Gulf of Alaska we all landed. There were 69 airplanes on the Poker Run this year (a record) and it was interesting to walk the beach and see so many airplanes with tricycle type landing gear here. Pilots infrequently land this type of aircraft on sandy beaches. A Cessna 185 on wheel floats even landed on the sandy beach at Hook Point. All the pilots gathered near the beach to get a group photograph. The next landing was only 10 minutes away in Cordova.

5. We landed our airplanes at the Municipal airport on Eyak Lake. This is a small gravel strip just outside Cordova, a small commercial fishing village of approximately 2,000 inhabitants (I lived in Cordova in 1972 working for the US Forest Service). Our next landing would be at Cordova Mudhole Smith Airport which is a few miles east of Cordova in the Copper River Flats. This is the jet airport that serves Cordova. Do you know of any other place with 2,000 people that has jet airport service? Alaska Airlines provides service west to Anchorage or east to Juneau, Sitka, Ketchikan, and Seattle on a daily basis.

6. The next flying is to the Copper River and then north up river. The entire floodplain on the Copper River was still covered with a foot of snow. It looked like winter! This was my first time as pilot in command flying over the lower Copper River. In July 1970, I and another kayaker had paddled down the Copper River from Chitina. This is a 110-mile journey on a beautiful glacial river with mountains on both sides. You can't paddle out through the mouth of the Copper River because it is too shallow. We exited the lower Copper River on one of its tributaries (Alaganik Slough) to the Gulf of Alaska. From here we paddled 10 miles west to the Eyak River and up the Eyak River (6 miles) to Eyak Lake Dam. We lifted our kayaks over the dam and paddled in Eyak Lake to Cordova.

7. It was great to see the kayak route from the air. The Copper River is unique. The lower Copper River enters Miles Lake and flows out the lower end. A very large glacier (Miles Glacier, which is 35 miles in length) calves into the lake. We paddled our kayaks near the terminus of the glacier and a large front section of ice on the glacier broke off, sending large chunks of ice into Miles Lake. This created waves several feet high. The roaring noise of the waves terrified us. We paddled hard toward the middle of the lake to get away from the big waves. We could not outrun the waves; they overcame us. We turned

to face the waves head-on in our kayaks. The waves were not a problem for the great Klepper kayaks (a canoe would have ended in a disaster) although I can still remember that loud roaring noise the waves made as they streaked across Miles Lake. A few miles downriver from Miles Lake we came upon the Childs Glacier, which forms the bank of the river for 2-miles on the west side. I do not know of another river that has a 2-mile-long ice bank that calves into the river. Very special indeed! The last part of our flight was up the Tasnuna River over Marshall Pass to Valdez. There are beautiful mountains and glaciers here—the mountains rise from sea level to over 8,000 feet.

8. The May Day Fly-In in 2010 was a great joy and I hope to be able to return for many more Fly-Ins in future years.

MEMORANDUM 6
SUBJECT: Advanced Training by Marc C. Lee*

June 18, 2014

1. Advanced Training by Marc C. Lee in July 2014 issue of Plane & Pilot Magazine covered the traditional ways to expand your aviation horizon. These typically are tailwheel endorsement, commercial and instrument ratings, seaplane rating, multiengine rating, aerobatic training, warbird flying and flying gliders. Alaskan pilots have other options to accomplish useful results.

2. We have the extraordinary pilots in the Great Land. They are among the best in the world. Why not take advantage of this amazing gift? That is what many pilots in Alaska do to substantially improve their aviation skills. This is accomplished by learning and implementing improved flying strategies and techniques developed by Alaska's distinguished pilots. The learning pilot takes command of the training and in time becomes a knowledgeable, innovative, well-disciplined and self-reliant pilot. This advanced training will make you the best pilot you can be—bar none. In addition, it will substantially lower your aircraft accident rate by a wide margin.

3. The inspiration in flying and training the Alaskan way is off the charts. The progression and journey in becoming a much improved pilot is one of the most cherished events in a pilot's aviation career. Once you get started,

* This narrative has been published in *Plane & Pilot* Magazine in the October 2014 issue. *Plane and Pilot* Magazine is a National and International Aviation Journal.

this becomes a challenging, self-motivating and career-long journey. You never stop learning. You never stop training and improving your flying skills. This ensures the highest pilot proficiency. I would hope additional pilots could take advantage of this incredible way to focus on your flying skills and greatly improve them. This is one of the preeminent ways to expand your aviation horizon. The pilot benefits are enormous—nothing else compares with the great rewards.

MEMORANDUM 7
SUBJECT: Flying by the Seat of Your Pants

March 30, 2014

1. Flying by the *seat of your pants* is the most mysterious flying technique in all of aviation. The reason for this is that it is so benign that you often don't even know that it is there. After trying to understand it and figure it out, it is so elusive that when you think you see it or feel it you are not certain you do. It is always difficult explaining to other pilots how to learn this technique. I try to explain to pilots that this is not a technique that you will quickly pick up. The best way to learn it is to understand the basis of the technique and then just go flying. Keep this technique on your mind and one day when you are least expecting it, this technique will show up and you will recognize it.

2. This technique is not often applauded by pilots nor is it always brought up in discussions on flying techniques. Nevertheless, learning to fly by the *seat of your pants* is one of the most important techniques used by Alaska's elite pilots for off-airport operations. It is the most accurate technique for determining your aircraft's flying performance. In slow flight, initial stalls can easily be detected and corrections can be made to prevent unintentional stalls. An even more basic use for flying by the *seat of your pants* is to be able to perform *precision landings*. Every landing by the Alaskan pilot must be made with the main wheels touching down at initial stall speed. This takes all of that excess and dangerous kinetic energy out of your airplane before landing it. The reliability and accuracy of this technique is what makes it so valuable. All variable factors such as wind speed and direction, aircraft weight with cargo loads and constant changing weights due to fuel burn, density altitude, and many others are all incorporated within the airplane that is showing the pilot its flying performance. This means that the information you are detecting is absolutely accurate. Your airplane does not lie.

3. Most pilots rely on an airspeed indicator to provide information on the proper speed to land an airplane. The airspeed indicator at low speeds is not very accurate. Other factors can greatly degrade the indicated airspeed accuracy and lead to false assumptions. Some of these are gusty winds, high density altitude, heavy cargo loads, and many others. All of these alter the reliability of indicated wind speeds and make flying in for a landing difficult and highly problematic. General Aviation pilots compensate for this inaccuracy by using the FAA recommended 1.3 Vso for flight speed on landing. Alaska's elite pilots cannot and will not land an aircraft with double the amount of kinetic energy in the airplane when there is another safe way to land the airplane at stall speed. Flying by the *seat of your pants* is used to precisely land your airplane every single time right at the initial stall speed. There is never an issue or a problem with landing your airplane at stall speed by relying on flying by the *seat of your pants* for detecting it.

4. For all of you who want a formal explanation of flying by the *seat of your pants*—here is it. It can be defined as flying an airplane without the aid of instruments and using only instinct, visual observations, feel and practical judgment. A second definition is flying by using all of one's senses—including lateral and vertical "G forces" transmitted to your derriere through the seat—to control an aircraft in flight. While the latter phrase may have been used in an uncomplimentary sense, it isn't always the case. Improvising and standard-izing everything in life probably isn't a good idea, instruments lie, and blindly following procedures can exacerbate a problem that situational awareness and instincts developed through experience could have nipped in the bud.

5. There is nothing quite as important in flying your airplane as being creative and learning to be your own self-reliant pilot. *Seat of your pants* flying will give you the best opportunity to accomplish this task. This way of flying is a developed art learned over a sufficient amount of time by self-training.

MEMORANDUM 8
SUBJECT: Safety Alert in 2003 by the NTSB

January 10, 2014

1. Title of the Safety Alert: *Prevent Aerodynamic Stalls at Low Altitude.* National Transportation Safety Board says pilots need to avoid this often deadly scenario through timely recognition and appropriate responses.

2. The problem happens when maneuvering an airplane at low altitude in visual meteorological conditions. Many pilots fail to avoid conditions that lead to aerodynamic stall, fail to recognize the warning signs of a stall onset and fail to apply appropriate recovery responses. Many stall accidents result when a pilot is momentarily distracted from the primary task of flying, such as while maneuvering in the airport traffic pattern, during an emergency, or when fixating on ground objects. Aerodynamic stall accidents fall into the "loss of control in flight" category, which is the most common defining event for fatal accidents in the personal flying sector of general aviation. Sadly, the circumstances of each new accident are often remarkably similar to those of previous accidents. This suggests that some pilots are not taking advantage of the lessons learned from such tragedies that could help them avoid making the same mistakes over and over again.

3. The NTSB Alert is very important because stall accidents happen way too often and kill too many pilots and passengers every year. The NTSB report was issued to alert pilots about this tradegy and hopefully to play a role in helping pilots reduce the rate of stall accidents to an acceptable level. Nevertheless, this will not happen because large numbers of general aviation pilots do not have the proper training and knowledge needed to avoid many stall accidents. NTSB acknowledges that the circumstances of each new stall accident are often remarkably similar to those of previous accidents. This validates that many pilots do not have the necessary skills and knowledge to prevent stall accidents. If the pilots had the proper skills and knowledge, the stall accident rate would be significantly reduced to lower levels than what is now occurring. Flight Instructors training general aviation pilots twice a year to practice stalls simply does not provide the effective training and knowledge necessary for many pilots to avoid unintentional stalls that lead to aircraft accidents.

4. General aviation pilots need a new strategy and training program to significantly reduce stall related accidents. It just happens that one of the Alaska's elite off-airport pilots Cardinal Rule for becoming the best pilot is Precision Landings. This is a two-step procedure that requires making selected or spot landings at initial stall speed. It requires the main wheels simultaneously touching down in a symbolic rectangular box that is 60 feet wide and 20 feet in depth and also the wheels touching down at initial stall speed. This type of landing technique provides pilots with the safest and shortest way to make off-field landings in natural terrain. Learning and training to make initial stall landings every time you land your aircraft will also significantly increase your

understanding about stalling an aircraft to a much higher level than what is available with a Flight Instructor at high altitude twice a year. Once a pilot learns to make precision landings at initial stall speed, the increase in proficiency and knowledge will allow pilots to significantly reduce unintentional stalls and related accidents. The Alaskan pilots have already proven many years ago that precision landings provide positive results not only in short field landings but also in avoiding unintentional stalls that lead to deadly accidents.

5. General Aviation Pilots would benefit substantially in reducing stall accidents if they learned the Alaska pilots' Precision Landings.

MEMORANDUM 9
SUBJECT: Landing Insights by Thomas A. Horne published in AOPA Pilot Magazine August 2010

July 1, 2014

1. Horne states that your skill at landing an airplane is your most heavily-judged piloting skill. He also pronounces that most accidents occur in the landing phase of flight. The majority is mishandled crosswind landings but there is a fair share of overshoots, undershoots, and ground loops. Additional articles in AOPA Pilot follow this introduction. These articles cover more prominent landing challenges.

2. As a long-time pilot flying the wilds of Alaska, I could not agree more with Thomas Horne's introduction on landings. With the other five articles published in AOPA Pilot on landings, I can't say I am in complete agreement. Before I review and comment on the AOPA Pilot articles on landings, it is important to be aware of my aviation roots. I was trained like most General Aviation (GA) Pilots with FAA Certificated Instructors. I began in 1975 with a multitude of instructors and learned many important flying techniques from each of them. This gave me the skills needed to safely fly and to obtain the Private Pilot License (PPL). After receiving the PPL, I wanted to learn how the extraordinary Alaskan pilots fly. I was aware of Alaska's distinguished pilots several years before I received my PPL. These astonishing pilots transported me and my recreational gear to remote locations in Alaska for kayaking, mountain climbing, backpacking, skiing and winter camping. I was shocked to observe the skills these pilots portrayed when landing on short gravel bars where no airplanes have landed before. The detailed evaluations from the air and the precision landings were incredible.

3. I communicated with as many of these highly talented pilots as I could locate. They showed me how to get started in learning the advanced training that is necessary for greatly expanding my aviation horizon. What they had were original flying strategies and techniques. These were absolutely necessary because the basic and conventional flying procedures were not sufficient for the challenging flying and landing in Alaska's remote backcountry. They told me to take command and go out and learn in my airplane all that I have studied prior to flying. Learn on your own. Self-training is the modus operandi. So off I went. I found it to be self-motivating and a career-long journey. You never stop learning. You never stop training and improving your flying skills. I have over 30 years of this self-style training and learning to be a capable pilot that can handle the unique challenges that wild Alaska has to offer. Much of what I have learned is not just for off-airport pilots landing in challenging natural terrain, but also for GA pilots that are landing primarily on airports and occasionally on airstrips. Advanced techniques from the Alaskan pilots will improve any pilot's flying skills and it will reduce your aircraft accident rate to near zero. The latter is the reason GA pilots should pay attention and adopt some of the best Alaskan techniques.

4. The first article after the introduction by Thomas Horne is *Shorts and Softs* by Dave Hirschman. He states the main variables you have to control in making short landings are speed and placement on the runway. Pilots should make a pre-selected touchdown point and they should make the touchdown at minimum speed. That will be sufficient on traditional runways; however, it is certainly in no way close to precision landings by Alaska's extraordinary pilots. They take precision landings to another level. They learn to simultaneously touchdown their wheels in a symbolic box (20 feet deep and 60 feet wide) and at initial stall speed. These precision landings restrain your aircraft so that it does not have sufficient kinetic energy to get out of control and crash and it places the wheels down at the end of the runway so that there is no chance of running off the landing area into rough terrain. This is the best landing technique that exists. It is not difficult to learn and it is a safe landing procedure.

5. Hirschman mentions that it is not necessary to fly a steep approach when making a short landing. Most of Alaska's top pilots make high and steep angle approaches to landing. The reason for this is it provides the best technique for being able to observe the target spot for landing. It also provides the shortest landing roll as the wheels (especially Alaskan Bushwheels) dissipate a large amount of kinetic energy when they plop down from a steep angle onto the

landing area. Braking is often not necessary when all of the excess kinetic energy is drained from the aircraft prior to landing. This ensures a short roll out.

6. Hirschman says that Lori MacNichol from Mountain/Canyon Flying in Idaho has been teaching backcountry pilots her own technique for landing. It involves picking an aiming point on the runway, setting the airplane's attitude, and precisely controlling airspeed with pitch and rate of descent with power so that the aircraft touches down just beyond the aiming point. MacNichol's landing technique is similar to the Alaskan pilot's precision landings although it is not the same. Landing just beyond the aiming point is not precise and uses up too much runway when landing on short strips. Landing in a small box is extremely precise and is always accurate due to the amount of training for this technique. Controlling airspeed when landing is important but not limiting your airspeed to the initial stall speed of the aircraft is not controlling kinetic energy to the fullest extent. The safest landing possible is placing wheels down on a selected target at stall speed. MacNichol's technique is probably sufficient for Idaho's lengthy backcountry strips but it is only half the effectiveness of the elite Alaskan precision landings.

7. Ian J. Twombly's article is *Get Crossed*. It covers the basics of crosswind landings. He talks about the two traditional techniques used for crosswind landings—side slipping and crabbing. The coverage is well presented although one major omission is that there was no mention of landing on one wheel when side slipping. This is the safest way to land an airplane in a crosswind. Landing on the windward wheel is so important that pilots should perform training exercises until they can perfect one wheel landings. One wheel landings are also the safest way to land and take-off on sloping beaches. Place the wheel on the upslope side of the beach and keep it tracking straight ahead until the aircraft's speed slows and the other wheel falls down to the beach. By this time the kinetic energy of the aircraft will be low enough that the airplane will not get out of control and cause problems. One wheel landings are highly useful.

8. Twombly recommends pilots increase final approach speed by half the gust factor and use partial flaps on windy days. I have learned many years ago that it is safe to land with full flaps and at initial stall speed regardless of wind conditions. I have over 30 years' experience landing taildraggers— many times in gusty wind conditions up to 45 miles per hour without a single mishap. This must be evidence that this is not a problem. The important

aspect of full flaps and landing at initial stall speed is kinetic energy management in your aircraft. You don't want one extra mile per hour in airspeed when landing because the kinetic energy increases by the square of airspeed (velocity). A small amount of extra airspeed increases the kinetic energy in your airplane by an enormous amount. The extra airspeed and the large increase in kinetic energy that is not needed is a major cause of airplanes getting out of control and crashing in landing operations. Avoid excessive airspeed in landing your airplane like the plaque.

9. Dave Hirschman second article is entitled *Cracking the Code*. Dave talks about how he learned to do wheel landings by holding off the airplane from touching down as long as possible. This may be a way to make wheel landings; however, there will be no precise landings on target with this type of technique. This will never be practical on short landing areas. If the airplane bounces back into the air when making a landing attempt—your landing speed is too fast. Even with too much kinetic energy in the airplane, you can still prevent bouncing back into the air by pushing the stick forward when the wheels touch down. The better way to do wheel landings is to land at initial stall speed—kinetic energy is too low for the airplane to bounce back into the air. The name of the game is controlling your landing airspeed.

10. A second article by Thomas Horne is entitled *Steady as she Goes*. This article emphasizes the importance of aircraft standardization and stabilization in landing patterns. Horne says this is the way to go. He discloses that he and most other pilots use this method for landings—I'll take predictability over a nasty surprise. I can only say that Mr. Horne evidently is not aware of the elite Alaskan pilot's non standardized and non-stabilized procedures for landing aircraft. Why do Alaska's best pilots choose this way of landing an airplane? It is simple, effortless, and it will produce flawless landings every single time you land your aircraft. Why would pilots choose a complicated landing procedure that makes near-perfect landings problematic and difficult to accomplish on a regular basis? I know this very well because I first learned to make standardized and stabilized landings early on with FAA instructors. It is much too complex, difficult, and too many upsetting variables to be a valuable and reliable way to land an airplane. Variable factors such as airplane cargo loads and unpredictable wind speeds make it even more difficult and problematic on making satisfactory landings. Alaska's elite pilots have used this simple landing technique for decades and it is their most important Cardinal Rule for flying in Alaska.

11. Landing an aircraft without all of these difficult obstacles is so simple and easy. I come in for a landing with no memorized or written down flying speeds and other parameters to follow. I am only concerned with placing the wheels down in my pre-selected box at stall speed. That is all I have to do. On final, I set up a proper aircraft attitude and speed with pitch control—regulate the aircraft's deceleration rate with the throttle. When you have trained for a short time you will learn how to compensate for all of the changes that have to be made in short order. It is not difficult making rapid changes when they are needed. If you are too high you side slip—too low you add a short application of power by proper throttle control. You don't get surprises because you have observed practically every condition an airplane can be in when coming in for a landing with an uncontrolled flying pattern style. Once you land your airplane in the box at stall speed—all other landing problems are automatically regulated. What could be more simple and effective than this? Nothing else comes even close to the Alaskan precision landings in the ease of performing the techniques and their consistent effectiveness.

12. A third article by Dave Hirschman on landing an airplane is *Stabilize This?* Don't fly like an old jet. Dave rejects the stabilized approach to landing GA airplanes as not necessary. Dave says that the stabilized approach was mandated in the 1960s by airline crews operating heavy, multi-engine, swept-wing transports with turbojet engines that take 10 seconds or more to spool up (from idle to full power). The GA aircraft with quick-reacting piston engines don't need stabilized approaches for landing. The engine can quickly react to all inputs for safe flying in the landing pattern. I agree with Dave—he got this correct. The stabilize approach is complexity with all the drama and difficulty without a reason. There is a much better way for controlling a landing aircraft—ban stabilized approaches, they are not necessary.

Summary. There seems to be considerable disagreement among GA pilots about landing insights. There would be additional agreement if pilots were knowledgeable not only in the standard FAA aviation doctrine but also in the elite Alaskan pilot's aviation sphere. Having knowledge in both aviation worlds would provide a well-informed foundation for comprehending flying procedures on a higher level. This would also provide a leading role in convincing GA pilots that there are much greater aviation approaches in advanced training than what most GA pilots rely on today. If GA pilots want to improve their flying capabilities and reduce the aircraft accident rate- major changes in flying strategies and techniques are essential.

MEMORANDUM 10
SUBJECT: Tabulating Takeoffs by Peter Garrison in Flying
Magazine December 2014

November 26, 2014

1. Peter Garrison's narrative calculating complex parameters for airplanes taking off on unlisted backcountry airstrips in Utah is quite amazing. The author describes multifaceted and difficult to understand ways to calculate parameters for takeoffs on these airstrips. He discusses a computer-aided program and *rules of thumb* for calculating takeoff distance, *Pilot Operating Handbooks* for cargo weight performance, and other ways for determining takeoff procedures. He says that the conclusions for some of these calculations can be inaccurate and unreliable. Galen Hanselman who created the guide books for these backcountry airstrips said he wished he had more to tell pilots desiring to land on these backcountry airstrips other than the *rules of thumb* found in Sparky Imeson's *Mountain Flying Bible*.

2. Well, there is certainly more to tell pilots desiring to land on these improvised and makeshift airstrips in Utah as well as all other backcountry airstrips across the globe. Why not learn how the elite pilots in Alaska conduct challenging short field landings in natural terrain? These are some of the shortest short field landings that exist. Alaska's elite pilots have taken short field operations to an exceedingly higher level when compared to calculated landings on backcountry airstrips in Utah and other U. S. Western States. The pilots that fly these extreme operations in Alaska would consider landing on backcountry airstrips in Alaska or anywhere else routine landings that would not be more difficult than landing on gravel airport runways in Alaska. Compare this with evaluating a short field landing site on a gravel bar from the cockpit of an airplane and making a decision to land where the pilot and no one else has ever landing before. This is what extreme flying in Alaska is all about and it is far more challenging and demanding than landing on a fixed and marked landing strip.

3. The most important factor to pick up on is that Alaska's extreme flying strategies and techniques will transform a pilot into the best self-reliant pilot he/she could ever become. The advanced training is extraordinary and the pilot will develop the highest pilot proficiency and will reduce their aircraft accident rate by a wide margin. Picking up and integrating some of the Alaskan pilot strategies and techniques will enable pilots to routinely fly into the backcountry

airstrips in Utah and the rest of the world with little or no difficulty. Training the Alaskan way would be the greatest aviation achievement for many pilots that spend the time and effort to transform and improve their flying careers.

4. The self-training that is necessary to incorporate the Alaskan strategies and techniques into the pilot's flying routine is straightforward—easy to learn and integrate. All of the complex and often inaccurate parameters discussed in Peter Garrison's article are not necessary with the Alaskan pilot training. Can you imagine the simple training without the need to calculate all of the parameters for takeoffs and landings? Can you imagine that Alaska's elite pilots ban standardized landing patterns and stabilized approaches when landing an airplane? These procedures are way too complex and unreliable to use in routine landings. Alaska's elite pilots use an unorthodox landing procedure that is simple and most effective—they come in for a landing any way you desire and learn to make quick changes when necessary. This is by far the easiest and safest way to land an airplane. The Alaskan training relies heavily on flying by the *seat of your pants* and does not require checklists or memorizing anything. This type of flying is a self-learned art by the pilot. The pilot can look at the short landing strip from the airplane cockpit and knows if it has sufficient length for landing and takeoff. No measurements are needs as this is a creative self-learned exercise. It is the most accurate way to fly an airplane. All the deceptive factors such as wind speed and direction, cargo weight, fuel weight, passenger weight and many others are all incorporated into the airplane. What you see, feel, and hear is absolutely an accurate reflection of the airplane's performance. Nothing could be a more simple and accurate way to land your airplane.

5. One of the most important Alaskan techniques to learn to land airplanes is *Precision Landings*. This requires placing the wheels down in a targeted 20 foot by 60 foot symbolic box and simultaneously touching the wheels down in the box at stall speed. These learned procedures will enable pilots to make routine and safe landings every single time a landing is made. There will be no need for *go arounds* or running off the end of a short landing area into rough terrain or vegetation that damages the airplane. Once a pilot masters *Precision Landings* all landings on short and rough airstrips will be easy to perform and in a safe manner. Landing at stall speed removes all excess kinetic energy in the airplane so that it does not have sufficient energy to get out of control and crash. The lower landing speed also reduces the ground roll by a substantial margin. Landing at stall speed is easy to execute and

is the safest landing procedure that is possible by a wide margin. Alaskan pilots have used this technique for landing airplanes for decades and it is one of the most important *Cardinal Rules* for flying in Alaska.

MEMORANDUM 11
SUBJECT: Short Field Ops by Budd Davisson in *Plane and Pilot* Magazine September 2014

August 24, 2014

So, how do we do it? It's a given that the stall speed is obviously too slow, ...

1. For Alaska's elite pilots that land at initial stall speed on every landing, the above statement in Plane & Pilot Magazine is very perplexing. In the past, Alaska's extraordinary pilots would just excuse this for a lack of understanding how pilots in the Great Land fly and go on with their daily business. I think the time has come that pilots not only in the Lower 48 States but from around the World should begin to become familiar and understand how Alaska's best pilots fly their airplanes. Our extraordinary pilots have some of the best flying strategies and techniques in the entire World. It would be highly beneficial if pilots around the Globe pick-up on what these Great Pilots have accomplished in refining traditional strategies and techniques. This allows Alaskans to become highly proficient pilots able to land their airplanes in challenging natural terrain. They also become safer pilots that have the essential skills necessary to reduce aircraft accident rates by a wide margin. All of these indispensable benefits would aid many other pilots from around the World in becoming highly improved pilots. Not all of these Alaskan pilot's strategies and techniques would be practicable for all GA pilots operating on airports and fixed airstrips; however, pilots could select the operational assets that they should add to their flying program to become a more proficient and safer pilot. Almost every GA pilot would certainly benefit by understanding and selecting useful Alaskan pilot operations.

2. To provide a broader understanding of Alaska's elite pilot stall landings I have written a narrative on the subject (Myths about Stall Landings). To recap; precision landings which includes initial stall landings is one of the most important Cardinal Rules for Alaska's exceptional pilots landing in off-airport operations. There is nothing as close to perfection as landing an airplane simultaneously on a selected target and at initial stall speed. A perfect landing every time the wheels touch down. The kinetic energy in the airplane landing

in this condition is profoundly controlled and it preserves the full length of the landing surface. The airplane can't get out of control with the lowered kinetic energy and the airplane can't run off the end of the landing surface in rough terrain. GA pilots would all benefit by learning this highly skillful technique for landing their airplanes. Aircraft accidents caused by Pilot Error in the landing configuration would be reduced so low that they would be removed from the list of primary caused accidents. What a huge worldwide difference this could make in landing airplanes safely. Problematic landings and making go-arounds would suddenly become beneficial lost skills in the flying world.

MEMORANDUM 12
SUBJECT: Paul Claus Reaffirms Claim to the Importance of Precision Landings

December 22, 2013

1. A feature in *Plane&Pilot* Magazine by Budd Davisson in October 2013 was *10 Best Pilots: The ability to make an airplane do the impossible is what separates the best from the rest.* Alaska's Paul Claus was named as the best or at least one of the best bush pilots. Paul was asked what makes a highly proficient bush pilot. Paul replied *The key is precision. You have to be able to consistently put the airplane right on the spot where you want it, at a minimum speed and that, in turn, means making every move as precisely as you can.*

2. The author's book has listed precision landings as one of the top Cardinal Rules for increasing pilot landing proficiency and reducing the aircraft accident rate by a wide margin. Paul's comment above reaffirms this claim. Precision landings are essential for safely landing aircraft on short and rough landing areas. It is important to remember that precision landings have to be properly understood and the training techniques have to be mastered before any rewards will be gained.

3. It is disturbing to find out that many pilots in Alaska believe that precision landings can be mastered by practicing short field landings. This is misinformation and it will not provide effective training for precision landings. Learning to fly short field landings will do little toward learning precision landings and will not transform pilot proficiency to the elevated level that is necessary for the shortest and safest landings. It may seem strange, but you don't practice short field landings to learn how to do precision landings. There is another significantly more productive way to learn precision landings.

4. The proper way to practice precision landings is learning to place the wheels down in a 20 by 60 foot rectangular-marked box at initial stall speed. Remember that both of these operations (wheels touching down in the box and wheels touching down at stall speed) have to be made simultaneously as the wheels touch down in the box. By mastering these two operations, a pilot will have become proficient at precision landings without worrying about the length of the landing roll. That comes automatically after the wheels touch down in the box at stall speed. Little or no braking is needed because most of the kinetic energy is drained from the aircraft prior to touchdown.

5. The information above is essential in providing pilots with a complete understanding of what precision landings are all about. It will take a sufficient amount of training to learn spot landings (landing with the wheels in the box) and additional training to learn how to perform proper stall landings. Nevertheless, both of these landing operations are comprehensively covered in my aviation book. After mastering precision landings, a pilot's landings will be substantially improved and the aircraft accident rate will be reduced to near zero.

MEMORANDUM 13
SUBJECT: Techniques for Landing Your Airplane

March 25, 2014

1. Most pilots have been trained by Federal Aviation Administration (FAA) certificated flight instructors on how to land an airplane. Takeoff and landing is the first flying techniques that are taught to a new pilot. Since landings are more complex and difficult to learn, more time is spent learning this technique. The conventional training for landings consists of techniques that are standardized for all aircraft—*one-size-shoe-fits all*. We have all heard *the landing is made in the approach*. This translates to making a good approach and you can be assured of a good landing. Instructors say it is important to arrive on the downwind at the appropriate elevation and speed. From this point on to landing at selected points in the flight pattern, the pilot must make a multitude of changes in speed, add flaps, change airplane attitude and learn to flare the airplane prior to touchdown. All of the selected speeds at the appropriate points in the flight pattern must be memorized or written down. The training for landing is certainly *flying by the book*. Creative flying in the flight pattern is considered poor technique and is forbidden.

2. The complexity of learning how to make landings by a certificated FAA instructor is found in an article in Plane & Pilot Magazine by Budd Davisson in May 2011. The name of the article is *Greasing It On: 20 Tips to get- 'er done*. From reading this article on landings, a pilot will understand that there are a multitude of items that must be mastered. If a pilot gets any one of these items wrong, it could result in an unacceptable landing and a go around. This makes it problematic for pilots to consistently learn and fly the landing technique that is taught by flight instructors. Nevertheless, it may be the best way to initially learn to land an airplane. This is usually the only training for landing an airplane for most pilots until they obtain their Private Pilot License (PPL). Most General Aviation pilots continue to use the instructor trained landing technique throughout their aviation careers.

3. A select number of pilots after obtaining the PPL continue along a different path on landing airplanes. An alternative landing technique that is far superior to the traditionally taught technique is one that does not require memorizing or writing down air speeds for specific points in the pattern nor does it require any pattern standardization. It is an unorthodox technique that is effortless and is extremely accurate and safe on landing an airplane. This alternative technique was developed by the elite Alaskan pilots many years ago because the traditional landing technique was not sufficient for routine safe landings. The following paragraph provides brief knowledge and understanding of this flying technique.

4. Alaskan pilots when landing in natural terrain learn to make precision landings. This is spot landing (selecting a target) and simultaneously touching the wheels down at stall speed. They also fly by the *seat of your pants*. With these 3 techniques, pilots do not need standardization when landing an airplane. Standardization is complex and a difficult task to perform on a consistent basis. There are too many variables—wind speed and direction, turbulent winds, cargo load weight, and many others that will interfere with making accurate precision landings. Approaching a landing at variable heights above the ground and variable speeds is not a problem. Pilots that fly by the *seat-of-your-pants* will quickly learn from watching the airplane and the landing target how to quickly change the airplane's flight path when it is needed. The precision landings were developed for landing in challenging natural terrain; however, the technique is the safest landing technique for General Aviation pilots landing at airports and on landing strips. Why would a pilot continue to use a complex landing technique

when the Alaskan pilot's technique is so simple, easy to perform, safe, and delivers a first-rate landing every single time one is made?

MEMORANDUM 14
SUBJECT: *The Lure of the Backcountry* by Budd Davisson in Plane & Pilot, January/February 2012

March 12, 2014

1. I know it is a little late; however, I have important information concerning your short article in Plane & Pilot Magazine. I would hope that future articles on this subject would include a basic understanding of off-airport flying in Alaska. This is the root of all off-airport flying. It should start from here and if you want to concentrate on Lower 48 off-airport flying then go ahead. Remember that the latter is profoundly different than how the off-airport pilots in Alaska train and fly for this venture.

2. The pictures in the article portray most of the airplanes with conventional tires. Where are the airplanes with Alaskan Bushwheels? Anyone landing off-airport in Alaska or anywhere else in the world with any knowledge of off-airport landings will certainly not have conventional tires—they will be equipped with Alaskan Bushwheels. Three pictures show tricycle-equipped aircraft. This type of aircraft is not the traditional off-airport type—it is exclusively the taildragger.

3. Training in the article is misleading and it sends the wrong message. There are no instructors that can provide the essential training techniques required for flying the safest off-airport operations. Although the training operations listed can provide a limited amount of useful training, the lion's share of training is substantially different for off-airport operations. The proper off-airport training established by Alaska's extraordinary pilots is *Self-Training*. It is in bold emphasizing its importance. Alaska's best pilots long-ago found out that this is the best way to become a much improved and self-reliant pilot. Pilots that have learned on their own can safely land their airplane time after time in challenging terrain without a mishap. Pilots that train this way are creative and frequently perform trial and error maneuvers to learn how to refine techniques. Pilots that think instructors can teach them off-airport operations are at best average pilots that are subject to a higher accident rate because they do not have the proper techniques and knowledge to fly safer operations. To summarize learning to perform

off-airport operations, it goes like this. Read, study, and talk to other pilots and learn as much as possible about flying off-airport. Then you have to go out in your airplane and practice what you have learned. This is the most potent way possible for learning. It takes lots of training on your own to become a proficient and safe pilot. If you train the traditional way with an instructor, the flying skills that are lacking will catch up with you many times over the years resulting in accidents that could have been easily avoided with the Alaskan pilot training. I have seen this play out in Alaska over and over during my 39 years as an active Pilot in Command. After reading the above, pilots will have the understanding and knowledge about the best training procedures for off-airport operations. They can choose the training they desire. They will now understand that their lack of choosing the best training will compromise their proficiency and cause accidents. It's the pilot's choice to become the best trained off-airport pilot or the other option is to be satisfied with being an average off-airport pilot that will have a substantially higher accident rate.

MEMORANDUM 15
SUBJECT: Reduction in the Excessive GA Accident Rate

September 25, 2014

1. The FAA and the NTSB in frustration acknowledge the excessive aircraft accident rate for GA pilots. Their records show that 80% of aircraft accidents are caused by pilot error. Many of the accidents are repeat accidents (the same kind of accident) that happen over and over again. They are continually reminding pilots that this is a big problem and that the high accident rate is not acceptable. These two agencies spend an enormous amount of time and effort to reduce the high accident rate to an acceptable level especially during the past 10 years. They hold a large number of safety seminars and they issue many pilot safety advisories and alerts on a yearly basis. Nevertheless, there have been little or no improvements over all those years in their attempt to reduce the aircraft accident rate. Their assessment of this high accident rate is that it is due to lack of pilot training and for pilots not paying attention to FAA and NTSB advisories and safety alerts.

2. Most GA pilots are trained by FAA certificated instructors. Advanced training after receiving the PPL to improve their flying skills is also provided by instructors. The training and the flying strategies including techniques that pilots use are involved in and are directly linked to the aircraft accident rate.

190

Not been able to see any changes in the large number of aircraft accidents over many years of attempting to lower the aircraft accident rate strongly indicates that the accident rate is consistent with the contemporary training and the flying strategies taught by FAA instructors. What FAA offers through certificated instructors is providing the large numbers of aircraft accidents. If you want significant changes to lower the aircraft accident rate to acceptable levels, you will have to offer changes to the current training style that includes flying strategies and techniques.

3. The elite Alaskan pilots offer the training and flying strategies that are necessary for changes in lowering the aircraft accident rate to acceptable numbers. The reason for this is due to the training style and the selection of the best strategies and techniques that come from both aviation spheres—both the FAA's aviation world and the elite Alaskan pilot's world. Self-training and integrating the best strategies and techniques from both aviation worlds make an enormous difference in pilot proficiency and a significant reduction in aircraft accidents from an improved pilot. This dramatic change in lowering the aircraft accident rate for all GA pilots is available by training like the elite Alaskan pilots.

MEMORANDUM 16
SUBJECT: Prevent Unintentionally Stalling Your Airplane

October 10, 2014

1. No Pilot wants to endure the dreadful consequences of unintentionally stalling an airplane. This can lead to stall/spin accidents with the airplane crashing on the ground. Stall/spin accidents are lethal as the kinetic energy in a moving aircraft is increased substantially with the gravitation pull of the earth as the airplane free-falls to the ground. The large number of injuries and fatalities caused by stalled aircraft accidents are sensible reasons for reducing the accident rate to acceptable levels for all flying missions.

2. Are there flying strategies that will prevent stall accidents? Absolutely there are and if followed they will for all practical purposes eliminate unintentionally stalling your airplane. The first step is learning where most of the stall accidents occur—takeoff/landing and turning operations. The next step is learning preventive measures and strategies in takeoff/landing and turning operations that will not place your airplane

in deteriorating conditions that will result in unintentionally stalling your airplane. Below are the Pilot Strategies that will keep your airplane from unintentionally stalling.

3. Avoid taking off in a steep climb (High Angle of Attack) for a prolonged duration of time. There may be a steep angle when the airplane takes off; however, after leaving ground effect—lower the nose and build up airspeed at a lower Angle of Attack. If you make a prolonged steep climb out on takeoff and the engine fails, the Pilot will likely not be able to lower the nose in time to regain flying airspeed and prevent stalling the airplane. The airplane will likely fall out of the sky instantly and crash on the runway. Heavily-loaded aircraft will also benefit substantially by lowering the nose after takeoff. This will build up airspeed which is essential after leaving ground effect. The wings generate less lift when they come out of ground effect. To counter the lower lift the airplane must have a higher airspeed. Lower airspeeds cause stalls.

4. Avoid steep turns with a high Angle of Attack especially with a heavily loaded aircraft. Shallow turns with a low Angle of Attack are a safer way. This can be easily accomplished by lowering the airplane's nose and making shallow turns. This will keep you safe and out of *Stall Country.*

5. Use the full length of the runway on short field takeoffs. Do not get airborne as soon as possible—aircraft flying speed is too slow. Use a substantial portion of the space that is available to remain on the ground so that when the airplane becomes airborne its flying speed will be high enough to climb out of ground affect. The wings produce less lift when coming out of ground effect. To prevent stalls when coming out of ground effect a higher airspeed is needed. Airspeed management on takeoffs is critical. Maintain sufficiently high airspeeds to keep your aircraft from stalling. This is a common mistake that causes many aircraft accidents.

6. Stall landings will help Pilots better understand aircraft stalls. Alaska's Elite Pilots make every landing at stall speed. Taking out every bit of excess kinetic energy prior to touching the wheels on the ground is one of the most important Cardinal Rules for safely landing aircraft on challenging natural terrain. When making every landing at stall speed a Pilot becomes intimately involved and exceedingly knowledgeable about stalls. Pilots landing at stall speed no longer are terrified with stalls but have a greater understanding of them. This helps greatly in recognizing stall conditions and it also helps in

understanding procedures in counteracting stalls.

MEMORANDUM 17
SUBJECT: How to Improve Your Flying Career

April 28, 2014

1. I have written an aviation book on flying and training in Alaska after 40 years as a Pilot in Command. One of the important reasons for writing the book is to provide comprehensive knowledge about Alaska's best trained pilots. Their flying strategies and techniques are extraordinary and combined with the FAA doctrine are far superior to FAA's training alone. Incorporating their features into your flying program will substantially increase pilot proficiency and greatly reduce your aircraft accident rate by a wide margin. The Alaskan pilots have proven their high standards with decades of flying and training in Alaska. Now for the first time an aviation book is written to describe these quality standards and to provide a contemporary training manual to show pilots how to adopt and train like the Alaskan pilots. Adopting the Alaskan pilot standards will make you an improved pilot with greater aircraft proficiency. The greatest value is that it will reduce your aircraft accident rate to near zero.

2. Although the elite pilots have developed their flying strategies and techniques for off-airport landing in natural terrain does not mean that these procedures are not valuable for GA pilots that only land on airports and developed and maintained airstrips. GA pilots will greatly improve their flying skills and their proficiency as a pilot by adopting many of the elite pilot's procedures. What traditionally trained pilot would not want to enhance his/her flying career with this valued upgrade?

MEMORANDUM 18
SUBJECT: Modern Avionics for Flying Taildraggers in Alaska

November 16, 2014

1. Global Positioning System (GPS) is a space-based satellite navigation system that provides location and time information. A *Garmin GPS 92* has been my sole modern avionics device for flying small taildragger aircraft in Alaska for over a decade. I use this GPS unit for bearing/track navigation, miles to destination, ground speed of aircraft, GPS position in longitude

and latitude, and to determine wind speed and direction. This information was not available prior to the modern GPS Technology. It makes navigation very accurate and easy to setup. It is a very useful addition for flying an airplane in Alaska.

2. Avionics has now advanced to Glass Cockpits with touchscreens or control keys. There are also many hand-held GPS panels and tablets for airplane navigation. The cost of the flat-glass panels for small airplanes can be in the $10,000 to $15,000 range. The cost of the hand-held devices is much less but they are usually over $1,000. It is amazing how many of these high cost items are being installed in GA aircraft. Most new aircraft are being built with glass panels installed from the factory. It would make one believe that these high cost panels and tablets are mandatory for flying aircraft today. The message seems to be is that your airplane is not fully equipped for safe flying without these modern GPS units.

3. The cost of my Garmin GPS 92 was about $400. It provides everything I need for safely flying a small taildragger in remote Alaska. I can't image what I would gain spending $15K for a Glass Cockpit over what I have with the Garmin 92. My airplane is used primarily for inspirational flying in remote Alaska. That means viewing all the magnificent wildlife and taking in the awe-inspiring character of the mountain and glacier country. I have no desire to be watching a glass panel the entire time I am flying my airplane. In addition, I am one of the many middle-class pilots that have an all-encompassing passion for flying. Nevertheless, fuel for flying is rapidly becoming a cost-prohibitive factor. I don't need another cost-prohibiting item such as the Glass Cockpit to dampen or kill my desire for flying Alaska.

MEMORANDUM 19
SUBJECT: The Thrill of Flying an Airplane

August 25, 2014

The joy of flight does not have to be based on your airplane having all the *bells and whistles* and the latest modification upgrades but much more importantly it should be based on pilot self-training skills necessary for flying the airplane safely. Without the skills of a proficient pilot—you are missing out on the most important and joyful aspects of flying an airplane.

MEMORANDUM 20
SUBJECT: Choosing the Perfect Flight Instructor

November 30, 2014

1. After obtaining the FAA's Private Pilot License (PPL) many pilots pursue ways to advance their flying careers. Flying magazine articles cover the traditional ways to expand your aviation horizon. These typically are tailwheel endorsement, instrument and commercial rating, seaplane rating, aerobatic training, and flying gliders and war birds. This advanced training will expand your flying career to a higher level but it will be no way close to the advanced training benefits a pilot obtains from training like the elite Alaskan pilots. This type of training will elevate a pilot to the highest level of proficiency and to becoming the best self-reliant pilot you possibly can be.

2. Alaska's elite pilot's *modus operandi* for training is that you train yourself—self-training. Therefore, it is understandable that the pilot is the perfect instructor for advanced training. Pilots that train the Alaskan way must take on an academic role in learning as much as possible. Knowledge is paramount for advanced training success. That includes reading as well as discussions from instructors and Alaska's elite pilots. Nevertheless, integrating the learning into flying the airplane needs to be accomplished by the pilot alone in his/her airplane. Self-training is the most potent way to learn any subject. It is a self-imposed creative learning process that becomes an art. It provides opportunities to fine-tune learned procedures and to tailor processes that are in equilibrium with the pilot's individual and natural traits. This is the definitive way to integrate your aviation knowledge into flying your airplane—nothing else comes close to the enormous benefits.

MEMORANDUM 21
SUBJECT: What Pilots should know about Multitasking

February 20, 2014

There are those out there that think they can multitask. They know it does not work well but they do it anyway. A study published in the New England Journal of Medicine in 1997 showed that using hand-held cell phones while driving a vehicle quadruples the risk of an accident. This is almost as dangerous as driving while drunk. Neuropsychologists have discovered that the conscious brain (normal waking state) can process only one task at a time—it has zero chance and no such ability for multitasking. It is important for pilots to get this correct because processes are disrupted while multitasking as your attention is focused elsewhere. This inattention and the time it takes to switch the mind back to the original task leads to accidents. Instructors teaching emergency procedures (partial engine loss, engine failure, forced landings, etc.) request pilots to review the inflight emergency check list. This is multitasking and therefore it is problematic for being the best way to handle emergency situations. There are many aircraft accidents in emergency situations where pilots were seriously injured or suffered fatalities due to failure to maintain flying the airplane to a safe landing. It is highly likely that many of these accidents are caused by distractions and inattention from multitasking. It may be a better strategy when facing a major emergency procedure while airborne to focus only on the most important issue—flying the airplane to a safe landing. All of the other issues such as announcing the problem on the radio, using checklists, or anything else can be taken care of after the airplane is safely on the ground.

MEMORANDUM 22
SUBJECT: Lower 48 Pilots Flying to Alaska

May 25, 2015

1. Pilots from the Lower 48 states flying to Alaska to obtain the distinction of being in the Great Land are quite amazing. Many of these pilots fly to Alaska so they can add the experience to their flying repertoire. Most of these pilots land at main airports and remain in Alaska for a few days before returning to the Lower 48 states. These pilots are flying through Alaskan airspace; however, they are gaining very little of what Alaska has to offer. A much better way of exceeding this effort is to take a commercial airliner to Anchorage. Once in Alaska, make arrangements to go flying with several experienced Alaskan backcountry pilots. After flying for three or four days in several taildraggers and landing in dozens of challenging backcountry areas, one will come away from the experience with a thorough understanding of what it is like to fly in Alaska. Most pilots will be impressed well beyond their expectations. Alaska is special with the exhilarating flying environment and the extraordinary pilots.

2. I was corresponding with a pilot/instructor from the Northwest U. S. about backcountry flying in Alaska. Descriptive narratives were sent by

E-mail on this subject but to no avail. Finally, *I said, the only way you are going to understand how we fly taildraggers off-airport in Alaska is to fly up here on a commercial airliner and go flying with us.* The Pilot did just that and I called it *Four Days of Flying Alaska.* This was the last week in June 2005. The pilot and his companion came up and I arranged two taildraggers for flights each day to backcountry destinations. In the four days of flying out of Merrill Field, we managed to make a multitude of landings on the Knik River gravel bars, Lake George backcountry landing areas, and fly over the Chugach Mountains at the head of Colony Glacier at 6,000 feet and land on a 400-foot sandbar at the mouth of the Coghill River in Prince William Sound. We landed at Bold airstrip on the east end of Eklutna Lake in Chugach State Park, in the tundra on top of Little Susitna Mountain at 2,900 feet above sea level northwest of Merrill Field, at Charlie's Bear Haven where we found brown and black bears, on a gravel strip on the west end of Beluga Lake near Mount Spurr, on a gravel bar near Strandline Lake, multiple landings on the coastal Susitna mudflats between the Susitna and Little Susitna Rivers, on the mudflats in Turnagain Arm near Seattle Creek, on an inactive mine site near Spencer Glacier on the Kenai Peninsula, and on the Twentymile River at the Head of Turnagain Arm of Cook Inlet. This was a wide-ranging circuit of 1,000 miles (11 flying hours in each aircraft) in taildraggers to the northeast, northwest, west, and southeast of Merrill Field in Southcentral Alaska. The flights were flown in 5 taildraggers; 2 Piper Super Cruisers (PA-12s), 2 Piper Super Cubs (PA-18s) and my Arctic Tern. The Seattle guests enjoyed the flights. They were amazed at the flying skills of the group of self-trained taildragger pilots that could land in so many places in the natural terrain. Nothing can compare with this type of firsthand observation of flying in Alaska. If the many pilots who fly their own airplanes to Alaska chose this type of aviation adventure in Alaska, I am certain that some of them would take the next step and learn to fly a taildragger Alaskan style. I can assure you that it is an unbelievable flying journey that you will take great delight in for the rest of your life. Once you get started, the challenge will become irresistible and you will do whatever it takes to continue the journey.

3. It has been 10 years since the *Four Days of Flying Alaska* for my Northwest friends. The flying record for the 4 Alaskan pilots who flew the mission in 2005 have since accumulated a grand total of 6,020 hours. This is an average of 151 hours per year for each pilot. We are all flying on a

regular basis in summer on Alaskan Bushwheels and in winter on skis. I am very optimistic in reporting that there have been no accidents for the 4 pilots and 5 airplanes during this 10 year span (one pilot flew 2 different airplanes on succeeding days). Two of these pilots fly difficult and challenging commercial flying missions. They fly hunters into remote game areas and haul out heavy loads of game meat from short landing strips. They also fly heavy cargo such as building materials for remote cabins. They often are compelled to fly in dreadful weather conditions. This data hopefully shows that well-trained Alaskan pilots flying challenging missions in the backcountry do not often wreck their airplanes. The primary reason is that we have the best advanced training possible for our flying mission. Hopefully, GA pilots will understand the value of Alaska's exceptional training program and will be able to select the strategies and techniques that can substantially improve their flying capabilities in becoming a better pilot.

MEMORANDUM 23
Subject: The Road to Success for the Best Advanced Training

May 1, 2015

1. If a pilot wants to know how to become a first-rate pilot, the response from one of Alaska's elite pilots would simply be self-training. If you can't agree on self-training to integrate new strategies and techniques into your flying program you are going nowhere in gaining the high proficiency that Alaska's elite pilots possess. You will only be an average pilot the remainder of your flying career. Self-training is the first step and it is essential if pilots want to become a first-rate pilot. Alaskan style self-training will provide the best advanced training possible.

2. The second standard that pilots have to agree on is to be an academic aviator. This means you must learn as much as possible about flying strategies and techniques by becoming knowledgeable from both the FAA's aviation doctrine and the Alaska's elite pilots sphere. Read FAA's Airplane Flying Handbook, Pilot's Handbook of Aeronautical Knowledge, and Weather Manual. Hold discussions with FAA certificated instructors as learning sessions. Read other books and manuals on advanced training. You must read current articles in aviation magazines such as *Aircraft Owners and Pilots Association* (AOPA), *Plane & Pilot*, and *Flying*. Pilots must also have a dialogue with Alaska's elite pilots to learn their strategies and techniques.

Minimal written material exists on the latter with the exception of my book that provides discussion on most of the important material for advance training.

3. The third standard is that you must select the best strategies and techniques you can find from both aviation niches that fit your individual style. Look for weak techniques in the FAA sphere that can be replaced by superior ones from the elite pilot's sphere. This will give pilots a rare opportunity to excel in proficiency and increase their advanced training to unexpected and gratifying levels. Pilots could not perceive early on in their flying careers that they could reach such lofty heights.

4. The fourth required standard is to take the learned knowledge and integrate it into your flying program. You must get in your airplane alone and accomplish this mission. This is the self-training part of advanced training. You'll be setting up this integrative exercise according to your own terms, your own personal traits, the way you like to do it. This integration by the pilot of the airplane—not by the instructor—is essential in obtaining the best results for advanced training.

5. The fifth required standard is that pilots must learn to fly by the *seat of your pants* so that precision landings can be made. Precision landings are made by placing the wheels down on a target and simultaneously at stall speed. Landing at stall speed is accomplished by *seat of your pants* flying.

6. The sixth standard is transferring the pilot's learned skills into flying as an art.

MEMORANDUM 24
SUBJECT: Alaska's Pilot Benefits to FAA and the GA Community

January 15, 2014

1. The Federal Aviation Administration (FAA) personnel and most General Aviation (GA) pilots operate entirely within their own aviation sphere without ever knowing what is inside Alaska's extraordinary off-airport pilot's sphere. My book was written for several reasons. One of the important reasons is to link these two aviation divisions. Alaska's elite off-airport pilots already know and understand the FAA and the general aviation world because they trained for their Private Pilot License with FAA certificated instructors. FAA and the

general aviation community have so much to gain if they would begin to learn about Alaska's best-trained pilot's world. They would learn how to improve pilot proficiency with better training techniques and they would greatly benefit by reducing their aircraft accident rate by a wide margin. I am attempting to do this from the top down. I don't have any famous claims. I know from others that this goal is almost impossible to accomplish. However, I am going to do everything I can to move my agenda forward. I am hoping that all of my aviation writing will show the aviation community that the Alaskan pilots have important training techniques and strategies that can be incorporated into general aviation pilots' current flying program to greatly improve it. The more books I sell, the greater the impact and the greater the chance that I will be successful. It is all about education. The knowledge gained along the way will validate the claims that are made above about the Alaskan pilot benefits.

2. I enjoy this type of endeavor. It keeps me busy and I know if I am fortunate this could be a transformative initiative in aviation in North America and really in the entire world. Learning and incorporating Alaskan pilot strategy and flying techniques into your aviation program will elevate the aviation world to higher standards and safety. If pilots are properly educated on the subject, they would all want what the Alaskan pilots have to offer. The rewards are too good to pass up.

MEMORANDUM 25
SUBJECT: Go / No-Go Decision Making

March 8, 2015

1. The use of Go / No-Go Decisions when preparing for a flight in Alaska is not very useful. The first obstacle is that we have inadequate weather reporting stations in Alaska. This means that the weather reports may be accurate, however; they also may be highly inadequate or any other way in between. There is no way to know the accuracy of the reports. In addition, current weather reports may not be available. When flying from Merrill Field to Iliamna 210 miles southwest you have to fly through Lake Clark Pass at 1,000 feet ASL. The weather report for the pass is that it is closed if the ceiling elevation is lower than 2,500 feet (1,500 feet above the pass). You don't need 1,500 feet clearance for safely flying through the pass. This will limit countless flights as the pass is below minimums for many days during the year. A 500 foot clearance of fog and clouds is more than enough for safely flying through the pass. Even 200 feet clearance is sufficient when

the fog or cloud layers are stable. In all my flights to Iliamna the pass has never being closed due to low clouds or fog totally obscuring the pass. Many flights over the years were made safely through the pass well below weather minimums.

2. The most logical way to prepare flight plans in Alaska is to check the weather along the route of your flight. Extreme weather that is absolutely not flyable may be a reason to hold off flying until the weather improves. An example of this is a weather report in the Lake Clark vicinity with gusty winds blowing 55 to 75 miles per hour and surface winds gusting from 25 to 35 miles per hour at the Iliamna airport. Pilots would not want to leave Merrill Field and fly to Iliamna with this type of weather. Nevertheless, most days the weather in Alaska is not that extreme and flights may be safely conducted. Marginal weather along the route or at the destination is often a given. This is the weather with low cloud ceilings, scattered fog layers, gusty winds, or combinations of all of these. The weather reports often will not provide accurate data for making a decision to fly or not to fly. Instead of cancelling the flight, pilots will assess the weather at their home base and make a decision to fly the route. After leaving the home base the marginal weather reported may be flyable or it may not be flyable. The pilot has to make this determination—continuing the flight or land the airplane—or a second option is to turn around and fly back to base. Even with no accurate weather data the pilot has certain advantages that will provide safely flying the airplane. One is that the most accurate weather reporting possible is the pilot looking out in front of the windshield. All you have to do for safe flying is learn safe flying weather conditions and the conditions that are not safe. Pilots have to be prepared to land or turn around when weather conditions are not flyable.

3. I have made many flights in marginal weather in Alaska and most of the time the destination was achieved without having to land the airplane or turn back to avoid unflyable weather conditions. A few weather conditions were too severe and did require landing the airplane or turning back and flying out of the unsafe weather. This was never a problem because my Arctic Tern is a small taildragger that can land and takeoff on a gravel bar that is 300 feet in length. There are many places to land taildraggers in Alaska so this makes it plausible. Larger airplanes and tricycle gear aircraft will have to be more closely relined to the Go / No-Go decision that is determined by the weather reports. Safely flying in marginal weather is just another benefit of flying a small taildragger in Alaska.

MEMORANDUM 26
SUBJECT: The White-Coat Syndrome in GrassRoots by Budd
Davisson in Plane&Pilot September 2014*

August 23, 2014

1. Thank you for discussing this torturous journey every two years for
pilots with hypertension arriving at their Doctor's office for a Third Class
Medical Examination. I know this all too well as I have been a victim of
this difficult and stressful problem for many years in the past. A recent Duke
University study found that 20 million Americans with a doctor's diagnosis
of hypertension (elevated blood pressure) don't have high blood pressure at
all. The study showed that 25% of all patients who have their blood pressure measured in the doctor's offices and hospitals are so unnerved by the
medical environment that their numbers temporarily rise an extra 15 points
or higher. This is called white coat hypertension and this false reading can
land you on a prescription drug. For pilots seeking a Third Class Medical—it
can cause you to fail the medical examination and stop you in your tracks
from flying your airplane. This is a big problem and many patients and even
doctors don't realize that this happens as often as it does.

2. Fortunately for most pilots, we can lower our blood pressure and avoid this
aggravating cyclic problem. Recent information has clearly shown that studies
find blood pressure drugs almost useless for the majority of patients. This is not
the best way to treat high blood pressure. Traditional doctors are missing the
boat as food and beverages are the biggest cause—and the very best cure—for
today's epidemic of high blood pressure. Food is the best blood pressure medi-
cation. You can lower your blood pressure into the safety zone with delicious
foods instead of expensive drugs that your chance of normalizing your blood
pressure is less than 50-50 and you will have to live with the nasty side effects.

3. There are currently many books written on the natural healing and lowering of blood pressure. I will mention four books that will provide all of the
information that you will need to help reduce high blood pressure to normal
levels. It does not work for every single person but improving what you eat
and how you live does work for almost everyone. Very few individuals will
not benefit from eating healthy foods. Foods can lower your blood pressure
naturally—while they help heal the damage that hypertension may have done
to your arteries, tissues, and organs. Drugs will not heal damaged arteries,

* This narrative was published in the December 2014 issue of *Plane and Pilot* Magazine.

tissues, and organs. These four books will help most to lower blood pressure to normal levels very quickly. Pilots that lower their blood pressure to normal levels will not have to be subjected to the exasperating feeling of failing their Third Class Medical every two years. Gone will be those annoying and frightful days. It will still be better if Congress passes the Bill on canceling Third Class Medicals for non-commercial General Aviation pilots. Below are the four books providing the straightforward blood pressure remedies.

Roy Heilbron, M.D. (2014). The 30-Day Blood Pressure Cure; *The Drug-Free, Step-By-Step Plan to Reverse Your Hypertension and Drop You Blood Pressure into the Safety Zone.* Bottomline Publications, Stamford, Connecticut.

Joel Fuhrman, M.D. (2011). *Eat To Live.* Little, Brown and Company, New York, N.Y.

Jonny Bowden, Ph.D., C.N.S. (2007). The 150 Healthiest Foods on Earth; The Surprising, Unbiased Truth about What You Should Eat and Why. Fair Winds Press, Beverly, Mass.

T. Colin Campbell, Ph.D. and Howard Jacobson, Ph.D. (2013). Whole; Rethinking the Science of Nutrition. Ben Bella Books, Inc., Dallas, Texas.

MEMORANDUM 27
SUBJECT: Alaska's Inadequate Weather Reporting System

November 18, 2014

Commentary: *Alaska Pilots Need No Weather Mysteries* by Tom George, Adam White and Harry Kieling. *Alaska Dispatch News.* November 14, 2014.

1. The referenced commentary cited the Washington Post's newspaper article republished in the Alaska Dispatch News on October 16, 2014 about Alaska's flying terrain not been mapped to modern standards. The article emphasizes that flying in Alaska can be perilous in adverse weather conditions. The commentary writers agree with the evidence on inadequate mapping but point out that there is an even more immediate danger for pilots flying Alaska. The most troublesome risk is an inadequate weather reporting system. Weather reports are one of the fundamental pieces of information that a pilot looks at before deciding whether to become airborne or to continue a flight especially in marginal weather conditions.

2. Alaska's weather reporting stations are few and far between when compared to the Lower 48 States. To have similar density as in the Lower 48 States, Alaska would need 2.4 times more reporting weather stations than are currently in place. A total of 133 automated weather stations are currently spread across Alaska. Better weather information to make more informed decisions is absolutely *life-and-death* critical. Pilots use weather forecasts to predict conditions during flight. The limited numbers of observations covering immense areas often results in pilots encountering unforcasted weather conditions that may lead to *controlled flight into terrain* (CFIT) accidents. Pilots need all the weather information available to make informed, educated and conscientious decisions about initiating and continuing flights.

3. All that has been expressed in the article is well stated and it does show that perilous mishaps can happen when the data that is necessary for adequate weather reporting is missing. It is not likely that the 180 weather reporting stations that would be needed to provide the same density coverage as the Lower 48 States will be constructed in Alaska anytime soon. What can be done to provide better weather reports? The commentary mentioned a small number of *A-Paid* weather reporting stations but disclosed that 5 of them were shut-down this summer. They also mentioned FAA's network of Weather Cameras spread across Alaska that provide day time views of the weather.

4. Meteorologists gather data to make weather forecasts in Alaska that may or may not be accurate. There are more inaccurate and missing weather forecasts in Alaska because of the widely scattered reporting stations. Nevertheless, most pilots in Alaska depend entirely on the weather forecasting and weather reports to guide their flying especially in marginal conditions when flying is difficult and problematic. Meteorologists are directing the pilot's critical decision making in continuing a flight or turning back when flying in low ceilings and other difficult weather conditions. Pilots depending on weather forecasting with the above mentioned quandaries are often subject to an unacceptable risk for aircraft accidents. Postponing flights in marginal weather for improving weather conditions may often require time delays to provide safer flying. This can be a great encumbrance and a huge waste of time when attempting to initiate a flight in Alaska. If the weather is rapidly changing while in flight, it can increase the risk of an airplane accident. Pilots depending entirely on the Alaska's weather reporting system may often be in risky conditions during periods of flying in marginal weather.

5. To counteract the inadequate weather reporting in Alaska an alternative flying plan is needed to address and offset these abnormalities. Alaska's elite pilots have tackled many of the challenging flying difficulties in Alaska and they have a plan for Alaska's inadequate weather reporting. These creative pilots use the Alaska weather reporting for basic flying guidance; however, decision making while airborne for determining outcomes on whether to continue flying or to turn back is made by the pilot. The pilot's decision is considerably more accurate than depending solely on problematic weather forecasts. What the pilot is attempting to accomplish is to interpret the weather and to predict the changes that will happen in the near future. This is a major deviation from most GA pilots depending entirely on weather reports. Nevertheless, what the pilot is viewing in front of the airplane is absolute reality—it is accurate, dependable, and is far more reliable than weather forecasts. The pilot in time will learn the difference between safe flying weather and unsafe flying weather. Once this is perfected, the pilot will be able to make very accurate and safe flying decisions. There will be no pressure to keep flying into IMC weather when forecasts are showing VFR flying conditions. It will be highly comforting to know that the pilot is in control and can be self-reliant in determining and implementing the highly important outcomes. Pilots making their own decision on the flying outcomes will be flying stress-free as all of the most accurate information is in close presence outside the airplane. Pilots always perform their very best when the responsibility is placed on their own shoulders. Alaska's elite pilots find the way that is effortless to implement and provides the safest and most reliable flying outcomes in marginal weather.

MEMORANDUM 28
SUBJECT: Weather-Restricted Valdez Fly-In and Airshow in 2015

May 11, 2015

1. Weather-related problems seriously affect Alaskan pilot's ability to fly their airplanes from Anchorage, Fairbanks, the Kenai Peninsula, Palmer, Wasilla, and Talkeetna to Valdez for the Fly-In and Airshow in one out of every 3 or 4 years. It appears the huge low pressure system in the Gulf of Alaska in 2015 created the most difficult conditions for flying to Valdez for any of the Fly-Ins. This is the 12th annual Fly-In and pilots were attempting to fly to Valdez on Friday, May 8, 2015. If we had good flying weather, this year's turnout in Valdez would likely be over 200 airplanes. Because of the horrible weather in 2015, only 40 airplanes made it to Valdez. Most of

the pilots from Southcentral Alaska that made it to Valdez had to struggle through this difficult flying weather.

2. I decided not to fly my airplane in the 3 hour flight from Merrill Field to Valdez in this atrocious weather. The biggest problem was fog and low ceilings in the mountain passes that stopped most pilots from continuing flight. Wind and turbulence was also a serious problem near Palmer, Gulkana Basin, and the mountain valley leading to Thompson Pass. While driving the highway from Anchorage to Valdez I was looking at the weather. It was marginal and windy almost the entire distance. The ceiling at Tahneta Pass was low; however, I could probably make it through the pass. Thompson Pass was fogged in with a few small corridors that may be safe for flying an airplane. When I reached Robe Lake which is 8 air miles southeast of the Valdez Airport the fog was on the ground. No way could I fly my airplane through this thick fog. I thought about what I would do if I was in my airplane. I would certainly not go back 20 miles to fog-clogged Thompson Pass. The only sensible option was to land on the Richardson Highway and wait for the fog to lift. When I arrived at the Valdez airport another pilot from Merrill Field had also just arrived. His name was Vern Ulmer. Vern told us that he was attempting to fly an airplane to Valdez but the weather was just too darn nasty. Vern said I am a 59 year Alaskan pilot and I choose not to fly. That made me feel like I also made the correct decision not to fly here. Tom George from Fairbanks and Marshall Severson from Anchorage usually fly their airplanes to Valdez for the Fly-In when the weather is not a problem. Both of them did not attempt to fly to Valdez this year. Paul Claus has most likely won more short-field competition events at Valdez than any other pilot. Paul flies a Cessna 185 and Piper Super Cubs. I was told that Paul and his pilots were flying to Valdez but were stopped short due to unflyable weather. I noticed 2 yellow Super Cubs landing and taxing to tie down at the airport. The airplanes were Jay Baldwin's cubs from Palmer, Alaska. I found out that he and his other pilot found that same fog down on the ground around Robe Lake. They landed the 2 cubs on the Richardson Highway to wait out the fog. After a short time Jay found a ride on the highway to the Valdez airport. The fog has lifted high enough for the cubs to get airborne and continue to the Valdez airport. I talked to a pilot which told me about 2 Cessna 170s and 1 Cessna 175 flying in a group of 3 from Fairbanks and their aggravating flight to Valdez. They flew straight to Thompson Pass. It was closed due to thick fog. They turned around and flew north again for the Tiekel River. They then flew east to the Copper River and south down the Copper River to the Tasnuna River and onward to Marshall Pass a 70 mile flight. Marshall Pass is often open when Thompson

Pass is shut down due to low-level fog. But today Marshall Pass was closed. They turned around and retraced their route to the Copper River and landed at Chitina Airport some 70 miles away. After some time they decided to try Thompson Pass again. When they arrived at the pass it was still closed. Highly frustrated, they found the Thompson Pass gravel landing strip and decided to land here and keep a close watch on Thompson Pass for an opening. After an unspecified amount of time the pass opened a little and they jumped into their airplanes and scooted through. They made it to Valdez without further weather hazards. This is exactly what pilots have to endure to fly to Valdez under these horrible weather conditions. I decided not to fly to Valdez not because I could not do it but because the stress and the extra time and uncertainly was too much. This would have been a miserable flight just like I expected.

3. The Short Take-Off and Landing (STOL) Competition on Saturday May 9, 2015 was very enjoyable to watch. There were few aircraft that made it to Valdez for the competition; however, there were some very interesting new aircraft that entered this year. A fairly large crowd of people from Valdez and others who drove cars from Southcentral Alaska were there to watch the events. The results follow.

Light Touring Class
First Place: Shawn Holley from Soldotna, AK (Cessna 170)
Take-off 76 feet; Landing 104 feet. Combined total 180

Second Place: Chet Harris from Anchorage, AK (Maule)
Take-off 98 feet; Landing 110 feet. Combined total 208

Heavy Touring Class
First Place: Kevin Doyle from Soldotna, AK (Cessna 180)
Take-off 105 feet; Landing 129 feet. Combined total 234

Second Place: Matt Conklin from Boise, ID (Cessna 180)
Take-off 112 feet; Landing 140 feet. Combined total 252

Alternate Bush Class (Experimental)
First Place: Bobbie Breeden from Sterling, AK (Modified Cub)
Take-off 24 feet; Landing 20 feet. Combined total 44

Second Place: Jon Bush from Anchorage, AK (Modified Cub)
Take-off 22 feet; Landing 29 feet. Combined total 51

Bush Class
First Place: Chuck McMahan from Gakona, AK (PA 18 Cub)
Take-off 62 feet; Landing 76 feet. Combined total 138

Second Place: Woodson Saunders from Anchorage, AK (PA 18 Cub)
Take-off 74 feet; Landing 135 feet. Combined total 209

Light Sport
First Place: Frank Knapp from Palmer, AK (J-3 Experimental Cub)
Take-off 21 feet; Landing 40 feet. Combined total 61

Second Place: Robby Pedersen from Oriental, NC (Just Aircraft)
Take-off 45 feet; Landing 67 feet. Combined total 112

MEMORANDUM 29
SUBJECT: Off-Airport Ops Guide by FAA

April 20, 2015

1. Alaska's FAA administrators wrote this 12 page *Off-Airports Ops Guide* published in 2010 to help pilots with techniques and procedures to improve safety for off-airport operations. FAA realizes that many pilots in Alaska desire to land their taildraggers off-airport. This desire is invigorated by Alaska's exceptional off-airport pilots. They are classified as legendary first-rate pilots.

2. The second sentence in the guide states: *It assumes that pilots have received training on those techniques and procedures and is not meant to replace instruction from a qualified and experienced flight instructor.* A sentence in the second paragraph reads: *Learning and practicing off-airport techniques under the supervision of an experienced flight instructor will not only make you safer, but will also save you time and expense.* From the beginning it is crystal clear that FAA is not communicating with Alaska's elite pilots. If they did, they would already know that there are no instructors that are capable of providing all the training necessary for this type of flying. The elite Alaskan pilot's modus operandi for training is Self-Training. You train yourself as this is the most potent way to learn any subject. The learning pilot takes command of the training and in time becomes a knowledgeable, innovative, well-disciplined and self-reliant

pilot. This type of training is what makes Alaska's off-airport pilots first-rate pilots. Prior to any training, pilots have to become knowledgeable about aviation operations. This is where the pilot talks to instructors, reads books and aviation magazines, and talks to Alaska's elite pilots. All of this knowledge is for learning purposes. After aviation knowledge has been gained, the pilot in his/her own airplane integrates the new learning into the pilot's flying program. A pilot will become the most proficient pilot by this way of training that is possible and the pilot will be capable of substantially lowering their aircraft accident rate. There are aviation businesses that specialize in teaching the fundamentals of off-airport flying. Two limited liability companies in Alaska are Above Alaska Aviation in Talkeetna, Alaska and Alaska's Cub Training Specialists from Palmer, Alaska. One company in the Lower 48 states is Andover Flight Academy from Andover, New Jersey. These companies can provide basic training for beginning off-airport pilots. However, the lion's share for becoming a proficient and self-reliant pilot is still on the shoulders of the pilot. These trainers know that they are providing a limited quantity of basic knowledge and encouragement for the hesitant pilot that is doubtable about training alone in their own airplane. Pilots should know that to obtain the prodigious rewards of Alaska's off-airport pilots—that you will never get there by training by instructors alone. There are no instructors that have all of the necessary strategy and techniques needed to train a pilot for these off-airport operations. The training is so repetitious that it would cost a fortune to have an instructor along on every training session. The most important point is that self-training in your own airplane is the most important consideration and duty for pilots in obtaining the first-rate flying status of Alaska's special pilots. The sooner a pilot breaks away from instructor training and establishes his/her own training program the better and the faster the progression will be for the pilot to become a complete and self-reliant pilot.

3. FAA discusses the techniques used for evaluating a new landing site from your airplane. It primarily tells you what to look for on the ground before going in and landing your aircraft. It leaves out the most important consideration. Pilots need a way to substantiate what they see from the air to what is on the ground. The elite Alaskan pilots make an evaluation from the air. When they land their aircraft, they measure the landing area, size of the rocks, height of the vegetation, how deep the swales are, and other important items. The measurements on the ground are facts that are

compared with the evaluation made while flying in the airplane. The next evaluation will be more accurate by using this comparison methodology. After using this technique over time, the accuracy from the evaluation in the airplane will substantially improve to a high rate. A pilot will not be surprised by an inaccurate evaluation that will cause difficulty when landing the airplane.

4. The manual provides this landing instruction. *Maintain manufacture's recommended speed or no more than 1.3 Vso all of the way to the touchdown unless wind gusts require more speed.* There is nothing more important in landing an airplane off-airport than the proper management of kinetic energy in the landing aircraft. Alaska's elite pilots safely land their airplanes off-airport by eliminating all excess kinetic energy prior to touching the wheels down on the ground or the runway. They do this by performing *Precision Landings*—one of their most important *Cardinal Rules. Precision Landings* are made by landing on a target (20 foot by 60 foot symbolic box) and simultaneously placing the wheels down in the box at stall speed. Alaska's elite pilots do not add additional speed in the aircraft if the wind is blowing—they land at stall speed. The extra speed in the aircraft is not needed. The 1.3 Vso Rule doubles the kinetic energy in a moving airplane when coming in for a landing. Many aircraft landing accidents in Alaska are due to pilots landing with excessive kinetic energy stacked in their airplanes. This facilitates the airplane in getting out of control and wrecking. There is no way to justify the 1.3 Vso Rule when Alaska's elite pilots have proven the worthy benefits from performing *Precision Landings* for decades.

5. The manual does not mention wheel landings. This is the preferred landing technique for most of Alaska's elite pilots. Wheel landings provide the best forward vision for a pilot landing an aircraft. Wheel landings also provide substantially more stability and control when touching the wheel down when compared to the three-point landing technique. *Precision Landings* are the safest way to land an airplane and they require employing the wheel landing technique.

6. The manual requests that pilots establish a go/no go decision point for takeoffs. Pilots can calculate 70% of your lift off speed, i.e., 50 mph x .70 = 35 mph. Check your airspeed as you approach the decision point and if you're less than 70% of lift off speed—abort. This is not what Alaska's elite

pilot use for taking off on a short runway. Hundreds of places in Alaska are not long enough for performing this technique. There would also be too many wrecked airplanes from aborting a takeoff due to insufficient aircraft speeds at the midpoint. Alaska's elite pilots learn what distances and conditions their airplanes can get off the ground. They use most of the takeoff surface so that when becoming airborne their aircraft speed will be increased to prevent stalling when coming out of ground effect.

7. The manual shows pilots how to determine the useful runway length by flying over it and counting the time in seconds. The aircraft speed correlates with the length in feet on the ground. Alaska's elite pilots have already learned by comparison methodology the distances on the ground while flying in their airplanes. These pilots have also taken this evaluation to a higher level. They make determining the length of a landing place on the ground an art. All they need to do is look at the landing place and they know the length in sufficiently accurate terms to make a safe landing.

8. It is obvious that FAA is providing this off-airport guide because many pilots in Alaska desire to make off-airport landings. Nevertheless, it is also quite obvious that FAA does not talk to Alaska's elite pilots to learn their flying strategies and techniques. FAA is presenting their own doctrine on how to perform off-airport operations. The problem is that FAA is leaving out most of the important strategies and techniques developed by Alaska's elite pilots. These pilots have many of the best short field flying techniques in the world and FAA is simply ignoring them. Many pilots would like to become an exceptional pilot by Alaskan style training, however; they will never come close to getting there with this flawed discussion on the techniques. FAA needs to inform their readers to accomplish their mission of becoming a highly proficient off-airport pilot requires selecting strategies and techniques from both the FAA and the Alaska's elite pilot's aviation spheres. Most pilots already have FAA doctrine because they trained with certificated instructors to obtain the Private Pilot License. What they don't have is Alaska's elite pilot strategies and techniques. These have to be obtained by talking to those first-rate Alaskan pilots or by reading the author's aviation book which provides most of the important strategies and techniques. Pilots will never make substantial gains in become a first-rate off-airport pilot without the desired techniques presented by Alaska top rated pilots. Any other way such as what has been presented in this manual is wishful thinking and it will never happen.

MEMORANDUM 30
SUBJECT: Letter to Alaska DOT About Closing Whittier Airport*

Alaska Department of Transportation and Public Facilities
Central Region Planning
P.O. Box 196900
Anchorage, Alaska 99519-6900

Re: Whittier Airport Proposed Closure

December 6, 2004

I would like to provide testimony concerning the proposed closure of Whittier Airport. Mr. Kip Knudson, Aviation Deputy Commissioner, DOT/PF provided an e-mail message dated November 23, 2004 to address the reasons why the state wants to close Whittier Airport. My comments are primarily to counter Mr. Knudson's reasons for airport closure. They are not based on common sense or facts. In addition, closing the airport would place a great burden on many pilots flying in Prince William Sound by taking away a very important relief landing area when Portage Pass is determined to be not flyable because of severe weather conditions.

The comment that closing the Whittier Airport will save lives and that the airport is the greatest risk to pilots and passengers is a good example of not understanding aviation users in Alaska. I am not aware of excessive airplane accidents or people killed at Whittier Airport during the past 25 years that I have been flying out of Merrill Field. Where are the facts? In addition, experienced tailwheel pilots who fly in Southcentral Alaska will not have a problem landing at Whittier. The Whittier Airport is magnitudes easier for landing than beaches, gravel bars, mudflats, and other short and rough landing places. Routinely landing on short and rough places provides high proficiency. The airport is plenty long and wide enough to be safe. I do recommend that it be used as a one-way airstrip, landing across the water on the approach and taking off toward the water. For experienced tailwheel pilots, this is very safe and a routine procedure on many of the airstrips that we use. Instead of saving lives, I firmly believe that the State would be endangering lives by eliminating a very important relief airport that may be needed when pilots approach Portage Pass in marginal weather conditions and determine that it is not safe to continue. If the pass is not flyable, Mr. Knudson recommends that a pilot should turn around and fly back to Chenega, Tatilek, or Valdez. I can assure you that the least desirable and most dangerous option is to turn

---

* Pilot's testimony helped to convince Alaska DOT&PF not to close Whittier Airport

around and attempt to fly back 75 miles across Prince William Sound to one of these airports. When the weather is deteriorating behind you as you fly west, turning around at Whittier and attempting to find your way back to one of these airports is certainly not advisable and often is not feasible.

Over the years, Whittier Airport has provided many pilots a safe place to land when weather conditions are too marginal for a safe flight through Portage Pass. If the airport were not available for use, many pilots would have no reasonable option but to continue in very marginal conditions in an attempt to fly through the pass. We will never know how many lives Whittier Airport has already saved. The fact is that there have been very few serious accidents (I can't recall any in over 20 years) from pilots either flying through Portage Pass or landing at Whittier Airport. This strongly indicates that Whittier Airport is playing a dominant role in keeping aircraft operations through Portage Pass safe. With that kind of amazing history, why would the State recommend closing such a vital landing area? Whittier is a poorly maintained airport so the State is not spending unavailable resources in its upkeep.

A pilot at the public hearing in Anchorage on December 2, 2004 described what he would do if he arrived at Whittier from the east in marginal weather and he could not fly through Portage Pass. This is assuming the State closed Whittier Airport. He said that he would either land in the Alaska Railroad Yard in downtown Whittier or on the road leading out of Whittier. These are not good choices and aircraft accidents are certain to result from the difficulty. His concluding statement was that lawsuits would certainly be filed as the accidents would be directly correlated with closure of the Whittier Airport. For the record, State DOT officials at the meeting said they are not aware of any, not even one, lawsuit stemming from aircraft accidents at Whittier Airport (the airport has been there for at least 35 years). Does this make a statement! It is obvious that it does.

For all the reasons discussed above, it is apparent that Whittier Airport serves an important and vital role as a relief airport for aircraft flying through Portage Pass. The facts are that it has served that function exceedingly well in the past, almost without flaw, and it must continue to be available in the future. There are many pilots from Kenai, Soldotna, Anchorage, Birchwood, Palmer, Wasilla and other places that fly their aircraft through Turnagain Arm to Prince William Sound through Portage Pass and then fly back again out of the Sound toward the west. These pilots depend on the availability of Whittier Airport being available for landing when weather conditions are marginal and flying through the pass is not safe. Please leave the Whittier Airport open.

William A. Quirk, lll, P.O. Box 212545, Anchorage, Alaska 99521

MEMORANDUM 31
SUBJECT: FAA's Runway Markings are Impractical for Learning Precision Landings

February 15, 2014

1. The Federal Aviation Administration (FAA) has developed a simulated bush strip within the confines of a larger, conventional gravel runway on airports at Fairbanks, Nenana, Wasilla, Palmer, Goose Bay, and Soldotna. These bush strips are to be used as practice areas for takeoffs and landings. The practice runway is 600 to 800 feet in length and 25 feet in width. White markings were used to provide visual identification of the landing strips. The FAA encourages pilots to use these strips to practice precision landings in a safe environment.

2. FAA should be applauded for realizing the value of precision landings developed by Alaska's extraordinary pilots for off-airport operations. These landings are one of these pilot's most important Cardinal Rules. Pilots need to be educated about the enormous rewards of learning to make precision landings. They also need to be educated about how Alaska's elite off-airport pilots conduct the training operations because they are the ones who have developed the techniques that provide the exceptionally useful results.

3. The proper place for conducting precision landings is on a gravel bar in natural terrain. Pilots can set up their own personalized markers on the gravel bar. A special locale that many pilots in Southcentral Alaska use for this purpose is the gravel bars on the Knik River. Pilots can select gravel bars on the river that are 800 to 1,000 feet in length—a few are 1,600 to 1,800 feet in length. These gravel bars are just as safe as the bush strips on the airports that were set up by FAA. On the natural gravel bars away from airport traffic distractions productive and efficient training can be accomplished.

4. The six airports in Alaska that are permanently set-up with markers for conducting short field takeoffs and landings do not provide an environment that is consistent with training for Alaskan off-airport pilots. It is unfortunate that the markers are standardized and offer only one fixed asset for precision landings. Pilots need to learn the options for markers and then choose their own set-up. Self-training is the *modus operandi* for Alaska's extraordinary off-airport pilots. The permanent markers are taking away the pilot's responsibility of being creative and setting up their own training program. There are several ways to set-up markers for precision landings. Many pilots use small

orange-colored cones or orange flagging material tied around cobblestones to create a rectangular box 60 feet wide by 20 feet deep at the end of the landing area. Creating your own set-up for precision landings is an important part of pilot development and proper progression as training advances. This provides the most potent way for learning and it helps pilots become confident that they can get the job accomplished. It is also important in providing a step-wise approach in helping to create a self-reliant pilot. You can't take away the pilot's responsibility for establishing their own training program because this significantly diminishes and degrades the value of the training.

5. Another fundamental limitation for the Alaska airport training set-up is that the training mission is ineffective for learning precision landings. The markers are set-up for pilots to fly in and practice takeoffs and landings. Practicing these operations has little similarity to the Alaska's pilots conducting training for precision landings. The airport exercises will not provide the proper training necessary to substantially increase pilot proficiency nor will it reduce the pilot's aircraft accident rate in Alaska to a significant amount. The Alaskan off-airport pilot training for precision landings covers a much more diverse aspect for training than practicing simple short field takeoffs and landings. The airport training is an exercise in futility that will not boost pilot proficiency in precision landings. The Alaskan pilot training techniques for precision landings that will provide incomparable beneficial results are shown below.

Training for Precision Landings by Alaska's Elite Pilots

a. Training for Alaskan of-airport precision landings involves two procedures. The first procedure in precision landings is to learn to make spot landings. The pilot has to select a place when coming in for a landing where the main wheels are to touch down. This can be the rectangular box, a willow bush adjacent to the touch down spot or a symbolic box as visualized by the pilot. The main wheels must touch down in the visually marked box every time a landing is made. Pilots must practice spot landings until this technique becomes flawless—nothing short of perfection on every landing is required.

b. The second procedure required for making precision landings is just as important as the first and it involves touching the main wheels down in the landing area at initial stall speed. This operation is essential in precision landings to remove all excess kinetic energy (energy in a moving object) from the aircraft prior to landing. Many aircraft accidents in Alaska are caused by airplanes coming in for a landing way above stall speed. This causes the airplane to touch down with an excessive overload of kinetic energy. The airplane under these conditions can easily get out of control and the pilot will not be able to recover. The huge amount of excess energy (often doubled when compared to initial stall speed) will ensure that when the airplane gets out of control it will crash with an enormous amount of damage. Taking out all excess kinetic energy by landing at initial stall speed has the exact opposite effect. This is a true blessing in disguise. The airplane is not likely to get out of control and crash because it does not have sufficient kinetic energy to do so. Initial stall speed landings also provide for the shortest ground run after touching down. Touching down at the slower speeds will require little or no braking. This will eliminate heavy breaking and nosing over aircraft in soft terrain when landing way above stall speed.

c. When practicing precision landings, it may be practical to take on one of the two techniques at a time and learn both of them separately with a high level of accuracy. After this initial effort, precision landings have to be practiced with both techniques (touching down in the box and touching down at stall speed) coming together simultaneously when the wheels touch down. This final phase is the ultimate goal in mastering precision landings.

d. The information above shows precisely the training needed for making precision landings. Both of these operations coming together simultaneously when the wheels touch down provide an impeccable rate of assurance in making routine safe landings. The benefits from learning to land aircraft in this manner are enormous. Pilots will be highly capable of safe landings on short and rough off-airport areas in natural terrain and will avoid aircraft accidents caused by highly energized aircraft getting out of control and crashing. Pilots will also benefit from precision landings when landing at airports by avoiding gusty wind and crosswind accidents caused by excessive kinetic energy stacked in their airplane. All excessive kinetic energy in an airplane is removed by conducting initial stall landings.

In summary, it would have been an effortless undertaking for FAA to inform GA Pilots to talk to Alaska's elite off-airport pilots about setting-up training for precision landings. However, the decision to place the training markers on the airports was most likely driven in large part by increased federal revenues for airport operation and maintenance that are due with increases in additional airport landings. Nevertheless, it cannot be overstated how important it is to learn to make precision landings by training like Alaska's extraordinary pilots. For decades, this has been the procedure for achieving the proper training that will deliver the maximum useful benefits. Substantially altering the training program will simply not be productive in learning to master precision landings. The message here is to use Alaska's best pilot training procedures for learning and practicing precision landings. Talk to Alaska's best off-airport pilots to learn how to conduct the training. It could not be simpler in learning the techniques.

MEMORANDUM 32
SUBJECT: The Challenge of Landing an Airplane in a Microburst

September 20, 2013

(Foregone conclusion—all hell breaks loose)

1. Flying into a microburst while landing my airplane on a remote airstrip in Southcentral Alaska was experienced in early September 2013. I did not choose to fly into a microburst; it was just there at the end of the runway when I came in to land. At the time, I did not have the knowledge to even recognize it as a microburst. It was annoying, somewhat terrifying; however, it was a great learning experience.

2. A father and his son came to Alaska to explore some of Alaska's outdoor activities. The chief pilot carried the father and I agreed to fly the son. Our flights over a 7 day period covered more than 1,000 miles of flying and landing in pristine environments from the Kenai Peninsula 100 miles south of Anchorage to the upper Susitna River drainage 60 miles northeast of Talkeetna. We set up tents and camped in wild Alaska. The weather was horrible with continuous low pressure systems moving through Southcentral Alaska. I preferred not to fly in the rain, low ceilings, and gusty winds blowing from 15 to 45 miles per hour. However, I was committed to helping my friend and his clients. They agreed to fly in this weather although it was not very much fun. We had a mission to complete and off we went.

3. Toward the latter part of the trip, we were flying northeast of Talkeetna near the upper Susitna River. It was getting late in the evening. We decided to turn around and head back to Talkeetna for the night. To our surprise, we were flying right into the teeth of a frontal system heading

217

our way. We were flying under the dark clouds at about 800 feet above the terrain. The winds picked up to 30-40 miles per hour. It was raining and the gray-streaked sky near the ground was becoming darker as we continued flying. In the next few minutes the visibility ahead was totally blocked—our chance of flying back to Talkeetna was slim to none. I talked to our lead pilot and convinced him that we should turn around and fly to a lodge north of the Susitna River that we had seen within the past half-hour. We turned around and headed northeast again. The lead pilot went in and landed at the private lodge. I stayed in the air while my partner talked with the staff at the lodge. After five minutes, I didn't get any negative signals not to land here. Hopefully, we will be able to stay here until the weather improves.

4. Now it was my time to land at this remote lodge. The airstrip was plenty long at about 2,000 feet. The east end was smooth compared to large stones protruding through the soil on the other end. Since the wind was light and not a factor, I decided to fly-in and land on the east end. As I turned the airplane to line up with the runway, I noticed a wispy dark-gray cloud hovering right over the end of the runway from ground level up to about 1,000 feet. The darkened cloud substantially dimmed my vision of the runway but not totally. I made a hasty decision to continue my attempt to land in these low-light conditions. As I approached the dark cloud at about 500 feet above the ground, headwinds increased dramatically. Although this was a strong headwind blowing at 25 to 40 miles per hour, it was not excessively turbulent. Landing an airplane into a strong headwind is usually not a problem. So I continued flying. When the airplane arrived in the center of the gray-streaked cloud, I was totally surprised to find strong vertical winds causing a dramatic downdraft. My airplane began to lose altitude at an alarming rate. I immediately lowered the nose in a steep pitched-down orientation and pushed the throttle in to full power. After a few seconds, the airplane was still losing altitude but at a slower and more manageable rate. At this time, I was not concerned about landing but making certain that these unusual conditions would not cause a loss of control leading to an aircraft accident. As my airplane came close to the end of the runway at about 100 feet above the ground, a strong tailwind appeared that was significantly decreasing aircraft performance by reducing the approach angle and increasing the ground distance needed for landing. This makes landing my airplane difficult

and highly problematic. After the airplane slowed down, I added half flaps then full flaps and pulled the throttle back near idle. If the airplane does not slow down sufficiently, I can make a go around and land a second time in the opposite direction with a head wind. As the airplane moved down the runway, the tailwind gradually decreased in speed and then the landing was possible. I landed in the middle of the long runway and used my brakes to stop near the lodge. I pulled the fuel-air mixture control all the way back and the engine shut down. Then I just sat in the airplane for a few minutes to unwind after this frightening experience.

5. When I exited the airplane, rain was coming down in a downpour and thumb-size hail began battering the fabric on my airplane. The noise from the hail was intense. The father's son in the back of my airplane was surprisingly calm throughout this difficult undertaking. He most likely thought that this was just a routine landing in a rain storm. We exited the airplane and quickly ran to the lodge for cover. I told everyone present that the landing was very difficult with all kinds of scary winds blowing at the end of the runway when I approached it. Although there were four pilots present, no one commented. Evidently, these pilots have not experienced landing an airplane in this dangerous weather condition.

6. It was not until I was home and looked up a microburst that I concluded, without a doubt, that my landing at the lodge involved flying through a classical microburst to reach the runway. This was an exceptional learning experience and I am not aware of other pilots flying through microbursts. Recently a pilot asked me "Would you land your airplane in a microburst again?" I told him no; I would not because they are potentially dangerous and they can be easily avoided.

7. Microbursts are small-scale downdrafts of great intensity that descend from a cloud base at 1,000 to 2,000 feet above the ground. They are often found in a low pressure frontal system that is moving through an area with rain and strong winds. They may be embedded in heavy rain associated with a thunderstorm or in light rain in benign-appearing virgas—wisps of rain that drop out of a cloud into air so dry that the rain evaporates as it falls. Its evaporation creates a column of frigid air that plunges. At several hundred feet above the ground the powerful downdrafts which can be as strong as 6,000 feet per minute begin to spread until, at near ground level, they are

entirely horizontal. Microbursts are typically less than 1 mile in diameter. Horizontal winds near the ground can be as strong as 50 miles per hour resulting in a 100 miles per hour wind shear (headwind to tailwind change for an airplane passing through the microburst). Microbursts are short-lived and seldom last longer than 15 minutes.

8. Microbursts are easy to avoid if pilots can first detect them and then keep a safe distance from them until they dissipate.

MEMORANDUM 33
SUBJECT: Density Altitude Chart for Ski Landings in Alaska

November 10, 2012

1. Density altitude is rarely a problem during the summer months in Southcentral Alaska because of cool summers with temperatures in the 50 to 70 degree Fahrenheit range and most landings being made in valleys with low to moderate altitudes. This means you don't need to calculate density altitude for most summer operations.

2. In the winter, aircraft may be landing at higher elevations because many places are available for landing ski-equipped aircraft. The density altitude chart below is developed for landing operations on skis during the winter. The chart shows proposed data based on Standard Atmospheric Pressure (29.92 inches of Mercury) and Standard Temperature at the selected landing location. The chart will help you understand how low winter temperatures greatly reduce the density altitude. When you land on Kahiltna Base Camp on Mount McKinley at 7,200 feet; at 8,400 feet at the top of Knik Glacier; or on the plateau near Mount Spurr at 10,000 feet—make sure you have a cold day (zero degrees Fahrenheit or colder) to reduce the density altitude. See the results in the chart.

3. To correctly determine the precise density altitude in your selected landing place, you will have to set your altimeter at 29.92 inches and read the current pressure altitude close to where you plan to land your aircraft. Then you'll need to obtain the outside air temperature (OAT). Use a density altitude chart to plot your precise density altitude with your inputs of pressure altitude and OAT. If you are landing at high elevation on a day with high density altitude, attempt to take off downslope. The distance required for takeoff is reduced by half in taking off on a 20 percent slope.

DENSITY ALTITUDE CHART FOR SKI LANDINGS IN ALASKA

Landing[1] (Feet)	Density Altitude[2] (Feet)						
	-20° F	-10° F	0° F	10° F	20° F	30° F	ST[3]
10,000	6,900	7,800	8,600	9,200	9,900	10,500	22°F
9,500	6,000	7,000	8,000	8,600	9,200	9,900	25°F
8,400	5,000	5,800	6,400	7,200	7,800	8,400	30°F
7,200	3,800	4,400	5,100	5,700	6,300	7,000	34°F
6,200	2,200	3,000	3,800	4,500	5,200	5,800	38°F
5,600	-500	800	3,000	3,700	4,300	5,000	40°F
3,200	-1,800	-1,000	10	800	1,200	2,000	48°F
2,000	-3,200	-2,200	-1,500	-800	0	700	51°F
1,000	-4,500	-4,000	-3,000	-2,000	-1,200	-800	55°F

[1] Elevation where you plan to land your aircraft. Data also used for pressure altitude.
[2] Density Altitude based on Standard Atmospheric Pressure and Standard OAT.
[3] Standard Temperature for selected landing elevations.

MEMORANDUM 34
SUBJECT: Safety When Moving on Glaciers

January 5, 2013

1. Storms in early winter provide adequate amounts of snow to fill in many small crevasses on glaciers. These so-called snow bridges are most often strong enough to support a man on cross-country skis or snowshoes and a ski-equipped airplane during the winter when the snow particles have been exposed to low temperatures to strengthen them. It is important to understand the pressure placed on snow bridges with different types of conveyance.

2. Table 1 below shows the moving or walking surface pressure in pounds per square inch for a horse's hoofs; a dog's feet; and a man's winter boot, snowshoe, and ski. In addition, the moving surface pressure is shown for my airplane on skis. It is difficult to compare dissimilar types of convey-ance. Horses and dogs, unlike humans, walk with two feet on a surface at a time. Humans, while walking, will have only one foot on a surface at a time. Furthermore, humans momentarily place full weight on the heel while walking. This smaller footprint (the heel) further increases the pounds per square inch for the foot by three times. A galloping horse and a running dog

221

and human will double or triple the surface pressure when compared with the walking pressures.

3. The data show that walking on glaciers with winter boots generates nine times more pounds pressure per square inch than walking on glaciers with snowshoes. Common sense dictates that after landing on glaciers you should put on snowshoes or skis before moving away from your aircraft. The calculations also show that your taildragger is the safest conveyance on the glacier. This is due to the large number of square inches on the two main Landes 2500 skis (1904 square inches) and the Landes tail ski (140 square inches) which totals 2,044 square inches. The weight of my loaded Tern with two passengers is about 1,600 pounds. That turns out to be only 0.8 pounds per square inch when the taildragger is parked or double that number (1.6 pounds per square inch) when moving on a glacier. It is great to know that the taildragger is the safest of most conveyances on glaciers and therefore it has the least chance of punching through a snow bridge and falling into a crevasse.

4. It is important to be cautious and to take measures in reducing chances for falling into a crevasse. It can be a very difficult task pulling a person out of a crevasse. Prevention is a prudent consideration. Pilots who land their airplanes on glaciers should carry the necessary equipment for extracting a person who has fallen into a crevasse. The equipment includes a climbing rope (9 or 11 mm diameter and 150 feet in length), ice ax, carabineers, pulley, Jumar ascenders, aluminum snow anchors, and a nylon seat harness. Training for extracting a person from a crevasse is also highly recommended.

TABLE 1. GROUND PRESSURE APPLIED BY DIFFERENT TYPES OF CONVEYANCE[1]

Conveyance	Pounds/Inch²
Horse (1,500 pounds with weight on 2 hooves)	60.0
Man (winter boot with weight on one heel)	20.0
Dog (75 pound dog with weight on 2 feet)	12.0
Man on Cross-Country Skis (weight on one ski)	2.3
Man on Snowshoes (weight on one snowshoe)	2.2
Arctic Tern on main and tailwheel skis (weight on all skis)	**1.6**

[1] Pressures calculated for animals walking and airplane moving over a snow-covered glacier.

MEMORANDUM 35
SUBJECT: Whiteout and Flat Light

June 3, 2008

1. Reference: *A Pilot's Guide to Aviation Weather Services in Alaska* published in July 2006 by the Alaska Aviation Weather Unit of the US National Weather Service (NWS), Anchorage, Alaska. Note the definitions of *Whiteout* and *Flat Light* presented on the back of the brochure.

2. The definition of a whiteout as presented in the NWS guide is unequivocally incorrect. First of all, whiteout is one word, not two words as the guide portrays. Second, defining a whiteout as being caused by blowing snow is absolutely without foundation. Blowing snow has little to do with a whiteout. It does reduce shadows; however, the snowflakes can totally block out vision. The terminology for naturally blowing snow is a *Blizzard*, not a whiteout. Whiteout is an optical phenomenon in which the snow-covered terrain blends into a uniformly dull sky reducing the visibility of shadows, clouds, the horizon, and so forth and one's sense of direction or distance[*]. Flat light is no more or less than another common word for whiteout. Whiteout and flat light are used interchangeably.

3. The misuse of the word whiteout is a gigantic embarrassment to Alaskans and also to mountaineers from around the world who come to Alaska to climb our challenging mountains. These individuals are intimately aware of whiteout conditions on Alaska's glaciers and they would cringe at the NWS definition. The greatest difficulty in navigation on Alaska's glaciers is the optical phenomenon caused by low cloud layers and light with greatly reduced visibility. This causes problems in navigation because it is difficult or impossible to discern or choose a proper route when one cannot see rises, depressions, holes, crevasses, and other obstacles on the surface of the snow-covered glacier. Whiteout conditions on glaciers in Alaska are common occurrences. Wind is for the most part a nonfactor in navigation on glaciers. If the wind is blowing hard enough to blow snow around, a mountaineer or pilot would probably not be active. The greatest challenge for a pilot is a mild whiteout, which many pilots will not recognize, and they would land in such conditions. They would all too quickly find out that a snow bank or a deep depression was concealed by the mild

---

[*] *Webster's New World College Dictionary*, 4th Edition. 2004. Wiley Publishing Incorporated, Cleveland, Ohio

whiteout. After touching down on skis, the pilot would only then see the snow bank—too close to avoid. Pilots in Alaska will land on glaciers and a few will run into a hidden snow bank or a depression because of mild whiteout conditions.

4. For the sake of individuals knowledgeable about the correct definition of a whiteout, please correct this deficiency in the brochure. We don't need to confuse or complicate matters for individuals who are learning or ones needing instruction.

MEMORANDUM 36
SUBJECT: Atypical Pilots Flying Taildraggers in Alaska

April 15, 2013

1. Airline Transport Pilots (ATPs) fly taildraggers in Alaska after retiring from a professional aviation career with a commercial airline. Why do retired ATPs move to Alaska and fly taildraggers? First, flying taildraggers and landing off-airport in remote places is one of the more challenging, interesting, and enjoyable flying experiences in all of aviation. The inspiration of flying Alaska with its vast uninhabited mountains, glaciers, and fjords and magnificent wildlife is also a powerful motivating force. And thirdly, the camaraderie of flying in Alaska is the best that can be found anywhere. With all three of these aviation attributes—who would not enjoy flying Alaska?

2. Recently, I have noticed that there are active ATPs that are flying taildraggers in Alaska. These ATPs are flying commercial aircraft based in the Lower 48 states. They have homes near the aviation hub where they fly from and a few have a second home in Alaska. Their commercial airline working schedule with lots of time off and their high compensation rate allows for this to be practical. I know of one ATP flying for a commercial airline in the southeastern states that not only has a home in Anchorage but owns a 5 acre parcel with a beautiful cabin on a lake northwest of Merrill Field. He uses a Super Cub on floats in the summer and skis in winter to fly to his cabin retreat with his wife and dog in tow. This is the ultimate aviation lifestyle. Not only living your professional aviation dream with having full time employment but having the best retirement-type of aviation experience in mid-life that is possible. It doesn't get any better.

3. Commercial pilots in Alaska that fly aircraft for regional airlines also fly taildraggers. These pilots have privately-owned taildraggers and fly them when they are not working on their commercial flying occupation. This flying combination provides the better of two worlds—full time employment in a career field and flying and enjoying the best type of aviation experience on your own time. These commercial pilots, like the ATPs, have lots of time off making the choice of flying taildraggers in Alaska a reality. What a fabulous aviation career this is?

4. There are still other pilots from the Lower 48 states and from European countries that fly taildraggers in Alaska. These are pilots that typically have a Super Cub stored in a hangar in Alaska. They will fly to Alaska several times a year on a commercial airliner and spend a week or more flying their Cub in wild Alaska. These pilots deserve very high marks for they have done their homework. They have learned the true value of flying in Alaska. What Alaska has to offer does not exist elsewhere and they want to take advantage of it. They also want to be part of Alaska's rich aviation legacy.

MEMORANDUM 37
SUBJECT: Arctic Tern Advocate

May 10, 2008

1. I attended the Alaska State Aviation Trade Show and Conference on Saturday and Sunday, May 3 and 4, 2008 at the FedEx Maintenance Hangar on Anchorage International Airport. I was disappointed when I did not find a booth for Interstate Aircraft Company, which has provided a display for the past several years. Nevertheless, I was elated to find out from Bill Diehl at the trade show that the amended Type Certificate for the new Arctic Tern has been approved by the FAA in 2007 and that Interstate Aircraft Company was bought by Mr. Charles E. Nearburg, an oil magnate from Colorado.

2. My interest in the subject comes from the Arctic Tern I purchased on August 8, 1997. I had flown a Piper Cub for the previous 15 years in Alaska. My Tern is on Bushwheels in summer/fall and Landes straight skis in the winter. The Tern has excellent off-airport (bush flying) capabilities that have allowed me to explore and safely land in hundreds of remote locations in Alaska. Many of these landings are first-time events where no airplane has landed

before. The Tern is a sturdily built airplane with an award-winning aerodynamic design that makes it a marvelous flying machine. No Airworthiness Directive (AD) has ever been issued for the airplane's airframe. The Tern is very stable while airborne due to its large-size vertical and horizontal empennage (tail assembly). The excellent stability at near stall speed allows pilots to make outstanding short-field landings. It has the most benign stall of any of the taildraggers. The wings hold steady in the stall (they do not drop off) as the airplane makes genuine deflections as the nose drops down and then starts flying again. It is easy to fly and handles extremely well in turbulent and gusty wind conditions. The mammoth-sized flaps are slotted and the combination helps to generate a slow stall speed of 32 miles per hour. The excellent visibility over the cowling allows great landing capability on short-field landings. The landing areas on Alaskan Bushwheels include river gravel bars, ocean and lake beaches, mudflats when dry, grass-covered sod, tundra, and mountain ridges and saddles. On Landes skis in winter the landing places are snow and ice-covered surfaces on lakes, glaciers, ice fields and on the top of mountain ridges. The additional space in the pilot's seat with 31 inches of shoulder width is very comfortable. The huge baggage area is a great asset not only the large 6 foot fiberglass cargo tray but also the large side door which allows the easiest loading and unloading of large items of any of the two-seat tandem taildraggers. Cruising speed at low power is 98 miles per hour with 26" Bushwheels. The dependable 160 horse power Lycoming engine provides sufficient capacity for excellent takeoffs and climbs. The fuel burn can be reduced to 7.2 gallons per hour with the engine properly leaned out.

3. I am very excited and optimistic that the new Arctic Tern will become a reality and that it will soon be built and available to pilots flying the remote backcountry. Manufacturing the new Tern will hopefully make it possible for all of us with the original Tern to have a ready supply of parts when we need an upgrade or replacement due to damage to our aircraft. Keeping the Tern alive is great news to all of us who fly them. Approximately 14 pilots are still flying the originally built Terns in Alaska. Seven pilots are flying the Arctic Tern in the continental US. Several other Terns are flown in foreign countries.

4. Alaska will play a crucial role in selling the first newly built Arctic Terns. This is because the first Arctic Terns were being built and flown in Alaska, and because of the Tern's outstanding flying characteristics

in the bush. This is an aircraft that serves Alaska well. Pilots flying the new Tern after a short period of time will be shocked at the great flying characteristics of the airplane and its suitability to access remote lands in Alaska. With highly respectable pilots in Alaska endorsing the Tern, sales will then spread elsewhere, especially in Canada, continental US, and foreign countries.

5. The Alaska State Aviation Trade Show and Conference sponsors the Alaska Airman's Association annual airplane raffle. Dan's Aircraft on Merrill Field built a Piper Super Cub for the 2008 raffle. Providing an airplane for the raffle presents an excellent opportunity to show and sell new aircraft. Attendance for the trade show was over 21,000 in the year 2007. This is a tremendous amount of exposure in the Alaskan aviation community. I hope Interstate Aircraft Company will offer to build a Tern for the raffle in the future. This would be a very positive step forward for the future of the Tern.

6. When talking with Bill Diehl, the designer and builder of the Arctic Tern in Anchorage from 1975 to 1985, at the trade show, I mentioned my Arctic Tern ski landing on the Kahiltna Glacier at 7,200 feet ASL at the Mount McKinley Mountain Climbing Base Camp on March 28, 2008. Bill countered with his over-the-top flight of Mount McKinley in his Arctic Tern (Lycoming O-320, 150 horsepower) on Easter Sunday. Bill had an oxygen supply and had a difficult time gaining sufficient altitude near the summit to fly over the top of Mount McKinley which is at 20,320 feet ASL. The air at 20,000 feet was thin and the engine had a greatly reduced amount of horsepower. Theoretically, engine horsepower would be diminished about 60 percent at this altitude. However, the cold air, which was well below zero Fahrenheit, helped to reduce density altitude. Bill said he was circling the peak with flaps employed trying to climb high enough to fly over the peak. He finally climbed high enough to fly over McKinley's summit. When he looked down at the summit when he passed over it, the height above the top of the mountain was only 50 feet. WOW! What an accomplishment.

7. All the best to Arctic Aircraft Company. You can count on many loyal supporters in Alaska.

MEMORANDUM 38
SUBJECT: Building Quality Airstrips in Alaska

August 16, 2009

1. The Cooperative Extension Service (University of Alaska) is trying to persuade pilots who are building airstrips to construct and maintain a grass-covered airstrip. Most airstrips in Alaska have a gravel base. The Cooperative Extension Service claims that grass-covered airstrips will save planes by avoiding problems caused by gravel.

2. From over 30 years of flying in Alaska and landing on all types of landing surfaces, it is abundantly clear that gravel surfaces are far superior to all the other types. This does not include paved surfaces, as this belongs in another discussion.

3. Anchorage International, Merrill Field, and Palmer Airports all have paved runways for commercial aircraft. These airports also provide unpaved airstrips for small aircraft. All of the unpaved airstrips have a gravel surface. The government can afford to build whatever type airstrip they want. They build gravel airstrips because they are superior to other surface materials, including grass. In addition, pilots support building gravel airstrips. Picking up gravel on these carefully prepared airstrips is a rare occurrence because the gravel is washed, graded, and sized. The proper size gravel is sufficiently heavy that in normal aircraft operations the propeller and tires do not pick up the gravel.

4. Grass-covered airstrips are expensive to build. The terrain has to be leveled, contoured for drainage, and maintained for months by mowing throughout the summer growing season. These airstrips are often soft, especially when wet due to prolonged periods of rainfall. If drainage ditches are not well designed, flooding occurs. Ruts and muddy conditions can occur if strips are repeatedly used when wet.

5. All the problems with grass-covered airstrips mentioned above are eliminated with gravel. One hour after long periods of prolonged rainfall, gravel strips have drained and the surface is firm and free of water. No splashing water and mud on your aircraft. No rutting on the surface of the airstrip. No flooded areas on the airstrip. Takeoffs and landings are shorter on gravel because of the firmer surface. Visibility of the ground conditions is far superior with gravel when compared to grass-covered airstrips which often cover-up obstacles such as logs, rises, swales, holes, and others.

6. The Cooperative Extension Service should not be promoting the building of grass-covered airstrips for aircraft use because of the cost and the inherent problems associated with grass strips. It is significantly more appropriate to promote the building of gravel airstrips in Alaska. Grass, however, may still have a role to play. The Cooperative Extension Service could research the best types of grasses that grow in a thin cover or scattered pattern over pit run gravel surfaces on established airstrips. This would bind and hold down the gravel so that it would be unlikely to get airborne and damage aircraft during takeoff and landing operations. This would provide relief for airstrips built with pit run materials. Pit run comes in many sizes and the rocks that can be picked up by aircraft are usually present. Pit run is commonly used on airstrips because it is readily available and the cost is low (usually paying only for loading and hauling).

7. Picking up gravel by the airplane propeller or tires while landing or taking off on gravel surfaces is a minor nuisance each and every pilot has to learn to deal with in Alaska. If you avoid it on your home landing field by having other surface types (grass, pavement), you will still have to live with it every day when landing off airport on river gravel bars and on beaches all over Alaska. A skilled pilot in Alaska has learned over time how to greatly reduce the damage of sucking up gravel into the propeller or setting gravel in flight by aircraft tires. Soft tundra tires help tremendously in this matter. The taller tundra tires also provide greater propeller clearance and reduce the likelihood of picking up gravel by the propeller. Learning the proper ground maneuvering of an aircraft is essential in avoiding gravel damage to your aircraft. And every so often, even experienced pilots, will nick the propeller by a rock. This is not the end of the world. You just file off the nick and properly dress down the propeller. Remember, propellers don't last forever. Every few years or sooner, a propeller will need to be taken off the aircraft and be reconditioned. This will effectively clean up all the nicks and balance the propeller. Eventually, the propeller will need to be replaced.

8. From the above discussion in paragraph #7, one can understand that landing on gravel in Alaska is a way of life. My aircraft is parked on a gravel strip and taking off and landing on it is my least concern or worry. The gravel bars on rivers or the ocean beaches are a much greater challenge in landing and takeoff without picking up gravel or sand. Nevertheless, landing on gravel and beaches is what provides much of the access to remote places in Alaska. If you avoid or don't land on gravel, you have eliminated

most of the access to the backcountry. If this is reality, we would not need Piper Cubs or all the other taildraggers we have in such plentiful supply.

MEMORANDUM 39
SUBJECT: Ski Landing Knowledge by Don Bowers[*]

March 10, 1995

1. **Metal Skag.** Helps to control aircraft on ice.
2. **Rear Cable.** Keeps the ski at the proper angle in flight.
3. **Front Springs or Bungee.** Keeps the ski in tension against the rear cable.
4. **Check Cable.** Keeps ski from dipping or drooping too far if the spring breaks or fails.
5. **A Drooped Ski.** A very serious event that can cause loss of control of aircraft because of the sudden pitch-down moment. Slow aircraft down and fly in an increased angle of attack.
6. **Ski Installation and Removal.** Requires only an entry in the Aircraft Log Book by an A&P.
7. **Essential Items to Carry in Aircraft While Ski Flying.** Snowshoes and snow shovel (absolutely mandatory). Compactor bags and duct tape.
8. **Ability of Skis to Slide across the Snow.** This is dependent on its ability to melt snow or ice crystals through the heat of friction. Skis then slide on the thin layer of water.
9. **Rough Ski Surface Can Be A Problem.** Scratched ski bottoms can reduce the slick factor. Frost, ice, or frozen snow can form on rough surfaces.
10. **Always Park Aircraft on Hard Packed Snow or on Existing Tracks.**
11. **Where You Tie Down Your Airplane, Always Place Wooden 2 x 4s Under the Skis.**
12. **If Skis are covered with Frozen Snow or Ice.** Only option is to free ice or frost from skis.
    • Use power and move rudder from side to side.

---

[*] Don Bowers was a pilot for Hudson Air Service in Talkeetna in the 1990s. Don was an author, teacher, and well-known veteran of the Iditarod Trail Sled Dog Race. He was also known for flying a Cessna 185 as top cover for Mount McKinley rescues, guiding the National Park Service's high-altitude Lama Helicopter through holes in the clouds to save mountain climbers in trouble. Don and three park service employees died in a tragic accident in June 2000. Don was flying the rangers from Talkeetna to Kahiltna Glacier base camp when horrific weather with extreme winds and poor visibility prevented his entrance onto the glacier. He flew west to clear the extreme weather; however, strong winds caused the plane to go down near the junction of the Yentna and Lacuna Glaciers. It crashed and burned. There were no survivors.

- Rock wings (helper on the ground shaking the wings).
- Use 2 x 4s and pry skis up. Scrape off frost, ice, or frozen snow.
- Cover skis with compactor bags and tie on with duct tape. The plastic bags will blow off in flight.
- Clear ice, frost, and frozen snow off skis by high-speed touch-and-goes.

13. **Ski Taxiing.** Keep skis moving briskly. Slow speed will allow ski to grab and to try to stop.

14. **Turns on Skis.** Turns should always be made to the left to take advantage of engine torque. Use moderate speed to maintain momentum when turning.

15. **Excessive Load on Ski Gear.** Do not place excessive load on the gear on the inside of the turn. Slow down to turn. Turns on rough surfaces need to be kept as slow as possible but fast enough to avoid ski grabbing and stopping.

16. **Turning Skis.** Apply power while pushing the desired rudder (stick forward) and nose-down elevator will make things easier by raising the tail at least partly out of the snow and allowing the propeller blast to hit the rudder, thus facilitating the turn.

17. **Be Careful When Turning on Skis.** Ski length allows it to put enormous twisting moments on the axle and gear leg, far more than a wheel. Too much speed or too sharp a turn will cause the inside ski to dig in. This can cause the gear leg to twist and collapse or snap off the axle.

18. **Skis Sliding Sideways.** Do not let the skis slide sideways on ice or snow. If they suddenly hit an obstruction, a ski can catch and flip the aircraft over or collapse the gear.

19. **Wet, Sticky Snow.** Wet, sticky snow is worse than mud for impeding a takeoff. Wet, sticky snow often happens at or above freezing temperatures.

20. **Side Load on Skis.** Light plane landing gear was not designed for high-intensity side loads that skis can cause. A ground loop on skis usually means major structural repair because the gear will probably be seriously damaged.

21. **Takeoff.** May have to lift one ski off at a time; sticky or old snow with a high resistance.

22. **Use Existing Tracks for Takeoff.** Alternative is to use snowshoes to pack a runway.

23. **Don't Land or Takeoff on a Dog-Leg Strip.** Too much side load.

24. **Snowmachine Tracks.** Watch out for buried snowmachine tracks crossing landing areas.

25. **The Safest Ski Landing was on a Packed Runway.**

26. **Open Snow Landings can be Fun but can Easily Cause Problems.**
27. **Overflow.** Overflow is more prevalent near inlets and outlets of lakes. Check for overflow by making a touch-and-go and come back to see if the tracks become darker—meaning water is seeping into them from below. Any indications of overflow require quick exit.
28. **Drifts.** Drifts can be a big problem and must be avoided for landings and takeoffs.
29. **Glare Ice on Lakes.** Be cautious when landing on glare ice on lakes. Lakes can freeze with cracks and pressure ridges that can grab skis.
30. **Avoid Flat-Light Landings (Whiteouts).** Avoid flat-light landings in open snow like the plague. Can't see a two-foot snow drift.
31. **Open Snow Landings.** Add power once on the surface to keep moving to a suitable parking area. First make a touch-and-go (or several) to establish a set of tracks. Make a left turn and a loop back to the takeoff position. Stop on the tracks heading back for takeoff.
32. **Can't Stop on Ice.** If you cannot stop on ice before hitting the shoreline of a lake, make an intentional ground loop by adding power, pushing the nose over, kicking full left rudder, pouring on the power to decelerate the by now backward slide. Chances are the ski will spin on the ice without grabbing and no damage will be done.
33. **Stuck in the Snow.** The most common king of stuck is when one ski digs in, creating a lopsided or unleveled aircraft. Solution—you'll need snowshoes and a shovel. Dig snow from under the high ski and make it level with the sunken ski. Dig ramps for skis back to the top of the snow pack. If snow is very deep, snowshoe a path to the runway. Propeller clear of snow.
34. **If Snow Swallows the Aircraft on Landing.** If snow has swallowed the aircraft on landing, it's time to put on the snowshoes. Stomp out a path to ski tracks or a whole runway if necessary. May need to shovel a ramp in front of the aircraft.
35. **Ski Landings.**
A. Look the landing area over thoroughly for a smooth surface. Don't land in areas with snow berms, wavy snow, depressions, holes, and other obstacles. Look for protrusions in the snow such as snow domes—they could be hiding a large boulder under the snow.
B. Always drag the landing area prior to making a final landing.
C. Determine the following snow characteristics before landing:
    1. Type of Snow:
       a. Light, dry powder snow;

> b. Dense, old, hard snow;
>
> c. Wet, sticky snow.
>
> 2. Snow Depth. What is the depth? How many inches do the skis settle down into the snowpack?
>
> 3. Snow Drag. Determine the snow drag or resistance on the skis; for example, is it low, medium, or high? This will affect takeoff distance.

D. If the snow is deep powder, wet sticky snow, or other snow conditions that will make for a difficult takeoff due to excessive resistance on the skis—drag the landing area two times longer than needed for normal takeoff. Then come back around and land short of your tracks—taxing ahead to the ski tracks. Takeoff will be straight ahead in the preset tracks. If there is limited landing space, you may have to set up two sets of parallel tracks. This is accomplished by dragging the two areas (not landing). Landing will be with a tailwind on the right-hand tracks so that you can make a left turn into the left-hand tracks. The takeoff will be into the wind on the left-hand tracks. (Item 35 by William A. Quirk, lll)

36. **Taking off Down-Slope.** Taking off on sloping terrain is a great equalizer for high-density altitude and tailwind problems. Your aircraft will need one-half the distance for takeoff on a 20 percent slope when compared to level ground. (Item 36 by William A. Quirk, lll)

Knowledge and Techniques for Ski Flying

Pilots must learn and understand the 36 guidelines to successfully operate a ski-equipped airplane. Remember that it is highly important not to just read and be aware of these items but to deeply understand the meaning of each one thoroughly. Go out and practice what they are telling you. And the most important consideration is to always remember to have a very active and thinking mind while out flying. Think about all these items that you have studied and learned and correctly incorporate them into your everyday flying skills. (William A. Quirk, lll)

MEMORANDUM 40
SUBJECT: Ski Flying on a Cold Winter Day

January 18, 2012

1. January 18 in the Anchorage area was forecasted as a sunny day with light winds. This could be a good flying day. The ambient temperature at Merrill Field at 8 AM was minus 18 degrees Fahrenheit. Quite cold; however, it may

233

warm up after the sun comes up. I prepared breakfast and by 10 AM, as the sun was coming up, I drove to Merrill Field. I have a two-step procedure to warm up the engine in the Arctic Tern. First, I have a heat pad glued underneath the oil pan that is plugged in overnight. This keeps the engine oil warm. I also have a 100-watt light bulb turned on inside the cowling. This lessens the chance that I will have a cold-soaked engine. Second, I plug in a small 1,000-watt electric heater that is inside the cowling. After 1 or 2 hours, this will warm up all parts of the engine and in particular the crankshaft. The cowling is sealed off with a well-insulated cover so that the engine compartment will retain heat. At 10:30 AM the ambient temperature rises to minus 10 degrees Fahrenheit. At 12:30 PM, the engine is warm enough for starting. The ambient temperature now has warmed up to 0 degrees Fahrenheit.

2. Preparing the Arctic Tern for flight involves removing the black nylon wing covers, the windshield cover, the propeller and nose cone covers, the horizontal tail covers and the engine cover. I rolled up all these covers with the exception of the engine cover and placed them in a 2-by-8 foot fiberglass snow sled. The engine cover is always carried in the Tern so it could be placed over the cowling to keep the engine from cooling down too fast when on the ground for any length of time. Now, I use a fulcrum and lever to lift the front and back part of the skis to remove the wooden 2-by-4s that keep the skis out of the snow. This would prevent snow freezing on the bottom of the skis. Frozen snow on the ski bottoms would keep the aircraft from moving forward, even at full throttle. I placed my daypack (lunch), a canister of water, and a nylon bag with warm personal equipment in the Tern. In the equipment bag are several pairs of gloves and mitts, ski stocking cap, winter hat with ear flaps, face mask, wool socks, and other warm gear. I also carry a tent with a winter sleeping bag, a stove and lightweight freeze-dried food to last for a week. The latter are always stored in the Tern as emergency items for a length of stay on the ground. I checked the oil level on the dip stick and walked around the aircraft to make an inspection and looked for anything that would need attention. I am now ready (after about an hour or two) to get in the Tern, start the engine, and go flying.

3. Another pilot was supposed to go flying with me today but he did not show up. Sunset was at 4:20 PM today, so I'd go flying alone as there was no time to wait any longer. I wanted to go to the glaciers in the Chugach Mountains but would change that destination to a flight to the north, where there are roads and homes scattered in the terrain. The latter was safer flying alone. On

a weekday, flying and landing on the glaciers, pilots would often see no other pilot. I had made many solo flights into the glaciers in past years; however, today I would want to be safer as I have not made a landing on a glacier in 2012.

4. I flew over Knik Arm of Cook Inlet and then north towards Big Lake. The ambient temperature flying at 1,000 feet above the terrain was minus 10 degrees Fahrenheit. I continued flying north beyond the road system until I reached the Willow Highlands 50 miles north of Merrill Field. I found a suitable place here and dragged the snow to see if the conditions were favorable for landing. The snow was soft and the skis penetrated about a foot. I came around again and landed short of my tracks so that I could take off straight ahead in the already established tracks. A takeoff is easier in set tracks versus taking off in loose snow. My first priority after landing was keeping the engine warm, so I quickly grabbed the engine cover out of the baggage compartment and placed it over the cowling. The temperature in the Willow Highlands at 3,200 feet elevation is minus 16 degrees Fahrenheit. I decided to stay here and enjoy the fresh air on a sunny day. From where the Tern was parked I can see the Talkeetna Mountains rising up on the east. Mount McKinley was clear and could be seen in the west.

5. I put my snowshoes on and headed out across the snow-covered terrain to a small hill. I climbed the hill and was awarded a splendid view of the surrounding plateau and mountains in the distance. The Tern was over a mile away and it looks as small as a toy airplane. I took a few images from the top of the hill and then snowshoed back down in my tracks to the Tern. Strolling through the deep powder snow was great exercise. When I reached the Tern, I checked the oil temperature gauge and it showed 130 degrees Fahrenheit. This was plenty warm and I'd have time to eat lunch before departing the Willow Highlands. I had small pieces of cheese, crackers, pecans, one half apple, and dates. After eating about half of my lunch, I grabbed the water bottle. No drinking water today—the water was a solid chunk of ice. This often happens on cold days like today.

6. I took my insulated engine cover off the Tern and placed it in the baggage compartment. I took off my snowshoes and stored them away. It was now 2:45 PM as I crawled in the Tern, pushed the throttle in halfway, and then started my trusty Tern. It roared alive at first crank. Merrill Field was 30 minutes away; however, I planned to stop and land on several lakes on the way home. I have always liked to make several landings on a flight from

home base to keep my proficiency levels high.

7. I flew across Big Lake and landed on a smaller lake just to the south. I got out of the Tern and looked around at the snow conditions on the lake, the cabins and the mountains in the distance. There was nothing more enjoyable flying and being able to land in so many places. After a short time on the lake, I got back in the Tern and flew south to Goose Bay. I went in and landed here on the snow-covered wetlands. This was close to Knik Arm with a great view of the Chugach Mountains.

8. I got back in the air again; it was now 3:35 PM and the sun was fading away on the western sky. The temperature took a nose dive and I'm flying at minus 20 degrees Fahrenheit. I was not cold because I was warmly dressed and my heater gave off enough cabin heat to keep my body core warm. However, I piloted my aircraft wearing gloves to keep the fingers and hands warm. I'd have time to land on one additional lake before flying back to Merrill Field. It would be Twin Island Lake, which was only 10 air miles from Merrill. The snow was velvety smooth and the landing could hardly be felt. There were really nice cabins here, accessible in the summer by floatplane and in winter by ski-equipped airplanes. It was cold here at minus 22 degrees Fahrenheit and I felt the cold stinging my face. I stayed here only a few minutes and flew off the lake. Now I proceeded to Merrill and wrapped up another typical winter flying day although this one was a little colder than most. I arrived back at Merrill at 4:10 PM only about 10 minutes before sunset. I needed to get back to Merrill before sunset as the landing strip has no lights and it is very difficult to land in twilight and almost impossible to land in the dark. I made it back and parked. It would take about one hour to put the Tern to bed. The darkness which was coming fast was not a problem as our parking apron has really good overhead lights. The lights automatically come on at twilight and they are already on and providing plenty of light, so this would not be a struggle. First chore was to place my electric heater inside the cowling so it would be ready for my next trip. Then I placed the insulated engine cover over the cowling. Next, I needed to use a fulcrum and lever to lift the front and rear part of both skis. Under the skis I place 2-by-4s to keep the skis from freezing to the snow. Then nylon covers needed to be placed over all horizontal surfaces of the Tern to keep snow and frost off. Last chore is to tie the Tern down so that strong winds won't move it around.

MEMORANDUM 41
SUBJECT: Next Ski Landing: Alaska's Legendary Mount
McKinley Base Camp

March 28, 2008

1. For years, ever since I put skis on my first airplane (Piper Cub) back in the mid-1980s, I wanted to fly into the Mount McKinley Base Camp (BC) on the Kahiltna Glacier. Eighty percent of the mountain climbers who climb to the top of the North American continent go into this BC. From BC, the climbers travel on skis or snowshoes to the top of Kahiltna Glacier and onto the west buttress of McKinley to the top. Approximately 1,200 climbers each season (many from foreign countries) come to Alaska to climb McKinley. Climbers enter Alaska by flying into Anchorage International airport and driving to Talkeetna, where they hire an air taxi to fly to McKinley BC. The BC is a 40-minute flight from Talkeetna. The airplanes are equipped with skis that have retractable wheels so the pilots can take off from the Talkeetna Airport on wheels and land with skis on Kahiltna Glacier. The ski landing site on Kahiltna Glacier is about 35 miles beyond the terminus of the glacier at an elevation of 7,200 feet above sea level.

2. Mount McKinley rises in elevation 19,520 feet from the terminus of the Kahiltna Glacier (800 feet) to its summit (20,320 feet). This vertical rise from the lowlands is unsurpassed anywhere in the world. At 63 degrees north latitude, McKinley is the highest big mountain closest to the Arctic Circle (66 degrees 34 minutes). This high latitude makes McKinley the world's coldest big mountain. (Mount Everest, the world's highest mountain, is located at 28 degrees north latitude which is the same as Tampa, Florida). McKinley is a permanently snow-covered mountain from its snowy summit down to 1,500 feet along its base. Five massive glaciers from 20 to 45 miles in length flow from high on the mountain to the lowlands. The lowest temperatures on McKinley are from November to April with average temperatures ranging from minus 30 to minus 70 degrees Fahrenheit recorded at the 18,200 foot level at Denali Pass. Nighttime temperature at the 17,200-foot-high camp in May when climbers are on the mountain frequently is minus 30 degrees Fahrenheit. McKinley is terribly unforgiving for inexperience, igno-rance, and poor judgment. Measured by any standard, McKinley is one of the world's great mountains with its awesome size, power, majesty, and stunning beauty.

3. Dee, John, and I agreed to attempt a fly-in and landing at McKinley Base Camp in mid to late March when the weather was appropriate. By this time of the winter, the temperatures at BC would not be too extreme and we would have longer daylight. Flight time to the BC is about 1½ hours from Merrill Field in Anchorage, Alaska. On Monday, March 24, after checking out the weather, we found good weather to fly into BC. Dee could not take off from work and I had difficulty finding John. By the time I reached John by telephone, we decided it was too late to go. From where my airplane was parked at Merrill Field in Anchorage, I could see McKinley's dome and it was as clear as a bell—no clouds anywhere. I had mulled over the thought of making the flight solo but couldn't quite make a final decision to take on this challenging endeavor alone. Great opportunity was blown. Only hope was that we would get another good flying day soon. On Friday, March 28, we had another suitable day that was not as good as Monday but it was good enough that we decided we should make an attempt. Again, Dee could not take off from work; that left John and me.

4. John was taking a friend with him in his Super Cub to a cabin on a small lake in the Susitna Valley halfway to McKinley BC. The plan was for John and his friend to go to the cabin first. They would install an electric fence around the cabin to keep bears soon coming out of hibernation from breaking in. I was to fly to the lake 1½ hours later and meet them. We would leave together for our flight to McKinley BC.

5. I departed Merrill Field at 11:40 AM Friday. When I arrived in the vicinity of the cabin where John had landed, I was at 5,000 feet elevation and fighting a 14 mph headwind. I decided not to go looking for the small lake because it would be difficult to find in a snow-covered landscape. Searching for the lake and having to climb again to 5,000 feet would burn up too much fuel. This would not leave me with sufficient fuel to continue to McKinley BC and back to Merrill Field.

6. If I was going to McKinley BC, it would have to be a solo flight. This is something I had wanted to avoid but often plans change due to circumstances beyond my control. Finally, I reached the terminus of the Kahiltna Glacier. It is the glacier that has the greatest length on McKinley. The glacial ice gently climbs for 45 miles from its terminus at 800 feet to 10,200 feet at Kahiltna Pass. I would need to follow the glacier for

35 miles to BC at 7,200 feet elevation. The flight up the glacier was impressive, with spectacular snow-covered mountains on both sides of the mammoth glacier that was 2 miles in width. Kahiltna Glacier near the BC opens up into a basin that is 5 miles wide. Surrounding the basin are these impressive mountain peaks: Foraker (17,400 feet), Crossen (12,800 feet), Kahiltna Peak (13,448 feet), Hunter (14,573 feet), and the awesome south face of Mount McKinley. Mount Hunter's elevation tops the highest mountain in the Lower 48 states, which is Mount Whitney at 14,495 feet. I located the BC landing strip as I could see airplane ski tracks on the glacier. Nobody is there! The wind was a light headwind so I went in and landed uphill on the sloping glacier. I was on the glacier at McKinley BC. WOW! Such a grand place to be with all the incredible mountains all around but as always, this is Alaska. Not so fast! Before I could start walking away from my Arctic Tern to take some images, I noticed the 10-12 mph breeze down glacier, the direction in which I would have to take off. This worried me because the tailwind deteriorates lift and the density altitude at 7,200 feet makes it even more difficult to lift off the glacier. The ambient temperature was zero degrees Fahrenheit at 1:20 PM, the warmest part of the day. Nighttime temperature would be about 20 to 25 degrees Fahrenheit below zero. I was hoping the winds would die down but also thought about if the winds picked up and I was not able to fly out. I did not want to put up my tent and spend the night here. That would require preheating the Tern's engine to get it started and concern about frost on the wings. If it started snowing, I might be here for several days. The safest procedure was to be on the glacier for a very short time and fly out of here before any drastic changes occurred. Frantically, I got a few amateur images and at 1:40 PM got back in the Tern and gently flew off the glacier, returning to Merrill Field. The takeoff was no problem as the 20 percent slope compensated greatly for the tailwind.

7. John flew in later but never found my ski tracks at Kahiltna Glacier. He did fly up the Ruth Glacier and landed at the Sheldon Mountain House in Ruth Amphitheater.

8. This was the last ski flight of the winter as the temperature at Merrill Field was 44 degrees and the snow was melting fast.

MEMORANDUM 42
SUBJECT: Ski Landing on the Top of the Harding Ice Field

January 24, 2010

1. Finally, after many years, I have succeeded on getting to the top of the amazing Harding Ice Field. Dee in his Piper PA-12 and I in the Arctic Tern landed on top of the Harding Ice Field at 3:20 PM on January 23, 2010. We landed our ski-equipped aircraft at 5,400 feet on the south end of the ice field. A second ski landing was made three miles southeast of the first landing at an elevation of 5,600 feet. The Harding Ice Field is on the Kenai Peninsula 80 miles south of Merrill Field (Anchorage, Alaska). The sunny day was unusually warm at 25 degrees Fahrenheit. The wind was light.

2. The Mountaineering Club of Alaska (MCA) sponsored a 30-mile ski trek every two- or three-years across the width of the Harding Ice Field (from east to west) in the 1980s and 1990s. This trek started in Seward, Alaska and participants were taken by boat to a glacier on the east side of the ice field. All skiers carried a fully equipped backpack (mountain climbing gear, warm clothes, food, stoves, and tents) for winter trekking. The route took skiers up a glacier beginning near sea level to the top of the Harding Ice Field at over 4,000 feet. From here the route went west down into the Tustumena Glacier, ending at Tustumena Lake. The party would be flown off the lake and taken to Homer, Alaska.

3. One of my primary outdoor recreational goals since joining the MCA in the late 1970s was to get on this trek and set foot on the Harding Ice Field. It never happened. The ski trek took about 4 to 6 days to complete; however, if fog rolled in or snow-storms arrived, the skiers were stuck in their tents until it was clear again. It is much too dangerous to be navigating with a compass on a snow-covered ice field and glaciers when you can't see where you are going. Chances of falling into a snow-covered crevasse increase significantly when visibility is restricted. It always seemed like I never found out about the next trek far enough in advance to schedule it. My work schedule with the federal government did not allow me to take leave from work on short notice.

4. Glaciers are plentiful in Southcentral Alaska near Anchorage. There are literally scores and even hundreds of glaciers in the Alaska, Talkeetna, Chugach, and Kenai Mountain Ranges in close proximity to Anchorage. Ice fields in Alaska are somewhat less common than glaciers and they have caught my attention.

There are only four large ice fields in the United States and the Harding is the largest contained wholly within its borders. The Harding is approximately 50 miles in length (oriented northeast–southwest) and 15 to 20 miles in width. The ice field spawns approximately 40 glaciers which flow down the sides of the ice field. The surface area of the ice field including the glaciers is approximately 1,100 square miles (704,000 acres). Compare this to the size of Rhode Island at 1,545 square miles. The ice field is a relatively flat ice-covered plateau surrounded by mountains. A few stray mountain peaks penetrate and rise above the icefield. These mountain peaks are called nunataks. The thickness of the icefield is estimated to be 1,000 feet. It was formed by thousands of years of colossal snowstorms blowing in from the moisture-laden Gulf of Alaska, dumping 400 inches or more of snow every year on the plateau. The pressure from the snow layers eventually forms ice. The ice cap or ice sheet is flat and does not flow like a glacier. This greatly reduces the likelihood of crevasses and makes it a safer ice environment to traverse on skis.

5. I have flown over the Harding Ice Field in the Arctic Tern about a dozen times in summer while flying on the Kenai Peninsula. The astonishing beauty of a flat ice sheet so vast and surrounded by snow-covered mountains is awesome. This has piped my interest to come back in winter on skis and land on the ice field. I have also taken visitors to Seward to fly over the ice field in summer. Dee and I made a flight on skis to land on the Harding Ice Field on March 17, 2007. But the ice field had other plans. A huge low-pressure storm with 100 mph winds had swept through the ice field previous to our flight. The winds had blown the snow on top of the ice field into rough waves. The low temperatures after the windstorm froze the wavy snow into hard ripples almost as hard as concrete. We tried at least six different locations to land on the ice field and every time we dragged the snow we could feel the snow rattling our landing gear. We did not land, as it was a high probability that the hard and rough surface would damage (break) our landing gear. We would have to return on another day under better conditions.

6. The Sargent Ice Field is the second one on the Kenai Peninsula. It is on the eastern side of the peninsula adjacent to western Prince William Sound. The ice field is also a huge ice sheet (35 miles long and 15 miles wide), a little smaller in size than the Harding Ice Field. Most of the ice field is lower in elevation (2,000 to 3,000 feet) when compared to the Harding (4,000 to 5,000). Dee, John, Pete, and I made two landings on the Sargent Ice Field on March 3, 2007. Dee and the author made two additional landings on

the Sargent Ice Field on February 23, 2008. The Sargent Ice Field and surrounding mountains are stunning and among the most striking in Alaska.

7. Landing on the Harding Ice Field is an epic and life-fulfilling event. The ice field is only a one-hour flight from Merrill Field; however, there are not many days the weather will allow you to fly there. It is also difficult to get accurate weather reports. This often means that halfway to the ice field the weather ahead (low clouds, strong turbulent winds) shuts down your plan. You will have to turn around and fly back to Merrill and try another day. Very few pilots land ski-equipped aircraft on Harding Icefield.

8. Many pilots in Alaska fly ski-equipped aircraft in winter. However, it is surprising how few of these pilots fly into and land their aircraft in remote mountain and glacier regions. Glacier landings are feared by many pilots. I fully understand the reluctance for this type of flying (midwinter, remote and intimidating). The vast mountainous and snow-covered glacier terrain takes your breath away and a chilling feeling surges through the brain. Pilots do crash in remote areas and all Alaskans are fully aware that you can disappear forever on these flights. Nevertheless, once you push forward and begin to explore this awe-inspiring wild country, there is no turning back. The vivid frontier is irresistible! "No humdrum of orderly life of social conventions or placid stream of regulated existence could ever satisfy you now or in the future", says A.T. Walden in *Dog-Puncher on the Yukon* (1928). I think that I have now reached a pinnacle of being a bona fide dyed-in-the-wool Alaskan.

MEMORANDUM 43
SUBJECT: Ski Landings Mount McKinley: Revisit to North America's Tallest Peak

March 21, 2010

1. Sean with his blue Piper J-3 and me in the Arctic Tern left Merrill Field in Anchorage, Alaska at 11:25 AM on March 21 to fly to and land on the glaciers at Mount McKinley in the Alaska Range. Approaching the terminus of Kahiltna Glacier we had headwinds up to 20 miles per hour. Flying up Kahiltna Glacier the winds subsided. Ski tracks were found 35 miles up Kahiltna Glacier at Mount McKinley Base Camp (BC). I went in and landed in the Tern at the 7,200 foot elevation on Kahiltna Glacier. Sean came in a few minutes later in his Piper and landed. I tried to taxi further up the glacier to allow for a longer distance on the glacier for a takeoff. However, the snow was

deep and had a very strong resistance. With full throttle I could not advance up the glacier. We were stuck on the lower part where the wind blew down glacier at 8 to 12 miles per hour. That was the direction of our takeoff. This meant a tailwind which was not good for takeoff. We thought there would be sufficient distance for takeoff with the tailwind but it still bothered me.

2. Sean and I covered our engines with insulated covers to keep them warm (ambient temperature was 10 degrees Fahrenheit) while we toured around the Kahiltna Glacier BC. We put on our snowshoes and climbed 500 to 600 feet in elevation up a ridge overlooking our airplanes. We took many pictures of the dramatic mountain and glacier landscape. After about one and a half hours we decided that it was time to move on. We had other plans on Mount McKinley as we wanted to also land on Ruth Glacier near the Sheldon Mountain House. Our takeoff with the tailwind was more an illusion than a problem as we both got off the glacier in a rather short run (about half of the space we had before crashing into massive crevasses lower down the glacier). The downslope ridge (20 percent) we were taking off on shortened the takeoff distance by 50 percent. This counteracted the negative tailwinds on takeoffs.

3. We would fly south about halfway down Kahiltna Glacier and then fly east through an 8,000-foot mountain pass to Ruth Glacier. The winds were turbulent and blowing over 25 miles per hour. I did not want to fly through that narrow turret of a pass and find out how strong the winds would be. We continued down Kahiltna Glacier until the mountain peaks were only 6,000 feet and we turned east here. The mountains were lower in elevation; however, the winds were still fierce. They began at 20 miles per hour and increased to 25 to 30, then to 35. Top winds were blowing up to 40 miles per hour and directly in the direction we were flying. Our ground speed slowed to 50 to 60 miles per hour. However, the strong winds were not turbulent so we kept going. It took a long time and used up our gas reserves bucking the headwind but we finally made it to Ruth Glacier. Once there the strong winds diminished to only 10 miles per hour. Great, landing on Ruth Glacier in the amphitheater looked promising. When we arrived at the Ruth Amphitheater, the winds were almost calm. There were many air taxis that had recently landed here and they had beaten down the snow. The landing would be quite easy. We went in and landed with no problems or apprehension. The landing elevation on Ruth Glacier is 5,800 feet above sea level. Walking off the packed-down area we found the snow to be 24 to 30 inches deep from a large snowstorm the previous week. Ambient temperature was 25 degrees Fahrenheit.

4. We found a well-packed trail that went up 300 feet elevation above our airplanes to the Sheldon Mountain House. This is a one-of-a-kind hexagon-shaped hut perched on top of a rock-and-snow-packed ridge surrounded by the Ruth Amphitheater. It provided a grand view of mountains and glaciers from the mountain house. We climbed up the well-packed trail in our boots (we did not need snowshoes) and found four people in residence. Three were Alaskans and one was from Sweden. They were in the middle of an eight-day trip. They skied cross-country each day on the glaciers around the Mountain House. We had seen their tracks flying in. They skied close to an almost vertical 1,500-foot granite spire sticking out of the glacier ice where the Great Gorge opens out into the Ruth Amphitheater. Some 30 years before, I had been with a small group of Alaskans that tented on the ice in the Ruth Amphitheater. We also skied underneath that great granite spire. We stayed about six days. At that time, when we were here in late March, the temperature was down to minus 20 to 30 degrees Fahrenheit each night. They said the weather this year was warm with night temperatures of 0 to 10 degrees Fahrenheit. The same people had been here last year in March and they said it was cold—like minus 20 degrees Fahrenheit at night. This shows the weather can vary greatly from year to year.

5. My first ski landing near Mount McKinley was March 28, 2008 at McKinley BC. The snow was better for landing in 2008 than in 2010. The ski-packed trail on the glacier ran further upslope and provided a longer run out for taking off in 2008. This was not the case in 2010 as the previous pilot had landed at the lower end of the glacier and this made for a short, problematic takeoff. The short takeoff with tailwinds and the fierce winds approaching Ruth Glacier made for challenging flying. Flying in Alaska also seems to have the condition that somewhere in your journey you will be severely challenged. If you plan to fly in Alaska, you have to get used to the challenge and be up to it. That is not to say that you should not make the right decision when Alaska is throwing too much for you to safely deal with. You have to know when it is time to turn around and cease your journey. The many Alaskan pilots who pushed on when they should have stopped and are no longer with us are always on my mind. There are more than a few pilots in Alaska who have disappeared in their airplanes never to be found again. I certainly don't want to be one of those—I want to live to fly another day.

6. Being able to fly to Mount McKinley and land on the glaciers near the huge mountain peaks in the Alaska Range is a life-changing flying experience.

Landing at two locations on the same day is an epic journey. The inspiration of walking on the glaciers under the snow-draped mountain peaks is overwhelming. This is a flying adventure that I could repeat every year in March and never tire. I am fortunate to be able to take advantage of this great opportunity. I am also fortunate to find pilots willing to fly with me on many of my most difficult trips. Being able to fly and converse with competent pilots greatly reduces the pressure a pilot bears when flying alone. It took Sean and me 4.3 flying hours to make this journey in March 2010. Mount McKinley BC is 129 air miles from Merrill Field—Sheldon Mountain House in Ruth Amphitheater is 125 air miles. These distances were read off the Garmin GPS 92 in my airplane.

MEMORANDUM 44
SUBJECT: Extraordinary Ski Landing on the Kenai Peninsula

March 13, 2011

1. Sunday, March 13 was a beautiful sunny day in Southcentral Alaska. I checked the weather and in particular the wind forecasts on the Kenai Peninsula. The northern part of the Kenai Peninsula showed wind at 5 miles per hour at Whittier (western end of Prince William Sound) and calm at Portage (eastern end of Turnagain Arm of Cook Inlet). This was a perfect day to go to one of my favorite glaciers—Spencer. Spencer Glacier is located on the northern end of the Kenai Peninsula 13 miles southeast of Portage and 52 miles southeast of Merrill Field in Anchorage, Alaska.

2. We decided to go to Spencer Glacier and look for places on the glacier where we could land our ski-equipped aircraft safely. Strong winds recently had blown the snow in drifts and created very hard snow that is not good for landing (you can break the landing gear on hard snow landings). Dee in his Piper 12 (three-seat Piper) was our leader. I'd be flying second in my trusty Arctic Tern. Tyler would follow me in his Piper 14 (four-seat Piper). This was Tyler's first winter on skis and it would be Tyler's first glacier landing. Flying is very relaxing having a skilled leader going first and relaying all important information to the other pilots. Group flying is the safest; however, many times pilots have to fly solo as other pilots are busy with jobs and family.

3. Dee circled over the upper part of Spencer Glacier and looked over the snow for a place to land. The wind was light and Dee dragged the snow with

his skis downhill so that it would be easy taking off and getting airborne again. The snow was loose and powdery and great for velvet-smooth landings. Dee went down and landed, I came in and landed and Tyler made his first ski landing. We were on the top of the left lobe of Spencer Glacier at 3,000 feet elevation. We were looking northeast toward Blackstone Glacier which falls all the way down to Blackstone Bay in Prince William Sound. In Blackstone Bay, we looked at Willard Island where Roy (my brother) and wife Janice camped a few years ago (we were kayaking in Blackstone Bay). To the west of us is the highly sculptured Carpathian Peak. Its elevation is 6,020 feet and it joins 35 other mountain peaks on the Kenai that are over 6,000 feet. The view in every direction from the top of Spencer Glacier is awe-inspiring. We took images with our point-and-shoot cameras and then flew away.

4. Our second glacier landing was at 4,000 feet on the upper part of Blackstone Glacier. This was the first time any of us landed on Blackstone. The snow was hard but we got in and out without any problems. The view of the surrounding mountains was simply marvelous. After leaving Blackstone, we flew to the top of the right lobe of Spencer at 5,000 feet. Dee dragged the snow and it was too hard for a landing. We had landed here several times in the past few years. The mountains here have snow pleats that are very scenic. We flew back to the top of Spencer on the left lobe and landed there at a different location than our first landing. We flew down to the toe of Spencer Glacier and landed on iced-covered Spencer Lake. The elevation here was 200 feet above sea level. We landed to get a close-up look at the calving glacier ice with beautiful green and blue colors. We flew back to Merrill Field and called it a day.

MEMORANDUM 45
SUBJECT: Ski Flying: Return to Mount McKinley

April 12, 2011

1. The snow had been melting fast at Merrill Field in early April and this would be our last ski flight in 2011. There was sufficient snow to taxi and take off even though only one half of the runway was snow covered. The snow had melted on the other half and it was all gravel. Sean and I talked about flying east and landing on the glaciers in the Chugach Mountains. That was until we saw the tip of Mount McKinley sticking up on the horizon. We immediately changed plans when we saw it was clear of clouds from Merrill Field to McKinley. McKinley is 130 air miles north–northwest of Merrill Field.

2. My first ski landing at Mount McKinley was a solo trip in late March 2008. The landing was at the Kahiltna Glacier Base Camp at 7,200 feet ASL. The next landing was on March 21, 2010. Sean in his Piper Cub went along on this trip. We landed at McKinley Base Camp and also near the Shelton Mountain House in the spectacular Ruth Glacier Amphitheater at 5,600 feet.

3. McKinley Base Camp was very beautiful on this day. It was slightly overcast with light winds and a pleasant temperature of 15 degrees Fahrenheit. A recent snowstorm had dumped 2 to 3 feet of powder snow on Kahiltna Glacier. There were no fresh ski tracks from other airplanes. My skis on the Arctic Tern sank from 12 to 15 inches in the deep snowpack. I set tracks on the glacier by dragging the snow flying downhill and then lifting off without landing. Then I landed flying uphill parallel to the top of the downhill tracks. I knew we would have to use my downhill tracks for takeoff to avoid the deep ski penetration in a takeoff in fresh snow. We sank about 2½ feet in the snow when we exited our aircraft. We both put on snowshoes and this made walking on the Kahiltna Glacier much easier. I still was gasping for breath with the lower oxygen levels at 7,400 feet above sea level. Mount McKinley (20,320 feet elevation), Mount Foraker (17,400 feet), Mount Hunter (14,573 feet), Mount Crossen (12,800 feet), Kahiltna Dome (12,525 feet), Mount Frances (10,450 feet), and many other lesser mountains were all in their glory on this magnificent day in April 2011. There were a few clouds up higher on McKinley and Foraker that made the light on Kahiltna Glacier sublime. Sean and I hiked around for about an hour then got back in our aircraft and headed back to Merrill Field. My Garmin GPS showed Merrill Field was 129 miles.

4. We left Merrill Field at 1 PM and returned there at 5:30 PM. As I approached the airport, I was shocked—all the snow had melted on the runway in the past 4½ hours while we were at McKinley. Nothing but gravel showed. I told the tower's controller we could not land at Merrill Field with straight skis and that we would have to land on the ice at Lake Hood near Anchorage International Airport. We called Lake Hood on the radio and went in and landed on Lake Spenard. We taxied on the lake ice to the transit parking area and tied our airplanes down with ice screws. It was now 6 PM. Sean's girlfriend picked us up and took us back to our vehicles at Merrill Field. We both went home and loaded up our Alaskan Bushwheels and a jack and headed back to Lake Spenard. Sean did not want to leave his airplane at Lake Spenard so I helped him swap out the skis for the wheels. After 9 PM when it was getting dark,

Sean took off on the lake ice and flew back to Merrill Field. I flew back to Merrill the next day. This was an exciting way to end the ski season.

MEMORANDUM 46
SUBJECT: Ski Landings on the Mysterious Root Canal Glacier

May 10, 2013

1. Finally, after more than 10 years, I was able to fly to Mount McKinley and land my ski-equipped Arctic Tern taildragger on the Root Canal Glacier. The flight was made with Sean in his Piper PA-14 on April 26, 2013. The top of the glacier where airplanes land is 7,800 feet above sea level and is near the granite rock walls of the Moose's Tooth. A pilot's first landing here could be unusually demanding. The flying approach elevation is 9,000 feet. The glacier landing requires flying over a snow-covered granite cap in center and through a narrow slot between the granite mountain walls on the left and the right. The landing is on a rising glacier slope near the bottom of the mountain wall in the background. This is a one-way landing and once you commit yourself, you must go in and land. Go arounds are not feasible.

2. Paul Roderick, an air taxi operator from Talkeetna Air Service pioneered landing on the Root Canal Glacier. The glacier is just below the Moose's Tooth on a ledge that plunges 3,000 feet steeply down to the Ruth Glacier in the Great Gorge. Paul conducts ski landings on the Root Canal in a turbine Otter. Every year mountain climbers from around the world have been flown into Root Canal Glacier where they camp out in tents and climb the steep almost 3,000 foot granite walls to the top of Moose's Tooth at 10,300 feet or takes the easy route to the top in the Ham and Eggs Couloir. They usually don't arrive here until mid-April. This means that there are no airplane ski tracks on the glacier in March. Usually the first week in April is the last week for flying out of Merrill Field on straight skis. That is why I have never been able to land here—no airplane ski tracks and no visible markers to see where to land. We received more snow in April 2013 in Southcentral Alaska than any previous year I can remember; we received more than 2 feet in east Anchorage. This April has also had much lower temperatures than normal, from 10 to 20 degrees Fahrenheit at night. The snow has remained and ski flying has been great during the entire month of April.

3. I was shocked at the sublime mountain attraction once we landed, got out of our airplanes, and started looking in all directions from nearly 8,000 feet

elevation on the Root Canal Glacier. We had a high in the sky perch where we could look to the northwest into the Ruth Amphitheater. We could see Mount Barrille (7,600 feet) which is near the Sheldon Mountain House, the Rooster Comb, Mount Huntington, and all six of the major peaks (Church, Grosvenor, Johnson, Wake, Bradley and Dickey) on the west side of the Great Gorge. These mountains have vertical granite walls of 4,000 to 5,000 feet protruding above the west side of the Ruth Glacier. We also had the most impressive view of the east face of Mount Hunter (14,580 feet). Mount Hunter is so special with the domed top which is glacier capped with huge amounts of fresh snow drifts. This is probably the most impressive view of Mount Hunter; its steep east face is an almost vertical buttress from the valley below until it reaches its domed top. The top of Mount McKinley was covered with lenticular clouds and could not be seen on this pleasant flying day.

4. Landing on the Root Canal Glacier has been sensational for me as it has removed the frustration of never being able to land my airplane here, walk the surface of the glacier, and seek out all the beautiful mountain peaks in the vicinity of Mount McKinley. Now I have done this and it has relieved a great tension I have had for a long time. I have always remembered what Mark Twain said: "Twenty years from now you will be more disappointed by the things that you didn't do than by the ones you did do. So throw off the bowlines. Sail away from the safe harbor. Catch the trade wind in your sails. Explore. Dream. Discover." Now I don't have to think about a great disappointment in my later years of not landing my airplane on Root Canal Glacier.

5. Sean, Scooter, Terry, and the author were planning another flight on April 28, 2013 to fly to Mount McKinley. The day was sunny and we could see the dome of McKinley from Anchorage. The afternoon winds for Anchorage at 3,000, 6,000 and 9,000 feet were forecasted to be 12, 17, and 19 knots respectively. At Talkeetna they were forecasted to be higher at 30, 27, and 28 knots respectively. Moderate turbulence was also forecasted for these areas. I commented that this would probably be a rough flight with some turbulence. You can do it but it probably will not be very much fun. Flying to McKinley with the strong north winds will be slow and will eat up a lot of gas. What does it mean once you get to the big mountains near McKinley? It could be windy and this could prevent landing there. This could be a wasted trip to McKinley. We decided to wait a while because FAA said the winds would probably subside as the afternoon went along. Terry dropped out but the rest of us decided we would go to McKinley on this sunny and windy day.

6. We departed Merrill Field in early afternoon. The surface winds were about 10 miles per hour leaving Merrill Field. The winds picked up to 15 miles per hour after crossing Knik Arm and flying north to McKinley. As we approached Big Lake the winds increased to 20-25 miles per hour. The winds kept increasing, at Red Shirt Lake the winds were up to 30-35 miles per hour. As we were approaching the Susitna River the winds were steady and the highest gusts were up to 40 miles per hour. Powerful updrafts and downdrafts were occurring frequently although it was not turbulent—only a light chop.

7. After passing over the Susitna River Scooter called to inform us he was turning back. He said the ground speed for his Piper PA-12 was only slightly over 50 miles per hour. At this rate, it would take 2 hours to reach McKinley. Sean and I decided to continue and hoped the winds would slow down and provide us with some relief. We could see the tops of Foraker and McKinley—they had massive lenticular clouds covering their summits. We wondered what this means lower down as we will be flying at 8,500 feet near McKinley. As we approached the Kahiltna Glacier, the winds slowed down to 20-25 miles per hour and upon reaching the terminus of the glacier, the wind was only 10 to 15 miles per hour. Ten miles up the glacier, the winds had completely stopped blowing, it was calm. As we approached the McKinley Base Camp at 7,200 feet above sea level, we could see a small lenticular cloud right there above the glacier; however, it was for the most part still nearly calm with only an occasional flurry of wind slightly buffeting our airplanes. The base camp is on a side glacier that flows into the Kahiltna Glacier. We took turns flying over the side glacier above the base camp. I was trying to look down at the base camp to see how many tents were there; however, the twisting and gusty winds made flying difficult. I had to concentrate entirely on flying—these snarling winds were dangerous and making a turn to get back to the Kahiltna Glacier had to be made with utmost caution. We both agreed that we would not land here today. The bottom of the squirrelly winds coming from that lenticular cloud above the Kahiltna Glacier was right down there at the base camp. I can't believe our luck runs out so close to where we want to land. We had light winds blowing only 1 mile before arriving at the Kahiltna Base Camp.

8. Sean recommended we fly to Ruth Glacier and check out the winds there. We could land in the Ruth Amphitheater at 5,800 feet or possibly make another landing at Root Canal Glacier if the winds and clouds would allow. We flew down to the lower end of the Kahiltna Glacier and then traveled northeast

to the lower part of the Tokositna Glacier. We crossed over snow-covered hills into the lower Ruth Glacier. The wind was light here at 6,000 feet. We decided to climb higher to check the wind. At 8,000 feet, the wind was still light. We flew to the Moose's Tooth and saw no clouds on the Root Canal Glacier. We decided to return here as we enjoyed our first landing so much. The snow surface on the glacier was the same as it was when we made our first landing two days previous—wind packed and hard. Our skis sank in the snow very little on landing. The light was different from the first landing and the multitude of mountain peaks that can be seen was ever so beautiful.

9. There were 6 tents with climbers camping out on Root Canal Glacier on April 26, 2013 when we made our first landing here. Today, there were 5 tents. We could see the tracks of the airplane that came in to take the climbers out. The ambient temperature was 10 degrees Fahrenheit. We talked to climbers—one lady from Detroit and two men from Japan. The Japanese climbers told us they had already ascended the Moose's Tooth and were planning a second climb on the Ham and Eggs Couloir before returning to Japan. When flying out of the Root Canal Glacier I counted approximately 20 tents on the Ruth Glacier in the Great Gorge. These are occupied by mostly rock and mountain climbers that scramble up the almost vertical granite walls of the nearby half dozen mountains with a topographic prominence of 4,000 to 5,000 feet. The number of tents on the Kahiltna Base Camp was only about a dozen. I surely thought there would have been more climbers there in late April. About 90% of the 1,200 or more climbers on McKinley each year fly into this base camp and launch their attack on the mountain from here. They climb McKinley in April, May, and June each year. This is the starting point for the classical West Buttress route, the least technical to reach the summit.

10. Our return trip to Merrill Field at about 5:30 PM was smoother flying than our flight to McKinley. The winds had greatly diminished by the time we headed back home. We picked up a tailwind of 10 miles per hour after leaving the mountains. The tailwind for most of the flight was from 10 to 20 miles per hour. I did not notice large updrafts and downdrafts like we encountered on our way north. These had all faded out with the diminished winds. Merrill Field still had snow packed runways when we arrived for landing although the snow was melting fast. This will be the last flight on skis this spring.

11. The ski flying season in the winter of 2012 and 2013 did not start out on a sound footing. We had many days with those notorious northeast winds

blowing too hard for flying. We also had days with low clouds and fog and snowy days which prevented flying. I had only 6.5 hours of ski flying by March 1, 2013. This was likely to be the lowest number of ski flying hours in the past 10 years or more. I usually average 55 hours of ski flying each winter. March 2013 had many days of great ski flying weather like it always has in past years. I accumulated 13 hours of ski flying in March. The large amount of snow in the first part of April and the low temperatures gave us the complete month of April for flying with straight skis for the first time that I can remember. I was able to fly 25 hours in April. This increased my total ski flying this winter to 44.4 hours by April 28, 2013. With the multiple flights to McKinley in 2013 and finally landing on the Root Canal Glacier—this ski flying season will be remembered as one for the ages.

MEMORANDUM 47
SUBJECT: Nordic Skiing in Alaska and the World

March 15, 2015

1. March 15, 2013 in Anchorage was sunny, low winds, and with an ambient temperature of 25 degrees Fahrenheit. This will be a grand day to fly 50 miles north of Merrill Field for a Nordic (cross-country) ski tour on the Willow Highlands. I fly northwest across Knik Arm at 1:35 PM and turn north toward Big Lake. The winds are blowing 10-15 mph from the northeast. There is light turbulence here; however, the Talkeetna Mountains up ahead will likely block these winds by the time I arrive in the Willow Highlands. The Willow Highlands are a large plateau above tree line at 2,500 to 3,500 feet ASL comprising about 6,000 acres. I am looking for a place to land near the Talkeetna Mountains on the northeast side of the Willow Highlands. I find a slightly sloping area and go in and drag the landing area to check on snow conditions. This area is smooth and the skis are not sinking into the snow more than 6 inches. I go in and land to the west with a 4 mph tail wind. I make a left turn into my ski tracks for a takeoff into the wind. I shut the engine down and cover it with my insulated cover. My altimeter shows the landing elevation is 3,250 feet ASL.

2. I take my wooden cross-country skis and bamboo ski poles out of my cargo bin. I place the toe of my boots in the pin bindings on the skis. A clip holds the ski on the boots. I grab my day pack and place it on my back. I go skiing for an hour and a half. I ski up a small hill. The skiing is excellent as the skis are sinking only 4" into fresh powder snow. Underneath the powder snow is a firm snowpack. The ambient
252

temperature is a comfortable 15 degrees Fahrenheit. The day is sunny with low winds—2 to 4 mph out of the east. There could not be a better day for cross-country skiing or a more peaceful place with absolute solitude than the Willow Highlands with the Talkeetna Mountains as a backdrop. The snow-covered mountains in the Alaska Range 90 miles to the northwest are plainly visible. McKinley, Hunter, and Foraker are the big three that dominate the mountain range.

3. When I arrive back at my airplane, I check the engine oil temperature and see that it has decreased from 150 degrees Fahrenheit to 130 degree while I was skiing. It is still plenty warm and I'll have time to eat lunch before continuing my flight back to Merrill Field. After eating lunch, I take the engine cover off and store it away in my cargo bin. My takeoff from the Willow Highlands was routine. On the way back to Merrill, I go in and drag several landing places on frozen lakes. They are all hard and the landing gear is rattling. I don't land at any of these places as this is hard on the landing gear. I continue onward and land back at Merrill Field at 5:10 PM.

4. Cross-country skiing is one of my favorite sports and Alaska has some of the best environments for this type of skiing anywhere. A skier can select outstanding snow conditions throughout the winter in forested lowland, hill, mountain, or glacier environments. There is no sport where one obtains such a complete workout as with cross-country skis. There is also the benefit of the tremendous ease in moving across vast tracks of terrain. Climbing mountains is several fold easier with skis when compare to climbing on foot in summer.

5. Most consider cross-country skiing a northern European invention that started in Scandinavia about 5,000 years ago. A pictograph in a cave in Norway 4,000 years ago shows a person on skis. In the 1960s a ski relic was found in a peat bog in northern Asia that was dated back 8,000 years. In recent years older pictographs and stone carvings have been found in the Altay Mountains in Central Asia that go back to at least 10,000 years and perhaps earlier. What a history for my beloved cross-country skiing.

6. I learned to cross-country ski in Alaska in Fairbanks in the early 1970s. Wooden skis and bamboo poles were used in that time period. My first skis were made in Norway. In later years, after cross-country skiing became more popular, the hickory supply for making skis began to dwindle. Newer skis

and poles were being made from fiberglass. I bought two pairs of the newer skis; however, I never liked them near as much as my wooden counterparts. They were always too slippery no matter what wax I used. I still have 6 pairs of wooden skis and select the pair needed for each occasion. You'll need a wider ski with more surface area for ski touring carrying a backpack up to 70 pounds. In the mountains above tree line with hard wind-packed snow, skis with medal edges are required so that the skis grip and do not slip. I have learned from the Norwegians that wax is not the best answer for preparing ski bottoms. Many Norwegians use only pine tar on the ski bottoms. Hot pine tar is applied by a heating torch as the tar penetrates the wood. Pine tar creates a tremendously flexible ski bottom that does not slip with multiple snow temperatures. On a few occasions, certain temperatures may cause the skis to be a little bit slippery. This is not a problem—all you have to do is to concentrate and improve your technique and the slipping will come to an abrupt halt. Out of shape, weak physical condition, and sloppy techniques cause most of the problems with losing traction while cross-country skiing.

7. I learned to cross-country ski in the mountains after joining the Alaska Alpine Club in the early 1970s in Fairbanks. We would drive 130 miles southeast on the Richardson Highway to the Alaska Range for weekend adventures including skiing, climbing, and camping overnight in tents. We would not go if forecasted temperatures were below zero Fahrenheit. However, temperatures often dropped well below zero several times after we were already there. One occasion I'll never forget is the 8 mile ski trip four of us made up the Canwell Glacier to an elevation of about 5,000 feet ASL. It was not real cold at 10 degrees and the wind was nearly calm. We set up our tents in the middle of the glacier. When we awoke in the morning, the wind was howling down glacier at about 15 to 20 mph and the temperature was 45 below zero. That was COLD. We all dreaded taking down our tents and loading our camping gear under these harsh weather conditions. It was slow and painful but we all endured the hardship. Skiing down the glacier was not as difficult because we had the heavy packs and we skied at a brisk pace that soon warmed us up. We were also lucky that the wind was to our backs going out.

8. The Northern Lights (*Aurora Borealis*) in Fairbanks in winter are some of the best in the world. Large numbers of Japanese tourists fly in to Fairbanks and stay a few days to a week in February and March when the Northern Lights are almost a nightly occurrence. Cross-country

skiers take full advantage of these colorful bright lights at night. I vividly remember skiing with no head lamp when the natural lights were out. Temperatures would be 10 above zero to 20 below zero at that time of the year. Fairbanks has many miles of ski trails, most are through forested tracks of land. There is nothing as spectacular as a ski trek at night when the Northern Lights are in full force dancing across the sky in many different colors.

9. Anchorage's Fur Rendezvous (Fur Rondy) is one of the largest winter festivals in North America. It is held in late February each year. The Fur Rondy World Championship Sled Dog Races are held along with other winter activities. Dog teams and their mushers complete 3 high-speed, all-out 25–mile loops over 3 days with the fastest elapsed time the winner. I took advantage of this 25-mile trail one winter during Fur Rondy when I skied the 25 miles in one afternoon. I remember that I was not real tired after skiing all those miles.

10. Alaska is fortunate to have America's all-time cross-country ski champion in Anchorage's Kikkan Randall. Kikkan, a three-time Olympian, has been on the World Cup Cross-Country Ski Tours in Europe for the past several winters. Kikkan won the World Cup sprint event in Lahti Ski Games on March 9, 2013 in Lahti, Finland which was her fourth World Cup win for the season and the 11th of her career. This win clinched the 2013 season's sprint crown for Randall—her second year in a row. As Nordic skiing royalty, Randall received her crystal globe as the World Cup's overall sprint champion for the second straight year, by none other than, King Carl Gustav of Sweden. Randall received another milestone in 2013 when she became the first American women to capture third place in the World Cup cross-country ski standings. The overall standings combine a skier's results in both sprint and distance races. Randall, 30, ranked No. 1 in the sprint standings and No. 10 in the distance standings, and her combined results placed her third overall. Last year, Randall finished fifth overall. Kikkan works very hard at training to be the best athlete she can be and is a phenomenal role model for women cross-country skiers in Alaska, the Lower 48 States, and around the world.

11. In 2015 Alaska had another women cross-country skier that came out on top. Anchorage's Holly Brooks won the 42nd American Birkebeiner in Hayward, Wisconsin on February 21, 2015. This is a 51-K (31.7 miles) Birkie Long Distance Classic cross-country ski race. Brooks finished 28.1

seconds ahead of the second fastest woman skier, recording a time of 2 hours 34 minutes and 51.9 seconds. Brook's claimed her second win in North America's biggest cross-country ski race—her first win of the Birkie was in 2012. Brooks lost in her first Birkebeiner in 2009 by a photo finish, finishing second by one inch. Brooks declined an invitation to spend another season with the U.S. Cross-Country Ski Team, opting to spend the season racing marathons—a choice that provides more flexibility than the World Cup Cross-Country Ski Races. The Marathon Cup consists of 9 races—the Birkie is the sixth in the series. In the first four marathons, Brooks registered two wins and two runner-up finishes to grab the series lead. Brooks skipped the fifth marathon in Estonia to prepare for the Birkie. Brooks will fly to Europe in early March to compete in the seventh marathon race in Poland. One week later she will compete in the eight marathon in Switzerland. The Marathon Cup final will be in Russia on April 11. Alaskans are all pulling for Brooks to win it all. She certainly has a good lead at this time. What a powerful skier she is. All the Marathon Cup races are from 40K (24.8 miles) to 50K (31.1 miles) in distance.

12. One other big breakthrough for American women in the World Cup Cross-Country Ski races in Falun, Sweden on February 24, 2015 was Minnesotans Jessica Diggins and Caitlin Gregg who took the silver and bronze metals. This made Nordic history for American women. No American woman had ever won a major championship metal in the long-distance cross-country skiing before this race in Falun. This was a 10 K (6.2 mile) free-style distance race. Charlotte Kalla of Sweden took the gold medal.

13. The only other World Cup Nordic metals won by American women are the 11 medals won by Kikkan Randall in the 1.2 K (0.75 mile) short-distance sprint races. Diggins teamed with Randall in 2013 to win the only American medal in the short-distance team sprint. This was a gold medal. It is great to read about Americans finally being able to compete and win metals in the cross-country World Cup and Marathon Cup races. American Bill Koch, the man who revolutionized Nordic skiing by ushering in the skating technique, won the overall World Cup title in 1982. He is the only American men's Nordic World Cup medal holder.

MEMORANDUM 48
SUBJECT: The Chilled Wolf and the Rambunctious Wolverine

December 26, 2010

1. It is just amazing the wonderful wildlife that lives next door to Anchorage, Alaska. On a flight from Merrill Field in downtown Anchorage on December 9, I flew east over a small ice- and snow-covered lake next to the base of the Chugach Mountains. Yes, right there was a beautiful sub adult gray wolf running across the lake. The wolf was light colored, speckled gray and white, and appeared silvery in the bright sun at 2 PM. I circled silver wolf, not up close, but at a distance so as not to disturb her. I wanted to know what the wolf is up to. Silver wolf began digging a small hole in the snow on the lake and then she jumped in and curled up in a circle with her tail wrapped tightly around her body. From the air, silver wolf was curled up into a perfect circle. This was an amazing sight to see and no one would expect to see such an elongated wild animal being capable of curling up into a perfect circle. Why did silver wolf do this? It is all about physics and cold weather. A perfectly round circle creates the smallest body surface area and therefore preserves the most body heat. This wolf was cold and curled up to rest or sleep. The temperature was zero degrees Fahrenheit at 2 PM. The overnight temperature was minus 10 to minus 20 Fahrenheit. Silver wolf probably had not had a meal in several days and was drawing energy from body fat. This would not keep silver wolf near as warm as having fed recently on a freshly killed moose.

2. Another flight in the Arctic Tern was made on December 12 into Ship Creek east of Merrill Field. Dee and his Piper 12 led the way. We flew up Ship Creek and turned east up the North Fork of Ship Creek. At the head of this drainage at 3,000 feet elevation near Moraine Pass, Dee spotted a young wolverine loping across the snow-covered valley. The Chugach Mountains rise up to over 7,000 feet in the North Fork Valley. The wolverine is a spectacular animal that very few people get to see because they exist only in wild, remote areas far away from human civilization. We were 22 miles southeast of Merrill Field in Chugach State Park. There were no roads or trails in this area.

3. The wolverine is an amazing animal as it lives in Alaska with the cold winters but it does not hibernate. It is active for most of the winter, covering miles and miles of territory searching for food which is primarily animal carcasses. It has an amazingly sensitive nose and can find animal carcasses under several feet of snow. It will dig them out and it almost always has a

meal even though other animals have cleaned all the meat off the bones. The wolverine will have a great meal just crushing the bones of a moose and eating the marrow. Wolves and other carnivores usually leave the larger bones whole as they don't have the powerful jaws of the wolverine. The wolverine does get out of the cold winter weather for short periods from a few days to a week or more by digging large tunnels in hardened snow banks. This is not hibernation, as the wolverine's body temperature and heart rate are normal while it rests and warms up in the snow tunnel. Then it goes out for a few days to a week or more searching all over again for something to eat in the cold snowy mountains. This is, no doubt, a very tough life.

MEMORANDUM 49
SUBJECT: Chronology of Wolf Sightings on Fort Richardson

December 20, 1997

Date	Wolf Sightings in 1997
Aug 2	Large dark gray wolf crossing Bulldog Trail on the South Post of Fort Richardson 1 mile south of Bunker Hill. Sighting was made in a vehicle while driving south on Bulldog Trail. Weight of wolf was estimated at over 110 pounds.
Sep 8	First aerial sighting of wolf pack near den site. Den site was located 1 mile southeast of Bunker Hill in the locality of 2 glacier kettles. Den site was on the west rim of north kettle. Large gray alpha male was sleeping in the bottom of south kettle. Black alpha female was in north kettle with 4 black pups. Female sleeping; pups playing nearby.
Sep 12	Alpha male and female with 4 pups found in north kettle.
Sep 19	Two black pups in north kettle.
Sep 20	Three black pups found in north kettle.
Sep 21	No sightings of wolves.
Sep 23	No sightings of wolves.
Sep 26	No sightings of wolves.
Oct 3	Alpha male and female with 3 black pups in north kettle.
Oct 4	Alpha male and female with 3 pups in south kettle.
Oct 12	Alpha female (black color) found in south kettle.
Oct 15	Alpha female was sighted in north kettle. First snow-fall in 1997 was 4–6 inches on Oct.14.
Nov 2	Two black wolf pups sighted on the west rim of north kettle.
Nov 16	Alpha female with 3 black pups sighted at sunset on west rim of north kettle.
Nov 29	Three black pups sighted at sunset on the west rim of north kettle.
Nov 30	One black pup sleeping in the snow on the west rim of north kettle. Pup was observed as a round ball curled up in the snow. This reduces body surface and conserves heat.

MEMORANDUM 50
SUBJECT: The Wildlife Legacy of Ship Creek

September 20, 2002

1. The Ship Creek drainage in the Chugach Mountains east of Anchorage is a protected watershed comprising 91 square miles (58,240 acres). Ship Creek was first protected in 1919 to safeguard the water supply for the City of Anchorage. Later it was afforded additional protection when the Army in 1941 constructed a timber diversion structure to take water from the creek. In 1952, the Army constructed the currently used Ship Creek dam and reservoir which is a 50-foot concrete structure supplying water for Fort Richardson, Elmendorf Air Force Base, and the City of Anchorage. In the early 1970s, upper Ship Creek was included in Chugach State Park and now has the highest order of protection under a wilderness classification. The long and continuously protected status of upper Ship Creek has precluded road building and vehicular use. This has preserved the wildlife resources and habitat in a natural state since people first lived in Anchorage to the present time. The only human activity in upper Ship Creek has been light recreational activities including hiking and backpacking, cross-country skiing and winter camping, and hunting on foot or horseback for moose and Dall sheep.

2. The core of wildlife resources in upper Ship Creek is only 12 air miles from downtown Anchorage. No other modern and progressive city the size of Anchorage can claim such a wildlife spectacle so close to an urban area. The vegetation resources in the Ship Creek drainage are excellent habitat for a wide array of Alaska's most magnificent wildlife. The Ship Creek drainage provides summer, fall, and early winter habitat for slightly over 200 moose. Predators associated with the moose herd include a wolf pack that remains year round in the upper Ship Creek drainage. Other predators found in Ship Creek are the lynx, pine marten, hawks, owls, and the golden eagle. Predators–Scavengers include 15-20 brown bears, a moderate density of black bears, wolverine, ermine, raven, and magpie. Other large mammals found in upper Ship Creek are Dall sheep. The population of sheep in Ship Creek has been as high as 375 and has averaged 258 in the early 2000s. Neotropical land birds nest in the Ship Creek drainage in the summer. A magnificent pair of white gyrfalcons was observed by the author on a flight in upper Ship Creek in June 1992. The upper part of Ship Creek supports a large population of beaver. Marmots, red and ground squirrels, and rodents complete the list of resident wildlife found in Ship Creek.

3. To maintain such an abundance and variety of Alaska's treasured wildlife, upper Ship Creek in Chugach State Park and Fort Richardson will need to be continually managed in the future for the long term sustainability of the animals and the habitat.

MEMORANDUM 51
SUBJECT: Wildlife Sighted in the Chugach Mountains

August 25, 2005

1. I conducted two scenic flights in the Arctic Tern on August 22, 2005 to fly a German schoolteacher and her 8-year-old son into the Chugach Mountains east of Anchorage, Alaska. The goal was wildlife and mountain–glacial scenery.

2. The first flight departed Merrill Field in Anchorage at 1PM. The flight plan was to fly a circuit up Eagle River, Whiteout Glacier (over the top), Lake George Basin, Knik River, Palmer, and then back to Anchorage. While flying up Eagle River Valley at 3,000 feet elevation, 4 brown bears were sighted in alpine habitat on Harp Mountain. This unusual sighting of bears consisted of a dark brown sow with three cubs that were 2½ years of age. Cub One was dark brown, the same color as the sow. The other two cubs had a color pattern that was different from the sow and Cub One. Cub Two had a coat of shimmering honey-blond hair on top and along its sides. Its rear end and belly were dark brown like the sow. Cub Three had a muted coat of blond hair on top and along its sides and also had a dark brown coloration on its belly and rear end. These bears were approximately 2 miles from Albert Loop Trail (near the Eagle River Visitors Center) in Chugach State Park.

3. Several groups of mountain goats in small numbers (4–7) were found in upper Eagle River drainage on the north side of the river. After passing over Whiteout Glacier, a black bear was observed on the mountainside in Lake George Basin. Continuing the flight to the southwest end of Lake George Basin, 14 mountain goats were observed on a mountain slope north of Sparrow Glacier. Seven additional mountain goats were observed on an ice-free ridge between the Glenn and Lake George Glaciers. On this same ridge on the Lake George side was a black bear sow with two spring cubs. Thirty-two mountain goats were observed on a west-facing mountain slope near the lower part of Lake George Glacier. Moose and trumpeter swans

were sighted in lake and wetland habitats in the Jim Creek Basin east of Palmer, Alaska.

4. The second flight began at 4 PM. We were able to fly only into the Eagle River drainage because of an approaching storm with high winds building up in the Chugach Mountains. We searched for the four brown bears and found them about a half mile east of the first sighting. We found another brown bear sow with two spring cubs (cubs that are about 7 months old) 1½ miles west of the 4 bears on Harp Mountain. We also sighted 2 single black bears lower down the slopes on Harp Mountain. Thirty-five Dall sheep were found further up Eagle River near Kiliak Glacier.

5. Summary of wildlife observed on the two flights—brown bears: 7; black bears: 6; mountain goats: 66; Dall sheep: 35; moose: 12; and trumpeter swans: 18.

6. The German visitors enjoyed the flights. These flights into the Chugach Mountains are to be cherished for the ages.

MEMORANDUM 52
SUBJECT: Amazing Wildlife in Eklutna River Valley

May 22, 2008

1. Thursday morning May 22, 2008 was a gorgeous day in Anchorage, Alaska. The day was mostly sunny on the coastal plain; however, thick masses of clouds covered the tops of the mountain peaks east of Anchorage in the Chugach Mountains. A flight could be made underneath the clouds in the Eklutna River valley. The forecasted light winds made it possible to take this flight and to view Alaska's magnificent wildlife. I also planned to land on Bold Airstrip in Chugach State Park 30 miles northeast of Merrill Field. I got the Arctic Tern ready and flew out to the Eklutna River which takes about 20 minutes.

2. Eklutna Lake Campground and Trailhead is on the northwest end of Eklutna Lake. Bold Airstrip is on the other end of the lake and is accessible by land on an 8-mile road reserved for hikers and All-Terrain Cycles. On approaching Bold Airstrip, the thick clouds covering the upper parts of the mountains were sufficiently high so that I could fly under them at 3,200 feet elevation and search for wildlife on the mountain slopes. I flew up the west fork of Eklutna River to the Eklutna Glacier. In this valley I found 6

mountain goats on the right side flying up the valley on steep rock faces. Another ½ mile up the valley was a large black bear on the mountainside. On the other side of the valley was a mountain peak called the Mitre (6,655 feet) which had almost vertical rock cliffs. On these cliffs were 14 mountain goats. Several of the goats were bedded down and surrounded in all directions by seemingly vertical rock cliffs. This was a sight to behold! I wondered how these goats got there and how they would depart. Did they ever slip and fall to their deaths while traversing the steep rock faces? Another large black bear was found further along on a forest-covered mountain slope.

3. Now I flew up the East Fork of Eklutna River. This was one of my favorite river valleys. It had three spectacular mountain peaks (the three Bs) in the 8,000-foot elevation range and many small glaciers in the upper end of the valley. It was also a wildlife haven for Dall sheep, mountain goats, moose, bears, wolves, wolverines, and other small mammals. On the backside of the Mitre were 6 mountain goats on very steep rock cliffs. At the head of the valley near Baleful Peak (7,920 feet) I found 10 mountain goats on rocky cliffs above lower Baleful Creek. Flying down the East Fork Valley, I observed 5 goats bedded down on the mountainside. On the lower slopes of Bashful Peak (8,005 feet) were 8 goats. Beneath the rocky cliffs of Bold Peak (7,522 feet) were 17 goats. Numerous black bears were visible in the east fork of Eklutna River. A majority of the bears were concentrated in a small area halfway up the valley. I found one large black bear on a south-facing mountainside along with a sow and yearling cub. Then I found a sow with two cubs of the year in the valley bottom near a large cottonwood tree. Also in the valley bottom near a lake was another black bear. On a north-facing slope a solitary black bear was found. One additional black bear was located on a mountain slope further down the valley. The wildlife totals for the East Fork were 46 mountain goats and 9 black bears. Dall sheep live in this valley but were not found today.

4. After flying out of the East Fork, I landed the Tern at Bold Airstrip. Chugach State Park (half a million acres) has provided two airplane tie-downs and two picnic tables. This is a great place for camping. I sat in the sun on one of the picnic tables reading the *Anchorage Daily News*. Two Canadian jays came by and I chopped some of my cashews with a Swiss Victorinox. The jays got the cashews and I got some close up images. I hiked down the airstrip to Eklutna Lake, then walked along the lakeshore for a while. Walking back down the airstrip I tossed large stone cobbles off the runway. It was a great day to be there in the sunshine with all the

spectacular mountains all around. In my two hours on the ground no one showed up at the airstrip. This is a favorite area for bicycle riders. They often ride from the trailhead parking to the airstrip (8 miles) and farther into the park to Eklutna Glacier which is 13 miles one way. Near Eklutna Glacier at Mile 12 is a large well-designed hut where the riders can stay overnight.

5. I was now flying out of Bold Airstrip with a 10 mile wind off the lake making the takeoff short and rock solid. On the way back to Merrill Field I'll fly the mountain slopes on the north side of Eklutna Lake and search for wildlife. Although there were no large rock cliffs in these mountains, I still found 6 mountain goats and one black bear on the mountain slopes. Farther along about halfway down the lake I flew into a valley and counted 48 Dall sheep in one flock. These were ewes and lambs. I did not find the rams, which should be together in their own band. A little farther down the lake I found 10 addition sheep on the mountainside. About 2/3 of the distance along Eklutna Lake I turned right and flew north up Yuditnu Creek and immediately located a large brown creature on the mountain slope above the creek. It looked like a moose from a distance. I figured I'd better circle and go around again and check this creature because I wanted to make sure what it was. On the next pass I could clearly see that it was not a moose but a beautiful sub adult brown bear. It was always so special to locate a brown bear and to circle a few times and see what the bear was up to. This bear was walking upslope searching for food. The bear had a dark brown belly, lower legs, rump, and a brown streak down the upper back, and dark brown on the shoulders. All other areas, the bear's sides and head, were light blonde or honey colored. This was a spectacular color combination and a sight to behold. In this same drainage I found 22 Dall sheep. Flying beyond Eklutna Lake I found several small groups of Dall sheep. These groups of sheep numbered 3, 8, and 4. The group of 8 was a band of rams. The total number of Dall sheep in the mountains on the north side of Eklutna Lake was 95.

6. I returned to Merrill Field and concluded another memorable day of flying into the Chugach Mountains. Wildlife totals for animals observed were 95 Dall sheep, 72 mountain goats, 12 black bears, and 1 brown bear. This makes living here so special and rewarding. Flying in the mountains is highly inspirational and being able to observe such a large number of Alaska's most magnificent wildlife on one flight is remarkable. When I stop flying, I will always have these fond memories that will be everlasting in my mind.

MEMORANDUM 53
FACT SHEET

APVR-RPW-EV | QUIRK / 384-3010

2 February 2004

1. MANAGEMENT OF MOOSE ON FORT RICHARDSON

2. BACKGROUND: Moose are the featured species for wildlife management on the Fort Richardson military installation. They are the largest, most dominant, and the most sought-after of the large mammals for hunting and for watchable wildlife. The primary source of information for moose management is based on composition data from aerial surveys conducted annually in November–December. The survey area consists of 90,000 acres and includes both military installations (Fort Richardson and Elmendorf AFB) and the Ship Creek Valley in Chugach State Park. Additional surveys are flown through the winter months to locate spatial concentrations and to determine the migratory status of moose in the upper Ship Creek Valley and on the Chugach Mountain slopes.

3. FACTS BEARING ON THE SUBJECT:

a. Over the past 18 years, the population of moose in the Fort Richardson herd has remained relatively stable at a projected population of 517 animals. The Calf:Cow ratio during this period (1986-2003) is 37 calves per 100 cows. This is somewhat higher than that of a typical moose herd in Alaska. The Bull:Cow ratio during this same time period is 50 bulls per 100 cows. This is a magnitude larger than any moose herd in Alaska because of the public's desire to maintain a greater number of bulls in the herd for urban viewing and photography.

b. The Fort Richardson moose herd is adequately productive to allow an annual hunt by permit lottery. Up to 35 muzzle-loading-rifles and 125 archery permits are issued annually. The early hunt begins the day after Labor Day (first Monday in September) and continues through November 15. The late or winter hunt begins December 15 and continues through January 15. The annual harvest of moose during the past five years has averaged 41 animals. The hunter harvest of moose along with natural and man-caused mortality—for example, winter starvation, predation by wolves, natural injuries, highway accidents, and other mortality—account for approximately 10 to 15 percent of the herd annually.

c. The Fort Richardson moose herd consists of a resident population of animals on the forested coastal plain of the military bases and a migratory population in upper Ship Creek and on the western slopes of the Chugach Mountains. The migratory population is in their upland habitat in late spring, summer, fall, and early winter. When the snowpack in the mountains reaches a depth of approximately 4 feet, usually by late January, a mass migration of moose set out for the coastal plain on Fort Richardson. The annual moose survey is usually completed in November when the migratory moose are in their upland habitat and can be easily distinguished from the resident moose occupying the coastal plain on the military bases. In past years, the resident population was larger than the migratory population; however, in recent years (since 2000) the migratory population has grown in number while the resident population has declined, resulting in the migratory population now representing the larger population of moose in the two groups. In 2003, there was a projected population of 394 moose in the migratory population and 257 animals in the resident population for a total projected population of 651 moose in the Fort Richardson herd. The shift in numbers of migratory and resident moose is thought to be from resident moose on the military bases joining the migratory moose on their return to the mountain habitats. The shrinking of the population of resident moose on the military bases is primarily due to the degrading and declining habitat on the coastal plain.

4. ACTION TAKEN: The Army's Environmental Resources Department at Fort Richardson and Alaska Department of Fish and Game in the Anchorage Regional Office have the responsibly for managing the Fort Richardson moose herd. Over the past 25 years, the Army has focused on habitat development and enhancement (creating new habitat areas and recycling over mature unproductive habitat), conducting annual and other winter moose surveys, and directing the annual moose harvest in the field. Alaska Department of Fish and Game has focused on jointly completing the annual moose surveys with Fort Richardson biologists and determining the number of moose hunting permits issued for harvesting moose on the military reservations and in the upper Ship Creek Watershed.

5. ACTION REQUIRED: Continue focusing on moose habitat development and enhancement by expanding the number of acres completed each year. Work closely with civilian and military personnel to provide an awareness of cumulative impacts that projects and training have on moose habitat degradation and interference with natural movements and migration.

265

MEMORANDUM 54
SUBJECT: Moose Migration out of the Ship Creek Valley

February 2, 2004

1. A large population of moose inhabits the upper Ship Creek Valley on Fort Richardson and in Chugach State Park during late spring, summer, fall, and early winter. When the snowpack reaches approximately 4 to 4½ feet in depth, usually by mid to late January, a large percentage of these moose migrate out of Ship Creek onto the Fort Richardson coastal plain near the Glenn Highway. Limited winter habitat east of the Glenn Highway causes these moose to continue to migrate to the west across the highway toward the Army and Air Force cantonment areas and off the south post of Fort Richardson into Far North Bicentennial Park. From the parklands, the moose disperse into the city of Anchorage. In the spring, when the snowpack melts away, this migratory moose population moves in an easterly direction back into the upper Ship Creek Valley.

2. The annual Fort Richardson moose survey conducted on November 15, 2003 captured the total number of migratory moose using Ship Creek in the year 2003. The total number was an estimated population of 287 moose (Table 1).

3. Additional aerial surveys were flown into Ship Creek during the winter months to determine the number of moose that remained and the number that has migrated out of the watershed. Results from an aerial survey conducted on December 25, 2003 showed that 116 moose (40%) remained in the Ship Creek drainage on this date (Table 1). A second aerial survey on January 25, 2004 showed that only 35 moose (12%) remained in the Ship Creek drainage on that date (Table 1).

4. Data from the aerial survey on December 25, 2003 showed that 171 moose (60%) have migrated out of Ship Creek by this date (Table 2). By January 25, 2004, 252 moose (88%) have migrated out of the Ship Creek drainage (Table 2).

5. In addition to Ship Creek moose moving out of the watershed, moose on the Chugach Mountain slopes adjacent to Ship Creek also migrate down onto the coastal plain on Fort Richardson. The total estimated number of moose on the western slopes of the Chugach Mountains on Fort Richardson is 81.

Surveys have not been flown over the mountain slopes to validate the number of moose remaining and the number that have migrated to the coastal plain. If the percentage of moose that have migrated out of Ship Creek were used to estimate how many moose have migrated off the mountain slopes, it would be 88 percent of 81 or 71 moose by January 25, 2004. Using the estimate from the mountain slopes, the total outmigration from Ship Creek and the slopes would be 323 moose by January 25, 2004. This is a large number of moose moving out of the Chugach Mountains to the lowlands. To find adequate food sources, these moose disperse onto the military bases and to many parts of Anchorage.

6. This has been a winter with higher than average snowfall and snowpack depths. The data in this report are typical of past years for these climatic conditions. In years with low snowfall, more moose tend to remain in Ship Creek for longer periods and for most of the winter. An aerial survey in Ship Creek on February 24, 2001 showed that 50 to 60 percent of the current migratory population was still present. A larger number of moose have not migrated out of the drainage because of low snowfall and shallow snowpack this winter.

TABLE 1. AERIAL MOOSE SURVEYS IN UPPER SHIP CREEK VALLEY[1]

SU[2]	Location	Estimated Number of Moose		
		Nov. 15, 2003[3]	Dec. 25, 2003[4]	Jan. 25, 2004[4]
1	North Fork	78	32	4
2	Main Stem (Headwaters)	78	7	1
3	Upper Valley (East)	49	42	11
3	Upper Valley (West)	12	4	6
4	Biathlon/Arctic Valley	43	20	8
5	Snowhawk Valley	27	11	5
	Total	**287**	**116**	**35**

[1] Data represent estimated moose populations from aerial surveys.
[2] Survey Units
[3] Data from annual Fort Richardson Moose Survey recorded by Jesse Coltrane, ADF&G
[4] Data collected from aerial surveys flown by Bill Quirk in his Arctic Tern taildragger

TABLE 2. MOOSE MIGRATION OUT OF SHIP CREEK 2003-2004

	Estimated Number of Moose		
	Nov. 15, 2003	Dec. 25, 2003	Jan. 25, 2004
Total # of Moose remaining in Ship Creek by date	287 (100%)	116 (40%)	35 (12%)
Total # of Moose that Migrated out of Ship Creek by date	0 (0%)	171 (60%)	252 (88%)

MEMORANDUM 55
SUBJECT: Moose Survey in the Upper Campbell Creek Drainages

November 17, 2003

1. An aerial moose survey was conducted on November 16, 2003 at 12:10 PM to document the number of moose in three Campbell Creek drainages in the Chugach Mountains 10 air miles southeast of downtown Anchorage, Alaska. The survey was flown in my Arctic Tern taildragger based at Merrill Field in Anchorage. The weather was sunny and cold. The ambient temperature was about 5 degrees Fahrenheit. There was light wind in the valleys with moderately brisk winds on the mountain slopes and ridge tops. Snow cover from the first snowfall of the year (November 8-11) was less than 6 to 8 inches. Although the mountain slopes blocked the sun, survey conditions were good especially in the subalpine habitats.

2. Three survey units (SUs) in the upper Campbell Creek watershed were surveyed (Figure 1). SU 1 was in the upper South Fork drainage of Campbell Creek. SU 2 was in the lower Middle Fork drainage of Campbell Creek. SU 3 was in three small unnamed drainages between Near Point (north) and Rusty Point (south) near the Wolverine Peak Trail. All areas surveyed were in Chugach State Park at elevations between 1,500 and 3,000 feet. Most of the areas surveyed were in subalpine habitats. A small part of the lower elevations (under 1,500 feet) was located in the boreal forest.

3. The total number of moose observed in SU 1 was 48; SU 2 was 46; and SU 3 was 26 for a total in all three SUs of 120 moose (Table 1). Flying time required to survey the three SUs was 48 minutes. An unusually large number of Bull Moose was observed in these populations. This would be expected

from a moose population that is not hunted. Moose in these drainages will move out of the subalpine habitats when the snowpack reaches 3½ to 4 feet in depth. The moose will move downslope through the Hillside and Basher residential areas into Far North Bicentennial Park and disperse into other areas in the city of Anchorage.

4. No attempt was made to obtain composition data, for example, cows, calves, small-, medium- and large-size bulls. Large numbers of cross-country skiers and other recreational users in the South and Middle Forks of Campbell Creek would have been disturbed by flying lower and circling each animal sighted. Low flying and circling is required for obtaining accurate composition moose data.

TABLE 1. MOOSE SURVEY CAMPBELL CREEK NOVEMBER 16, 2003

Survey Unit	# Moose Observed	Habitat(s)
1	48	Subalpine
2	46	Subalpine and Boreal Forest
3	26	Subalpine
Total	120	

MEMORANDUM 56
SUBJECT: Moose Survey MacKenzie Farms

November 24, 2006

1. A comprehensive aerial moose survey of the MacKenzie Farms was conducted beginning at 3:02 PM on November 23, 2006. The MacKenzie Farms are located 14 miles northwest of downtown Anchorage, Alaska. The survey provides data showing the number of moose using this important wintering habitat.

2. In 1982, in a joint project by Alaska Department of Natural Resources, the Agriculture Action Council, and the Matanuska-Susitna Borough sold 14,772 acres and built the main access roads into the property. Thirty-one farms were established, 19 dairy and 12 hay farms. Approximately 12,736 acres of forests were cleared with bulldozers so the farms could be established. After five years, many of the farms became unprofitable and were abandoned. By January 2000, only 3 dairy and 4 hay farms remained

operational (Steve Trickett, personal communication). Approximately 55 percent or 7,075 acres of the developed MacKenzie Farms have reverted to early successional deciduous vegetation due to lack of cultivation. The early-succession birch, cottonwood, aspen and willow saplings have become exceptional moose habitat. Moose from as far away as 30 to 40 miles migrate to the MacKenzie Farms during the winter months to take advantage of this bountiful food supply.

3. The survey was flown in my Arctic Tern taildragger based at Merrill Field in Anchorage, Alaska. Total flying time for the survey was 1 hour and 10 minutes. The weather was sunny and cold with an ambient temperature of 14 degrees Fahrenheit. Snow cover was complete; however, it was only a few inches in thickness. All the snow came in a few snowstorms about one month before (late October). The temperature since the snowstorms has been consistently low averaging in the 10s and 20s. At no time during this one-month interval has the temperature risen above freezing. Sightability for observing moose on this survey was no better than average due to the dull snow cover (old snow) and the vegetation which was not snow covered.

4. The survey area was divided into four equally sized quadrants delineated by Guernsey Road oriented north and south and by Holstein Avenue oriented east and west. Surrounding the farming area is the mature native black spruce coniferous forest containing scattered birch and aspen trees.

5. Moose were surveyed in each quadrant and the results show that a total of 181 moose were observed at the MacKenzie farming area on November 23, 2006 (Table 1). The estimated number of moose based on a 90 percent sightability factor is 202 moose in the MacKenzie farming area. The 10 percent correction factor allows for moose bedded down and not sighted during the survey.

6. Other early winter surveys show estimated moose numbers were similar to the November 23, 2006 data (Table 2). One exception is the October 24, 2001 data, which show estimates were high (371 moose). Heavy snowstorms in early and mid-October 2001 created a snowpack up to 30 inches deep. The deep snow cover triggered a large migration of moose to MacKenzie Farms. The snowpack was only a few inches deep on December 22, 2000 and December 19, 2002. The maximum number of moose wintering at

MacKenzie Farms is typically found in January and February each year. Peak numbers at that time are estimated at 544 to 728 moose.

TABLE 1. MACKENZIE WINTER MOOSE SURVEY DATA—NOVEMBER 23, 2006

Quadrant	# Moose Observed	Estimated Moose Population[1]
NW	50	56
SW	18	20
SE	68	76
NE	45	50
Total	181	202

[1] Based on 90% sightability factor of observed moose

TABLE 2. MACKENZIE EARLY WINTER MOOSE SURVEY DATA[1]

Quadrant	Dec. 22, 2000	Oct. 24, 2001	Dec. 19, 2002	Nov. 23, 2006
NW	54	99	69	56
SW	54	51	76	20
SE	87	160	83	76
NE	30	61	36	50
Total	225	371	264	202

[1] Data is estimated moose population based on 90% sightability factor

MEMORANDUM 57
SUBJECT: Moose Survey MacKenzie Farms

February 22, 2001

1. A comprehensive aerial survey of the MacKenzie Farms was conducted at 10:25 AM on February 18, 2001 to record the number of wintering moose. The weather was clear with high overcast skies and a slight breeze from the north. The ambient temperature was 18 degrees Fahrenheit. Good survey conditions were found with a complete snow cover. Snow depth was approximately 2 feet. The survey was flown in my Arctic Tern taildragger based at Merrill Field in Anchorage, Alaska.

2. The results of the MacKenzie Moose Survey are shown below in Table 1.

TABLE 1. MACKENZIE MOOSE SURVEYED ON FEBRUARY 18, 2001

Quadrant	# Moose Observed	Estimated Moose Population[1]
NW	218	242
SW	112	124
SE	231	256
NE	95	106
Total	656	728

[1] Based on a 90% sightability factor

3. In the northwest quadrant, moose were spatially distributed as follows: 72 moose observed in Section 35 north of Ayrshire Road; 22 moose observed northeast of the Little Susitna access road; and 124 moose observed south of Ayrshire Road. The two areas north of Ayrshire Road comprise approximately 700 acres while the acreage south of Ayrshire Road is approximately 3,800 acres.

4. The snowstorm that dumped approximately 2 to 3 feet of snow on Southcentral Alaska on February 11 and 12, 2001 was the largest of the winter. It triggered a mass migration of moose to Mackenzie Farms. Moose observed on the December, January, and February surveys totaled 203, 313, and 656 animals, respectively. The big snowstorm resulted in more than doubling the number of moose wintering at MacKenzie in January 2001 from 313 to 656. The February survey was conducted 6 days after the snowstorm.

5. A large number of snow machines operate on the north side of MacKenzie Farms. A parking lot for vehicles pulling trailers for snow machines is located on the north side of Ayrshire Road east of Guernsey Road. In this parking lot were found 110 vehicles. The parking lot was full and another 52 vehicles were parked along Ayrshire Road. If the 162 parked vehicles averaged two snow machines per vehicle, the total would be 324 snow machines. They have a large area to operate in north to Big Lake (6 miles) and west to the Susitna River (15 miles). It is surprising that on winter surveys I have not seen any of these snow machines running through the MacKenzie Farms. Evidently, the snow machines are not chasing MacKenzie moose on their wintering grounds. The only disturbance to moose which has been observed on the winter surveys is from snowshoe hare hunters. Because there is not much dense cover at MacKenzie, two hare hunters can alarm and cause

moose from a large area to run out of the immediate area of disturbance and relocate a half mile or more away. The extent of this low-impact disturbance is unexpected and would not be understood except from aerial observation.

MEMORANDUM 58
SUBJECT: Moose Survey near Big Lake

February 17, 2011

1. An aerial survey was conducted on the north and east sides of Big Lake on February 17, 2011 at 2:35 PM to determine the number of moose wintering in the area that burned in the Miller Reach fire in 1996. The survey was flown in my Arctic Tern taildragger based at Merrill Field in Anchorage, Alaska. The day was partly sunny with a high overcast. The ambient temperature was 15 degrees Fahrenheit with a light wind blowing from the northeast. The snowpack was 1 to 2 feet in depth. Survey conditions for observing moose were average. The flying time for the survey was 1.6 hours.

2. Surveying the burned area is easily accomplished as the trees that burned in the fire are charred and many are still standing. The charred trees are blackened and are easily distinguished from living trees from the air. The 1996 fire burned 32,000 acres and was sufficiently hot in many areas to destroy part or all of the organic and duff layers which lie on top of the soil surface. This resulted in exposing mineral soil. Hardwood seed naturally broadcast by the wind fell on the mineral soil and germinated. It has been 15 years since the burn and the early succession hardwoods, for example, willows, birch, and aspen are flourishing and producing excellent winter moose habitat.

3. The survey area was divided into three parts as follows: (1) North and northeast of Big Lake to the Little Susitna River, the Parks Highway, and the Big Lake Road comprising 14,720 acres; (2) Lucille Creek drainage from Big Lake Road south to Hollywood Drive comprising 7,040 acres; and (3) East of Big Lake and south of Hollywood Drive comprising 10,240 acres. The three parts totaled 32,000 acres or 50 square mile Sections.

4. Results show that 218 moose were observed in the northeast part; 90 moose were observed in the Lucille Creek part; and 155 moose were observed in the east part. A total of 463 moose were observed in the three areas (Table 1). Sightability during the survey was average. With 85 percent

sightability on the survey, the total estimated population of moose in the burned areas near Big Lake would be 533 moose. This is a new high total number of moose when compared to previous years.

TABLE 1. MOOSE SURVEY DATA, BIG LAKE, ALASKA (FEBRUARY 17, 2011)

Survey Area	Observed Moose	Estimated Moose[1]
Northeast of Big Lake	218	251
Lucille Creek Drainage	90	104
East of Big Lake	155	178
Total Number of Moose	463	533

[1] Using sightability factor of 85%

5. Results on a survey conducted on February 8, 2008 showed an estimated total of 471 moose (Table 2). The wintering moose numbers in the Big Lake burned area are up substantially from past years. The estimated population of moose in the Big Lake burned area in February 2001 was 322. The following year, in 2002, showed an estimated population of 393.

TABLE 2. MOOSE SURVEY DATA, BIG LAKE, ALASKA (FEBRUARY 8, 2008)

Survey Area	Observed Moose	Estimated Moose[1]
Northeast of Big Lake	184	239
Lucille Creek Drainage	130	169
East of Big Lake	48	63
Total Number of Moose	362	471

[1] Using sightability factor of 70%

6. It is worthwhile to know how many resident and how many migratory moose use this burned area near Big Lake. Additional surveys in late winter after most of the moose have moved to their traditional summering grounds and surveys in early winter before the migrating moose have returned will be necessary to answer the question. The surveys in the summer, without snow cover, are almost useless as the sightability would be expected to be too low to be of any value. Surveys at MacKenzie Farms after the first snowfall in October and surveys late in the winter have shown few moose recorded. This indicates that MacKenzie has high moose numbers during the winter. It is an important moose wintering area that is almost totally abandoned in summer.

MEMORANDUM 59
SUBJECT: Moose Survey near Big Lake

February 26, 2013

1. An aerial survey was conducted on the north and east sides of Big Lake (24 miles north of Anchorage) on February 25, 2013 beginning at 3:30 PM to determine the number of moose wintering in the area that burned in the Miller Reach fire in 1996. The survey was flown in my Arctic Tern taildragger based at Merrill Field in Anchorage, Alaska. The skies had a thin overcast. The ambient temperature was 30 degrees Fahrenheit with northeast winds blowing 10 to 15 miles per hour. The snowpack was 1 to 2 feet in depth. Survey conditions for observing moose were average. The flying time needed to complete the survey was 1.9 hours.

2. The survey area was divided into three segments as follows: (1) North and northeast of Big Lake to the Little Susitna River, the Parks Highway and the Big Lake Road totaling 14,720 acres (23 Sections); (2) Lucille Creek drainage from Big Lake Road south to Hollywood Drive comprising 7,040 acres (11 Sections); and (3) East and southeast of Big Lake and south of Hollywood Drive comprising 10,240 acres (16 Sections). These three segments total 32,000 acres or 50 square mile Sections.

3. Survey results in February 25, 2013, with a grand total of 956 estimated moose, show an all-time high for wintering moose at Big Lake (Table 1). The number of moose wintering at Big Lake has increased substantially (almost doubled) from the numbers found here 10 year ago. The number of moose at Big Lake in 2013 has increased by 80 percent over the estimated number of moose on February 17, 2011 (Table 1). Increases in the number of moose in 2013 were found in all three survey areas; however, the greatest increase was in the area north and northeast of Big Lake where the increase was 106 percent. The moose numbers increased in the Lucille Creek part by 60 percent and in the east and southeast part of Big Lake by 53 percent. Other surveys in the Big Lake burned area in previous years showed 330 moose in February 23, 2002; 545 moose in November 7, 2003; 471 moose in February 8, 2008; and 533 in February 17, 2011.

4. The landform of the burned area near Big Lake consists of repeating long and narrow swales (up to a mile in length) parallel to long and narrow gently sloping uplands (plateaus) which rise in elevation north and northeast of Big

275

Lake from 10 to 50 feet and rising from 50 to 200 feet east and southeast of Big Lake. The swales are depressions supporting the growth of wetland vegetation. The less wet or moist areas in the swales may provide suitable conditions for the growth of hardwood vegetation. The soils on the ridges are well-drained and support the growth of hardwood saplings consisting of birch, aspen, cottonwood, and willow. These plateaus support the high value moose winter habitat in the Big Lake area. The hardwood species have been flourishing and their biomass has increased several folds over the years since the fire in 1996. The large numbers of moose that come here in this emerging winter habitat are thought to be moose that formerly wintered in the riparian habitat in the much-braided Susitna River drainage. Evidently, the quality and quantity of the moose habitat in the Big Lake area is better than the riparian habitats in the Susitna River. Moose will switch winter habitat areas when they find one that is more productive than the one that they currently use.

5. Additional surveys are needed to determine the number of moose that remain in the Big Lake area year-round. Also needed is information on moose migration corridors. It is likely that a large number of moose that winters at Big Lake moves out of the area when the snow melts in April. These moose migrate to their summer, fall, and early winter habitat. Migrating moose wintering at Big Lake likely come from the northwest and north (Susitna River) and from the northeast (western mountain slopes of the Talkeetna Mountains).

TABLE 1. MOOSE SURVEY DATA, BIG LAKE, ALASKA

Survey Area	Observed Moose		Estimated Moose[1]	
	Feb. 17, 2011	Feb. 25, 2013	Feb. 17, 2011	Feb. 25, 2013
Northeast of Big Lake	218	450	251	518
Lucille Creek Drainage	90	145	104	167
East of Big Lake	155	236	178	271
Total Moose	463	831	533	956

[1] Using Correction Factor of 15%

MEMORANDUM 60

SUBJECT: Moose Survey Alexander Creek Drainage

February 28, 2000

1. A comprehensive survey of the riparian area of Alexander Creek was conducted at 3:30 PM on February 26, 2000 to record the total number and distribution of moose using this important wintering area. Alexander Creek is a small drainage that flows into the lower Susitna River below Susitna Station. The creek begins at Alexander Lake which is approximately 50 air miles northwest from downtown Anchorage. The survey was flown in my Arctic Tern taildragger based at Merrill Field in Anchorage. Total flying time for the survey was 40 minutes. The sky was overcast and there was a gentle breeze. The ambient temperature was 26 degrees Fahrenheit. The depth of the snowpack was 1 to 2 feet and was continuous. Sightability for locating moose was excellent.

2. The survey results show that 63 moose were observed in upper Alexander Creek drainage from Alexander Lake to Wolverine and Sucker Creeks and 125 moose in lower Alexander Creek, which empties into the lower Susitna River. The total number of animals observed for the entire creek was 188 moose. The estimated or projected population was conservatively calculated to be 207 moose for the entire Alexander Creek drainage. This was based on a sightability factor of 90 percent. Moose bedded in adjacent forests that were not observed would easily account for this discrepancy.

3. The total number of moose found in this drainage was surprisingly high, as the riparian area of Alexander Creek is very narrow. A heavily used snowmachine and dog mushing trail goes right up the creek from the Susitna River to Alexander Lake. Moose are bedded near the trail, as they do not find it feasible to climb the bluff away from the creek to get away from snowmachine traffic. There are numerous cabins and lodges on the lower 5 miles of the creek. The moose using this drainage notwithstanding the human intrusion have learned to adjust to the heavily used motorized trail and appear to be wintering fairly well.

MEMORANDUM 61
SUBJECT: Early Winter Moose Survey in the Palmer Hay Flats

November 6, 2001

1. An aerial survey was conducted at 3:25 PM on November 3, 2001 in the Palmer Hay Flats and vicinity (lower Matanuska and Knik River drainages) to record the total number and distribution of moose using this important wintering area. The survey was flown in my Arctic Tern taildragger based at Merrill Field in Anchorage. Total flying time was 1 hour and 10 minutes. The sky was overcast, the winds were light and variable from the south, and the temperature was 26 degrees Fahrenheit. The snowpack was continuous with a depth of approximately 12 to 15 inches. Overall sightability for locating moose was good.

2. The results of the November 3, 2001 survey showed that a total of 74 moose were observed in the Palmer Hay Flats and adjacent areas (Table 1). The greater number of moose observed on this survey were most likely resident moose. Census data show that the snowstorms in October 2001 were not sufficient to trigger a mass migration of moose to these wintering grounds. The area with the largest number of moose observed on this survey was in moderately good quality winter habitat southwest of Palmer and east of the Glenn Highway along the west side of the lower Matanuska River floodplain.

TABLE 1. MOOSE OBSERVED IN THE PALMER HAY FLATS AND VICINITY[1]

Survey Area	Moose Observed	
	Feb 21, 2000	Nov 3, 2001
Lower Knik River Drainage	20	4
Lower Matanuska River Drainage	15	12
Palmer Hay Flats (E of Glenn Hwy)	61	42
Palmer Hay Flats (W of Glenn Hwy)	179	16
Totals	275	74

[1] Includes the lower Knik and Matanuska River drainages

3. Most of the migratory moose that utilize the Palmer Hay Flats and vicinity concentrate in the area west of the Glenn Highway. The February 21, 2000 survey showed 179 moose in the Palmer Hay Flats west of the Glenn Highway compared to only 16 on this survey (Table 1). The November

3, 2001 survey data represent only 10 percent of the February 21, 2000 numbers. This shows that significant numbers of moose have not migrated to the Palmer Hay Flats after the snowstorms in October 2001. The data for the wintering grounds on the Palmer Hay Flats and vicinity contrasts sharply with the data from the Mackenzie Farms. A survey at MacKenzie showed that 334 moose were observed on October 24, 2001. This represents about half of the total migratory moose that would be expected to utilize MacKenzie at peak times in winter.

4. The Palmer Hay Flats and vicinity represent critical escape habitat for wintering moose which migrate out of their local area when a deep snowpack covers up the food supply and the expenditure of energy moving through the deep snowpack becomes prohibitive. In years with shallow snow accumulation when the snowpack does not build up to high levels greater than 4 feet, few moose would be expected to migrate to the Palmer Hay Flats.

5. The Palmer Hay Flats with their poorer quality and meager quantity of habitat draws migrating moose when the snowpack reaches intolerable levels in the local area. The attraction of the Palmer Hay Flats for moose is the snowpack depth, which remains shallow throughout the winter and rarely builds up to great depths because of lower annual snowfall and frequent Chinook winds from the Knik River Valley that sublimates the snow.

6. The wintering habitat at MacKenzie is strikingly different from the Palmer Hay Flats and vicinity in that it draws a large number of animals early in the winter when snow depths are not sufficiently deep to trigger mass migrations of animals. The reason for the difference in these two wintering areas is that MacKenzie, unlike the Palmer Hay Flats, has prime winter habitat composed of high biomass felt leaf and Scouler willow along with birch saplings growing in productive soils. Moose arrive early at MacKenzie because the habitat available is superior to what they would have if they remained in their local area. MacKenzie is an important winter habitat area that attracts large numbers of moose throughout the winter. The Palmer Hay Flats attract moose escaping the deep snowpack whenever that occurs.

MEMORANDUM 62
SUBJECT: Wildlife Paper on Urban Moose in Anchorage, Alaska

An Urban Wildlife Classic in Anchorage, Alaska

William A. Quirk, III*

July 20, 1999

An urban wildlife classic consisting of a high-density moose population in a heavily used recreational area was observed in the winter of 1999 near Service High School in the southeastern part of Anchorage, Alaska. To obtain a better understanding of how moose use the area, aerial surveys of the animals were conducted in midwinter (January and February) and a field reconnaissance of the vegetation and soils were completed in April and June. While this wildlife classic is happening here, it is thought to be repeated often in other urban areas in Anchorage. This phenomenon has not been previously reported. The purpose of this paper is to provide insight into how moose utilize winter habitat and intermingle with humans in an urban environment. This is important in learning how to effectively manage the large number of urban moose inhabiting the Anchorage Bowl.

The area of interest is a previously burned forest consisting of approximately 80 acres in size located east of Service High School (Figure 1). The area is intercepted by numerous trails which were constructed prior to the burn to provide a training area for the Service High School cross-country ski team. The trails in the burned area have been expanded over the years and they have become popular and heavily used not only by student athletes but also by Anchorage residents for skiing in winter and hiking in summer. A trailhead and large parking area was constructed for public access to the trail system which lies within Far North Bicentennial Park.

This urban wildlife classic shows the compatibility of wildlife completely integrated into a high-use recreational area without apparent deleterious results to either the moose or to the recreational skiers. The fire removed the forest and allowed the willows and other hardwood shrubs to flourish, creating excellent winter moose habitat. Pockets of high-value habitat are usually discovered by moose. This burned area was no exception. In a high-use recreational area, moose would normally feed when trail users are not present and bed down in adjacent spruce forest when recreational

* William A. Quirk, III, is a Biologist/Ecologist with the US Department of Defense at Fort Richardson, Alaska. Bill is also a 24-year Alaskan pilot with his Arctic Tern taildragger based at Merrill Field in downtown Anchorage, Alaska. The views expressed here are his own.

users return. Avoiding recreational users may have been the strategy early on; however, the moose have learned to adapt to the regular patterns of trail users. Trail users have a consistent pattern of moving through the area on the trails. Rarely do they get off the trail system and penetrate into moose habitat areas. Moose have learned over time that trail users pose no real threat to them. Trail users see moose on occasion when one gets up from its bed and feeds nearby or walks on the trails. However, recreational users have infrequently reported encounters or problems with moose in the area or on the trails. It is obvious that moose using the burn area are not harassed by trail users. This is unlike other areas in Anchorage where moose are continually being harassed by barking dogs, moving vehicles on streets and roads, and children throwing snowballs.

Four intensive aerial surveys were conducted to determine the number and spatial orientation of moose using the previously burned area. The aerial surveys were flown in my Arctic Tern taildragger. Flying time was approximately 8 minutes for each survey. The number of moose observed in the burned area on the first survey on January 8, 1999 was 18. Additional surveys on February 22, 26, and 28 found 15 moose on each survey. All surveys were flown between 1 and 2 PM. The number of moose observed in the burned area represents a very high density of moose using a limited winter habitat area. Most of the moose observed were bedded down in the burned area farthest from the ski trails. A few moose observed were bedded down close to the trails. Only 1 to 3 moose were observed bedded down, on each survey, in the adjacent forest surrounding the burned area. Numerous skiers were observed on all survey days using the trails in the burned area.

The field surveys were completed to determine habitat composition and browse production and utilization. These tasks were determined by ocular estimation (eyeballing) from representative areas within the burned area. The vegetation in the burned area was accessed along the trails on cross-country skis in early April. The soils and the amount of moose pellets in the burned area were evaluated in June to obtain a better understanding of the productivity of the site.

The vegetation in the burned area represents outstanding moose habitat consisting of a dense mixture of Scouler willow, aspen, and birch saplings growing on a highly productive site. The early succession vegetation came back after a fire in the 1980s removed a mature black spruce forest. The native forest also contained mature aspen groves and a few widely scattered mature paper birch trees. Willow was in the understory on the forest floor; however, it did not provide high-value moose habitat as woody shrubs cannot flourish in a closed-canopy spruce forest. The vegetation currently growing in the burned area is on a gently sloping terrace with a northwest aspect between 400 and 500 feet above sea level. Aspen and paper birch saplings from 4 to 10 feet in height dominate the woody plants in the burned area. Scouler willow grows in widely scattered clumps. The density of the deciduous saplings that came back after the burn is exceedingly high due to the exposure and warming of the surface or mineral soil, the release of nutrients from the burned trees, the lack of graminoids (grasses) and the relatively deep loamy soils that create a mesic site for vegetative growth. Aspen saplings grow in almost pure stands in the wetter sites found in depressions and swales. Paper birch saplings dominate and are very dense on drier slopes and ridge tops. Scouler willow clumps can be found growing in most areas with the exception of the wettest and driest sites. A small percentage of the woody saplings (primarily paper birch) have escaped heavy browsing and are 15 to 20 feet in height. Small spruce trees from 4 to 10 feet in height are growing back at moderately high densities. A second generation of spruce seedlings, 2 to 3 feet in height, is present in the understory. The spruce in the burned area is primarily black spruce; however, white spruce was found growing on some of the better-drained sites.

Browsing intensity and utilization in the burned area were evaluated in April and were found to be extremely high. The available stems on the willow and aspen saplings were being browsed at 95 percent and higher on almost all plants. The paper birch saplings were being browsed at a much lower rate of 40 to 70%. Birch stems in this area were not nearly as preferred as were willow and aspen. Approximately 40 percent of the escaped paper birch saplings were ridden down and broken in half by moose so that they could be browsed on the terminal branches. Breaking down of such a high percentage of escaped birch saplings indicate a shortage of winter food supply. The severely browsed willow and aspen saplings in the burned area also showed a shortage of winter food supply and the need for development of additional moose habitat in adjacent areas.

The June field survey showed that some of the pure stands of aspen saplings were experiencing high mortality with many stems lacking in chlorophyll and leaves. Most of the Scouler willow was severely browsed in winter, however, no plants could be found that were experiencing mortality. Some of the birch saplings also showed severe browsing, but like Scouler willow, they did not show signs of mortality. The field survey clearly shows that birch and especially willow can withstand repeated over browsing for many years and still continue to produce stems and leaves during the growing season to sustain life. However, with such intense browsing, the biomass of willow and birch would be quite low and would not provide an adequate food source for the large number and high density of wintering moose using the burned area.

The burned area was a highly productive site for vegetative growth because of the unusually deep and loamy textured surface soils. Unlike most of the forest soils in lowland areas around Anchorage that are very shallow and have a high content of glacial deposited parent materials (coarse sands, gravel, cobbles, and stones), the burned area escaped the Pleistocene glaciers and had more time to develop the deeper, more productive surface soils. The organic horizon in the burned area was destroyed in the fire and sufficient time had not been available for it to be replenished. The soil in the A Horizon was about 2 to 3 inches in thickness and is a dark brown fine silty loam. The B Horizon consisted of about 8 to 12 inches of light reddish brown loam which gradually grades into the C Horizon of courser textured loam. A limited amount of gravel-sized material was found just below the A Horizon and a few cobbles were found in the B and C Horizons.

The soils in the burned area were surprisingly free of coarse stone materials and therefore are able to retain a large quantity of moisture for plant uptake and growth. The number of moose pellets on the ground was very high. The pellets are broken down by weathering agents and biological processes and are incorporated into the soil, providing primary fertilizer nutrients for plant growth. The burned area would be considered a mesic site where plants have sufficient quantities of moisture and nutrients to provide a lush growth.

This wildlife classic shows that under certain conditions large ungulates such as moose are compatible with high-use recreational areas. The urban moose found in Anchorage have over time learned how to coexist with humans in residential and high-use recreational areas that provide suitable habitat. Wildlife biologists, land managers, planners, and others have had little or nothing to do with making this possible. The moose have determined how to live with people in an urban setting to a very high degree. In the burned area, it is working very well and changes to reduce or eliminate use by moose are not needed. Where moose and human interaction are causing problems, for example, ski trails in Kincaid Park, the development of habitat in adjacent areas could be accomplished to attract and keep moose away from the trails and other problem areas. Enhancement of over mature and decadent moose habitat and the development of new habitat are well documented and have been successfully demonstrated for the past 25 years (since 1974) on the Fort Richardson military reservation adjacent to Anchorage. The same techniques used there could be applied in the Anchorage Bowl with an assured success.

The winter moose population in the Anchorage Bowl is estimated at 800 to 1,000 by Alaska Department of Fish and Game (in the management plan, "Living with Wildlife in Anchorage"). With such a large population of moose in the city, the wildlife classic east of Service High School most likely repeats itself many times over in other parts of Anchorage. It is not obvious and well known because aerial surveys in the city that could reveal shared high density moose concentrations with high human use areas have never been flown.

Jan Buron, the Service High School cross-country ski coach, said that there are more moose this winter near the ski trails than observed in past winters but that there have not been any problems. The coach said trail users with poor skiing skills, such as small children, would be most vulnerable to getting out of the way of moose that may be on the trails. From all indications, it appears that the bedded moose are well adjusted to the skiers and that the skiers and the moose are compatible in this area.

The information in this paper can be useful in helping to formulate the moose management section in Alaska Department of Fish and Game's wildlife plan "Living with Wildlife in Anchorage." Great strides could be made with the preparation and implementation of a moose management plan that focuses on clear tasks to be performed in the proper sequence. Below is a straight forward and step-wise listing of tasks to facilitate the development of a Moose Management Plan for the Anchorage Bowl.

1. Conduct Annual Moose Surveys
   - Aerial surveys in November and December
   - 100 percent coverage of moose habitat areas in the Anchorage Bowl
   - Data collected for determining composition, total population numbers, and spatial location of high density moose concentrations
   - Annual report
2. Conduct Random Moose Surveys
   - Aerial surveys throughout the year to accomplish specific objectives
   - Aerial searches to locate high density moose concentration areas
   - Aerial reconnaissance to obtain spatial orientation of important habitat areas in the Anchorage Bowl
   - Report for each survey or reconnaissance flight
   - Overlay of high density moose habitat areas on vegetation base map
3. Develop a Moose Habitat Map for the Anchorage Bowl
   - Use vegetation base map to delineate and classify habitat areas.
   - Determine vegetation composition of moose habitat areas.

- Determine vegetation age class, condition, and biological productivity of habitat areas.
- Determine nutritional quality of habitat for moose utilization.
- Prepare moose habitat map for the Anchorage Bowl.
4. Determine Land Status of Moose Habitat Areas
   - Overlay moose habitat areas to show land status (ownership).
   - Prepare final map.
5. Determine Moose Movement Patterns and Migration Corridors
   - Attach satellite transmitters on moose.
   - Conduct a multiyear study to monitor daily movements, migration routes, and patterns.
   - Prepare final report.
6. Initiate Moose Habitat Enhancement and Development Projects
   - Review moose habitat areas and land status map to determine appropriate areas for habitat improvement projects.
   - Reduce moose/human conflicts in the Anchorage Bowl by developing habitat enhancement projects similar to Fort Richardson.
   - Prepare action plan for moose habitat improvement projects.
7. Revise/ Redevelop the Moose Management Plan for the Anchorage Bowl
   - Utilize the data and knowledge collected in the previous six tasks.
   - Prepare revised plan.

MEMORANDUM 63
SUBJECT: Modus Operandi for Flying Wildlife Surveys in Alaska

September 25, 2012

1. The traditional way of flying wildlife surveys in Alaska is with a pilot flying the airplane and a biologist recording the survey data. A nontraditional way of flying wildlife surveys in Alaska is with a pilot–biologist flying the airplane and recording the survey data—a one-person operation.

2. The Super Cub is the traditional aircraft used to conduct wildlife surveys in Alaska. Other two-place aircraft are used; however, they are used less often than Super Cubs. Larger and heavier aircraft are occasionally used for flying wildlife surveys in Alaska. These are four-place aircraft and frequently include the following Cessnas: C180 and C185 taildraggers and C182 tricycle gear aircraft. Helicopters are seldom used for flying wildlife surveys in Alaska because of noise and prohibitive operational costs.

3. The Super Cub taildraggers or equivalent airplanes are best suited for wildlife surveys in Alaska because of the low flying speeds, low noise emissions, low cost of flight operation and maintenance, tighter turning operations, and safer off-airport landings in case of emergencies. The larger and heavier Cessna four-place aircraft are much less suitable for wildlife surveys in Alaska because of the high noise emissions which disturb wildlife much more than the Cub, because of the higher flying speeds which result in lower sightability of wildlife, the difficulty and safety of making tight circles around moose for accurate surveys, the higher costs for operation and maintenance of the aircraft, and the difficulty of finding suitable landing places in remote areas in case of emergencies.

4. Flying wildlife surveys in Alaska as a pilot–biologist—a one-person operation—has several advantages over a traditional two-person operation (pilot and biologist). First and foremost, flying the airplane is much safer with lighter overall weight of the aircraft. The cost savings of a one person operation compared to a two-place team is considerable. The third advantage of the pilot–biologist survey operation is that it requires no coordination with a second person. This is paramount in reducing complicated scheduling of surveys with another person. Combined with adverse weather conditions, scheduling surveys with another person can become a difficult and frustrating task. The flexibility of the one-person operation provides a tremendous advantage over the two-person team.

5. In having been involved in both the one-person and the two-person operation for flying wildlife surveys in Alaska, I would opt for the one-person (pilot–biologist) as being the better way to manage this type of flying requirement. Some say it is unsafe for a pilot to fly and survey wildlife at the same time. In 25 years of flying wildlife surveys in Alaska in a one-person operation, I've never, not once, found this to be a problem. I like the solitude and time for contemplation while flying wildlife surveys in Alaska. This provides an environment better suited for concentration on the task at hand and stress-free flying of the aircraft. Flying surveys whenever the pilot chooses to fly without consultation with a second person is a tremendous relief in reducing the complexity and difficulty of the task. The wildlife survey by a one-person operation would provide a better overall survey because the pilot–biologist will have a clearer focus and concentration on the task and would have no interference or distraction from a second source. The accuracy of the survey and the finding of the highest number

of wildlife have a lot to do with placement of the aircraft in the proper position for locating the wildlife targets. It is much easier and more accurate to position the airplane for pilot observation versus attempting to position it for the person in the backseat of the aircraft. For all the above reasons, the one-person operation for conducting wildlife surveys will prove, in the long term, to be the best by a large margin.

MEMORANDUM 64
SUBJECT: Brown Bear Survey in Trading and Redoubt Bays

July 10, 2000

1. I conducted a comprehensive aerial survey in Trading and Redoubt Bays on the northwestern side of upper Cook Inlet at 2 PM on Saturday, July 1, 2000 to record the number and distribution of brown bears in the coastal wetland habitat. I flew the survey in my Arctic Tern taildragger. The sky was slightly overcast with sunny intervals. The ambient temperature was 65 degrees Fahrenheit.

2. The survey was flown between 350 and 500 feet above ground level sufficiently high so as to not disturb bears. The survey was flown in a continuous coverage pattern from Nikolai Creek on upper Trading Bay southwest along the coastal marshes to Cannery Creek on lower Redoubt Bay. All bear observations were within 1 to 1½ miles of salt water.

3. The bear observations were recorded on U.S. Geological Survey maps on the scale of 1 inch to the mile (Figures 1 and 2). The symbols on the maps are summarized and explained in Enclosure 1. The survey results conducted on July 1, 2000 showed the total number of brown bears observed in the coastal wetlands in Trading and Redoubt Bays was 46 (Tables 1 and 2). Trading Bay showed 15 bears and Redoubt Bay 31. Composition of the bears for the two bays is shown below in Tables 1 and 2. The criteria used to determine bear composition are described in Enclosure 2.

4. The spatial distribution of bears in the coastal wetlands on the western side of upper Cook Inlet shows that predominantly sows with cubs are using the coastal habitat in Trading Bay (Table 1). All bears observed in Trading Bay were sows with cubs with the exception of one adult found south of the McArthur River. The sows may be selecting marginal habitat along the Trading Bay coast to avoid encounters with adult male bears

that could be lethal to the cubs. Brown bears in the coastal wetlands of Redoubt Bay show a more uniform composition and double the number of bears using the Trading Bay habitat (Table 2). Thirty one (31) bears were observed in Redoubt Bay while 15 were observed in Trading Bay. Redoubt Bay appears to be the choice and most preferred coastal habitat of the two bays.

5. I surveyed the Redoubt Bay coastal wetlands for brown bears in early July 1989. The aerial survey consisting of a narrative with a map showed the location and numbers of bears found (Enclosure 3). The numbers and the locations of the bears in the coastal wetlands in the 2000 survey appear to be similar to the 1989 survey data results. The bears apparently come down along the coast annually in mid to late June for a few weeks to feed on sedges prior to feasting on salmon later in the summer.

6. This survey was conducted near mid-day on a warm sunny afternoon. I wondered how many bears had temporarily departed the coastal wetlands at midday for the inland brushy areas to seek cover and escape the heat. The survey, therefore, is a snapshot in time and may grossly under estimate the true numbers of bears using the coastal marshes in Trading and Redoubt Bays. Multiple surveys on the same day and throughout the bears' use of the coastal habitat are needed to obtain accurate data for determining bear density and the total number of bears in this coastal habitat. One conclusion that should be drawn from this survey is that there are a sufficiently large number of bears using this habitat to establish it as a 'keystone habitat' for the brown bears of Trading and Redoubt Bays. Active management to protect the habitat and the bears while they are present should be a goal of the land manager.

7. Inventorying brown bears in most habitats is difficult or impractical because brush and forest cover prevent detection of sufficient numbers of bears to provide accurate data. The coastal wetlands of Trading and Redoubt Bays provide an exceptional opportunity to gather composition data on a large number of bears in mid-summer due to excellent survey conditions without brush and other concealing cover. Surveys under these conditions result in observation of a large percentage of the bears present during the survey. The aerial surveys can be very efficient and conducted in about 1½ hour's flying time. The surveys could provide the most comprehensive data for the brown bears inhabiting these areas and could possibly provide reliable

trend data representative of the entire brown bear population between the coastal areas and the mountains.

8. One concern I observed while flying the survey was the proliferation of cabins in the coastal areas in both bays where the bears are feeding. Newly constructed cabins can be seen each year. This year was no exception. The cabins are mostly recreational cabins (duck and goose hunting); however, some cabins are utilized by commercial fishermen in the summer months. There was a float plane in a small lake near a recreational cabin near the mouth of McArthur River (Figure 1). Although this area contained a very large number and high density of bear trails through the grasses and sedges, not one bear was observed within a 2 mile radius around the human occupation. The survey also shows that bears seem to be avoiding high quality habitat along the lower stretches of the major rivers, for example, McArthur River in Trading Bay and Big River in Redoubt Bay. There were no bear trails or bears in these areas. To a lesser extent, this also applies to the coastal areas along the lower Kustatan and Drift Rivers in Redoubt Bay. The commercial fishermen occupy cabins on the large rivers and the constant traveling by boats from the cabins to the fishing grounds in Cook Inlet potentially creates sufficient disturbance to displace the bears from these important summer habitat areas.

9. Another concern is the amount of aviation traffic that overflies the Trading and Redoubt Bays during the summer months. During the survey I saw one large single-engine, float-equipped aircraft flying south at approximately 150 feet AGL over the coastal wetlands 2 air miles northeast of the Big River. One adult bear underneath the plane's flight path became highly annoyed and started running, then stopping, and turning in small circles to search for the source of disturbance. After the survey was completed, the author landed on a gravel strip near Nikolai Creek for a 15-minute break. Perhaps a dozen aircraft passed over, the lowest flew at about 1,000 feet AGL. For the most part, air traffic was not causing disturbance problems for the bears. The questions that need to be answered are how much disturbance is acceptable? How much should be tolerated for the well-being of the bears?

10. The greater part of the coastal wetlands in Trading Bay is included in the Trading Bay State Game Refuge. The most productive and largest extent of the coastal wetlands of Redoubt Bay from the Kustatan River to Drift River is included in the Redoubt Bay State Critical Habitat Area.

The Seward Sectional Aviation Chart shows coastal wetlands and mud-flats that are included in the Trading Bay and Redoubt Bay Sanctuaries (Figure 5). Pilots are requested to avoid flight in these sanctuaries below 1000 feet AGL during waterfowl migration periods in the spring and fall. Although there are some guidelines and restrictions for migratory waterfowl in the coastal areas of these two bays, there don't appear to be any for the bears.

11. Perhaps with sufficient data on where the bears are concentrated and the timing of their use of the coastal wetlands of Trading and Redoubt Bays, education could be provided to cabin users, commercial fishermen, and airplane pilots to ensure the bears are not harassed or displaced from their important summer habitat. Information and recommendations about human presence in the coastal habitat when the bears are present could be added to the Trading Bay State Game Refuge and the Redoubt Bay State Critical Habitat Area brochures. Information and recommendations could also be added to the Seward Sectional Aviation Chart for the existing sanctuary areas which are along the coast near salt water. The revised brochures and aviation charts with added bear information could be the beginning of an important public awareness effort to benefit the bears when they are concentrated near the coast of Trading and Redoubt Bays in early to mid-summer.

Symbols Used on Maps to Identify Brown Bear Composition

Single or Lone Bears:	Sow with Cubs of the Year:	Sow with Yearling Cubs:
A Adult Bear	Sow + 1 (C)	Sow + 1 (YR)
A(Y) Sub Adult Bear	Sow + 2 (C)	Sow + 2 (YR)
	Sow + 3 (C)	Sow + 3 (YR)

Enclosure 1

Physical Characteristics used to Distinguish Between Classes of Brown Bears[1]

Adults
Large Body Size
Large Body Length
Large Head
Small Ears

Sub adults
Smaller Body Size
Short in Length
Small Head
Large ears
Fluffy Fur

Sows with Cubs
Obvious

Cubs of the Year
With Sow
Small Size

Yearling Cubs
With Sow
Larger Size
Fluffy Fur

[1] No attempt was made to identify Adult and Sub Adult Bears.

Enclosure 2

TABLE 1. BROWN BEARS OBSERVED IN THE TRADING BAY COASTAL WETLANDS[1]

July 1, 2000	
Bear Composition	**Number(s)**
Sow + 2 (C)	3
Sow + 3 (C)	4
Sow + 3 (C)	4
Sow + 2 (YR)	3
Adult	1
Total Bears	**15**

[1] The bear observations listed above are in sequential order in which the Survey was flown from Nikolai Creek southwest to the McArthur Flats

Composition Summary of Bears at Trading Bay	
Bear Composition	**Number(s)**
Adults	1
Sows with Cubs	4
Cubs (C)	8
Cubs (YR)	2
Total Bears	**15**

TABLE 2. BROWN BEARS IN COASTAL REDOUBT BAY[1]

July 1, 2000	
Bear Composition	Number(s)
Sow + 3 (YR)	4
Sow + 3 (YR)	4
Adult	1
Young Adult	1
Young Adults (Siblings)	2
Adult	1
Adult	1
Sow + 2 (YR)	3
Sow + 2 (C)	3
Adult	1
Sub adult	1
Sub adult	1
Sub adult	1
Sow + 1 (YR)	2
Adult	1
Adult	1
Adult	1
Adult	1
Adult	1
Total Bears	**31**

[1] Bear observations are in sequential order from the Kustatan River southwest to Cannery Creek

Composition Summary of Bears at Redoubt Bay	
Bear Composition	Number(s)
Adults	9
Sub adults	6
Sows with Cubs	5
Cubs (C)	2
Cubs (YR)	9
Total Bears	**31**

MEMORANDUM 65
SUBJECT: Wildlife Paper on Brown Bears in Ship Creek

The Brown Bears of Ship Creek, Southcentral Alaska
William A. Quirk, lll[*]

December 12, 2002

The Bears of Ship Creek. Numerous bear survey reports in upper Ship Creek from the 1980s to the present have been written by the author to document the findings. Most of the bear observations that were documented were those of brown bears, as the Ship Creek Watershed is excellent brown bear habitat and relatively high densities of brown bears live here. The brown bears would tend to discourage black bears from using the area and limit their density in the Ship Creek drainage. Another reason for the low number of black bear observations is the difficulty of observing them from the air in their forested habitat. Brown bears are found in forest habitat; however, they spend more time in subalpine habitats than black bears and therefore are more readily observed. The few black bears that were seen over the years were observed predominantly in subalpine vegetation zones where sightings are greatly facilitated. Most black bear observations over the years were made as incidental sightings as the main goal of the surveys was to document the brown bears in Ship Creek.

The initial brown bear surveys conducted in the 1980s and early 1990s had limited value as there was no method or guide for determining composition data and ultimately the density or total population of bears in the Ship Creek Watershed. Individual bears were not classified as to age and sex. Repeat surveys in the same area could not distinguish between bears on one survey versus bears on successive surveys. All this has changed with the excellent video presentation prepared by biologists from the Alaska Department of Fish and Game (ADF&G) and Yukon Territory in Canada. The videotape "Bear ID, Take a Closer Look" was produced by Yukon Renewable Resources in 1990. From reviewing the tape several times and applying the lessons learned when locating brown bears on aerial flights, the author has learned to identify individual brown bears with a high level of proficiency (Enclosure 1). With this new skill, bear composition data can be collected on multiple flights on different calendar dates into the same

---

[*]William A. Quirk, III is a Biologist/Ecologist with the US Department of Defense at Fort Richardson, Alaska. Bill is also a 27-year Alaskan pilot with his Arctic Tern taildragger based at Merrill Field in downtown Anchorage, Alaska. The views expressed here are his own.

area to record information which can be useful in determining the total population of brown bears in a defined area.

Brown Bears in Ship Creek in the Year 2000. A series of random surveys were flown into the upper Ship Creek watershed during the summer and fall of the year 2000 to observe and record the brown bears inhabiting the area. Typically, the entire watershed was flown on each survey. The new skills of brown bear identification as to age and sex made it possible to identify and record all brown bears observed during the surveys. The objective was to determine the feasibility of observing a sufficiently large number of brown bears living in a well-defined geographic region to obtain useful spatial and composition data for management of a brown bear population. As the surveys were being conducted in the summer and into the fall of the year 2000, a relatively large number of brown bears were being located, characterized, and recorded. This was my first attempt to systematically survey the brown bears in a well-defined region. There have never been a summer and fall like the year 2000 for obtaining useful bear data from Ship Creek. The promising results from collecting valuable bear composition data is what prompted me to prepare this report.

Brown Bear Data in Ship Creek in the Year 2000. A total of 13 different brown bears were observed, characterized, and recorded in the upper Ship Creek Watershed in the year 2000 (Table 1). Incidental sightings of black bears in Ship Creek in the year 2000 were also recorded and are included in this report (Table 1). The locations of the brown bears were documented on a U.S. Geological Survey map with a scale of 1:63,360 (Figure 1). The locations of black bears observed in Ship Creek in 2000 were also shown on a U.S. Geological Survey map (Figure 2).

Significance of Brown Bear Data in Ship Creek

A. Spatial Distribution of Brown Bears in Ship Creek. The numerous aerial surveys over the years show that brown bears can be found in all areas of the upper Ship Creek watershed beginning at the western flanks of the Chugach Mountains near the Fort Richardson dam to the headwaters of the main stem, Ship Lake, the North Fork, and all areas in between. Brown bears are also often found in many side drainages leading into the main valleys of the Ship Creek watershed. Results in the year 2000 show that sighting locations were made from near Alpenglow Ski Lodge, up Ship Creek Valley to its headwaters on the main stem, and at the head of the North Fork. The latter two sightings were found in side valleys off the main stems. It is also apparent from the numerous surveys over the years and especially the year 2000 that the most important local area as determined by the large number of sightings is on the eastern slopes of the Ship Creek Valley approximately 6 air miles up the valley from the Chugach State Park trailhead on Arctic Valley Road. This would be considered a core area or the "heart" of the brown bear habitat in the Ship Creek Valley. It is the most important critical habitat area in the entire Ship Creek watershed for the bears. Surveys in the year 2000 showed 8 brown bears in this so-called heartland habitat (Figure 1). Composition of bears in this area were a dominant male, a sow with three cubs of the year, an adult female, and two sub adult bears (siblings). All of these bears observed were spatially located in a 2 mile area along the 1,500 to 2,000-foot contour of the eastern slopes of Ship Creek. Temptation Peak looms high on the horizon across Ship Creek to the west of this area.

B. Composition of Brown Bears in Ship Creek. The composition of the 13 brown bears observed in the Ship Creek watershed in the year 2000 include one dominant male, one sow with two cubs of the year, one sow with three cubs of the year, two sub adult males, one adult female, and two sub adult bears (siblings). Although the entire population of brown bears in Ship Creek would not be expected to be limited to the 13 sightings in the year 2000, the composition shows a nearly complete and logical number of bears in a defined region of this size. There are no glaring holes of expected data that are missing that can be readily identified. Recruitment into this population from the survey data show five cubs of the year and two sub adults (siblings). This indicates a healthy brown bear population with two sets of cubs of the year, one with three cubs and the other with two. The two sub adult bears being added to the population in Ship Creek show a healthy continuity between the cubs of the year, the sub adults, and the adults.

C. Population of Brown Bears in Ship Creek. When Dave Harkness was an ADF&G biologist for Game Management Unit 14C, which includes the Municipality of Anchorage, the military bases, and Chugach State Park, he often responded to the question of how many brown bears may be in the Ship Creek drainage by saying that perhaps a half dozen bears lived there. Dave's information was based on flying into Ship Creek to conduct annual

Dall sheep surveys. Over the years this became the best number anyone had for this drainage. From the survey data collected in 2000, we can see that this previous "best estimate" is far from accurate. A conservative estimate of the number of brown bears living in Ship Creek based on observing 13 bears in the year 2000 would be a total of 15 to 20 bears. The high density of brown bears in this watershed would indicate that this is prime habitat with excellent food sources for the bears.

D. Brown Bear Migration and/or Movement out of Ship Creek. The aerial surveys over the years do not show or indicate that there is a large migration of brown bears from the upper Ship Creek population down onto the coastal plain on Fort Richardson. For example, there is no indication from sightings that large numbers of brown bears move out of upper Ship Creek during the summer months downstream to feed on salmon along lower Ship Creek (downtown Anchorage) or at Sixmile Creek on Elmendorf AFB. There are modest numbers of brown bears on Campbell Creek during the salmon runs in late summer that likely are coming from the Ship Creek population of brown bears. Regional movement of bears from Ship Creek show that a small number do move down Ship Creek along the corridor at the Biathlon Range on Fort Richardson and onto the coastal plain lowlands on the Army Base. The few brown bears observed on the coastal plain on Fort Richardson were sibling bears probably looking for new ranges to explore.

E. The Effects of Moose Hunting on the Brown Bears in Ship Creek. In the 1980s and the early 1990s, frequent Defense of Life and Property (DLP) brown bear kills in Ship Creek were reported to the ADF&G. During those times, hunters used horses in Ship Creek to haul out the meat after shooting a moose. Brown bears were attracted to the kill sites and some of the brown bears were shot. Since the late 1990s and to the present time, very few hunters are now taking horses into Ship Creek for moose hunting. The younger generation of hunters does not think the boggy trail into Ship Creek is suitable for horses. Presently, there remain a small number of hunters that go into Ship Creek on foot for moose hunting. The meat is hauled out in a backpack. Only a few moose (as few as two or three) are taken each hunting season in Ship Creek since 1999. As a result of this change, the moose population in Ship Creek has doubled in number and no DLP brown bears have been reported killed from 1999 through the hunting season in September 2002. Hunters also backpack into Ship Creek to hunt Dall sheep, which are located primarily in the upper reaches of the main stem and the North Fork. There has been no evidence that sheep hunters are killing brown bears in Ship Creek.

F. The Effects of Recreational Users on the Brown Bears in Ship Creek.
A trailhead at approximately 2,200-feet elevation on Arctic Valley Road provides a parking area and entrance to a trail leading down into Ship Creek and Chugach State Park. Hikers and backpackers typically traverse Ship Creek to Indian Creek Pass and continue down Indian Creek to Turnagain Arm. This is a 22-mile trip and usually takes two to three days. The trail follows the valley bottom and many areas are wet peat bogs. In some areas the trail is faint and difficult to locate and follow. In other areas brush is a problem. Due to these limitations, the trail is used by a small number of recreational users in summer. During the winter months, cross-country skiers use the trail to traverse Ship Creek and continue to Indian Creek and the Seward Highway on Turnagain Arm. Most of the skiers take tents and spend one night camping on the traverse. If a ski trail is recently broken, skiers can travel the entire 22 miles in one long day. For the long, dark nights in winter, skiers use headlamps for finding their way. The light recreational use with small numbers of individuals is not known to have serious consequences for the brown bears in Ship Creek. In the mid to late 1980s, Chugach State Park was contemplating the construction of a "high-volume" recreational trail into Ship Creek. This could have serious and detrimental consequences for the brown bear population in Ship Creek. Evidently, the extensive funding for the construction could not be obtained and the trail was never built. If future plans call for trail construction into Ship Creek, wildlife impacts would need to be carefully examined and the trail route and the modus operandi for trail use would need to be compatible with maintaining the irreplaceable wildlife resources in Ship Creek.

Summary and Conclusions

The objective of the aerial surveys into Ship Creek was to determine the feasibility of observing a sufficiently large number of brown bears living in a well-define geographic region to obtain useful and accurate spatial and composition data for managing brown bear populations. The surveys conducted in Ship Creek in the year 2000 have provided insight as to the type of spatial and composition data that can be collected from aerial surveys. Whether or not this is the type or quality of information that is needed to manage brown bears populations in Alaska remains in the judgment of my peers in the field of bear biology. If this aerial technique is useful and workable, as I believe it is, it could be used in many other areas in Alaska. My hope is that this is the first of many opportunities of collecting useful data for the management of brown bears in Alaska.

Flying wildlife surveys in Alaska for over 20 years has taught me that a high degree of caution is needed in performing aerial surveys. It is critical to fly a geographical area ample times to become completely familiar with the nuances of the area and to be very creative in determining how to proceed with flying surveys to capture useful wildlife data. What has worked well in Ship Creek may or may not work well elsewhere. If most of the principles used in Ship Creek are followed in conducting aerial surveys in other areas in Alaska, fine-tuning will always be necessary to ensure the best methods are utilized.

The type of aircraft is also critical for flying quality wildlife surveys. A high-performance, backcountry tandem taildragger is the aircraft of choice. Slow flight (50 mph) and turning in shallow arcs are necessary for determine the distinguishing features of brown bears.

Afterword

A bear biologist in Alaska has indicated that the data from my bear surveys cannot be used to determine the number of bears in a locality because the surveys cannot demonstrate a measure of statistical reliability—it is not possible to duplicate the results that I have obtained. I have always believed in the thinking that all data has significance—certainly some data collected has more reliability that other data collected. In this situation, my bear data has to be compared with no other available bear data.

This "hard science" opinion is discussed in the recent book Super Brain (2010) by Deepak Chopra, MD and Rudolph E. Tanzi, PhD, Random House, Inc. Dr. Tanzi (Professor of Neurology at Harvard University and Head of the Alzheimer's Genome Project) says that "Hard science is proud of its status in society, but I have witnessed firsthand that this pride can extend to arrogance when it comes to considering the contributions of metaphysics and philosophy to developing scientific theories. This broad dismissal of anything that cannot be measured and reduced to data strikes me as incredibly narrow-minded. How can it make sense to dismiss the mind, however invisible and elusive it may be, when science is entirely a mental project? The greatest scientific discoveries of the future often begin as pipe dreams of the past."

TABLE 1. BROWN BEARS OBSERVED IN UPPER SHIP CREEK—2000

Date	Brown Bear(s)	Location
July 6	1 Sub adult Male	Upper Main Stem
July 7	2 Subadults[1]	Temptation Peak
September 7	1 Adult Female	Temptation Peak
September 15	1 Sow + 2 COY	Organ Mountain
September 16	1 Sow + 3 COY	Temptation Peak
September 17	1 Sub adult Male	Alpenglow
September 29	1 Adult Male	Temptation Peak
Total	**13 Bears**	

[1] Sibling Bears

Date	Black Bear(s)	Location
June 11	1 Mating Pair	Biathlon
July 6	2 Adults[1]	Upper North Fork
July 22	2 Adults[1]	Jct. North Fork
Total	**6 Bears**	

[1] Sightings on July 6 and July 22 were probably mating pairs of black bears that had recently separated. They were observed 100-200 yards apart.

MEMORANDUM 66
SUBJECT: Brown Bears on the Karluk River (Kodiak Island)

June 30, 2001

1. I organized a sport fishing trip by inflatable raft on the Karluk River during the period June 14 through 19, 2001. Phil Pierce from Virginia and Gene Deal from Colorado were my guests. Red salmon (sockeye) were plentiful in the river and we caught many silver beauties on flies with a flyrod from Karluk Lake 18 miles downriver to Karluk Lagoon. King salmon were scarce in the river and only two kings were caught. Both kings had already changed to spawning colors. This was my first float trip in 21 years on the Karluk River that silver-colored kings were not plentiful on the lower 11 miles of the river from French Camp downstream to Karluk Lagoon.

2. The Karluk River with king and red salmon in bright silver colors in mid-June has been the most enjoyable wilderness fishing river imaginable. We fly a commercial airline from Anchorage to Kodiak and hire a float plane

from Kodiak to Karluk Lake, a one hour flight. We booked dependable Steve Harvey in his Grumman Widgeon for many years. Every year I organized a trip with two to four cohorts to float the 18 mile long river and fly fish for reds and kings. The Karluk River is shallow and chest waders provide protection from the icy water when fishing the energetic reds and horse-bucking kings. For their size from 4 to 8 pounds, red salmon are among the hardest-fighting fresh water fish. Catching reds on a number 6 or 8 fly rod is a super delightful experience. The kings (weighing from 15 to 45 pounds) are one of the most challenging fresh water fish caught on spinning rods. However, on the Karluk River most of us opted for a number 10 or 11 fly rod. My old faithful is my Sage Number 11 which has never shattered when bending under enormous pressure with a feisty king. When a king takes your fly, there is no way to hold it. You run up and down the river following the king until the fish tires; then you reel in and slowly exert pressure to slow the fish down. Now it depends on who gets tired first—the fish or the fisherman. This will determine whether or not you will bring this king to shore. It is not unusual to battle a king in the Karluk River for half an hour or more.

3. The numbers and locations of brown bears observed on the Karluk River during the June 2001 float trip from the lake to the lagoon are shown in Table 1. Brown bears are thick in this part of Kodiak Island; however, mid-June is during the breeding season and the bears are away from the river in more peaceful environments. The bears flock to the river in July and feast on tired and dying red salmon. The average number of bears I have observed per year floating the Karluk River from 1975 to 1998 is 4. River-fishing trips on the Karluk were not made in 1999 and 2000. The large number of bears sighted in 2001 (12 bears) is the largest number on all my 21 float trips down the river. The weather was sunny and warm for the entire river trip in 2001. No rain! Very little wind! This is very unusual weather for Kodiak Island.

TABLE 1. NUMBERS AND LOCATIONS OF BROWN BEARS ON THE KARLUK RIVER IN JUNE 2001

Date	Time	Bears and Location
June 14	9:20 PM	Sow + 3 Yr. cubs on the NW side of Karluk Lake
June 16	12:40 PM	Mating pair 1 mile downstream from Big Bend
June 16	4:20 PM	Sub adult female at French Camp
June 16	5:05 PM	Sub adult Male at French Camp
June 18	12:10 PM	Sub adult male ¼ mile upstream from ADF&G Weir
June 18	10:10 PM	Sow + 2 Yr. cubs near Karluk Airport
		Total Number of Bears Observed: 12

MEMORANDUM 67
SUBJECT: Surprising Bear Survey in the Ship Creek Watershed

October 10, 2005

1. On some days it seems like all the bears are out on the mountain slopes. They are not difficult to locate and on these days it is likely that you can observe a record number of bears in the area being surveyed. This glorious day was Friday, October 7, 2005. The aerial survey began at 5:48 PM in my Arctic Tern taildragger based at Merrill Field in Anchorage, Alaska. The flying was completed in 1.3 hours. The first area surveyed was on the western flanks of Site Summit. Occasionally a brown or black bear can be found here. I looked over the slopes and did not find any bears. As I was leaving the area, my eye caught something in the landscape. I made a complete circle in the Arctic Tern and came back around and lo and behold, there were the black bears that I had been looking for since early July when they were sighted at McVeigh Marsh within ¼ mile of the Glenn Highway. The black bear sow had three spring cubs. This is the first black bear sow with three cubs I had observed on Fort Richardson since flying surveys during the past 20 years. I circled and managed to get digital images of the bears.

2. Now flying to Ship Creek and the home of the majestic brown bears in the Chugach Mountains. I observed three solitary adult brown bears on the eastern mountain slopes of Ship Creek opposite Temptation Peak. All these bears were in subalpine habitats at elevations from 1,500 to 2,600 feet above sea level. The bears were feeding on blueberries and other types of vegetation on the mountain slopes. Distance between bears varied from ¼ to 1 mile. The winds were blowing 20 miles per hour as I flew up the north fork of Ship Creek. The winds produced turbulent flight so I turned around and headed for the western slopes of Ship Creek near Temptation Peak. Bears are usually found here.

3. While flying at about 3,500 feet elevation, I located brown bears below on a large knoll at almost 3,000 feet elevation. I circled and got a good look at the sow with three spring cubs (cubs of the year). The bears were in deep shadows and in small creek drainage along the southeast end of Temptation Peak. I could not circle comfortably in the Tern and could not get any images with the camera. I'd hoped to see them again in a better location. I observed a brown bear sow on October 1, 2005 with three yearling cubs

on the eastern slopes across Ship Creek from here. Sows with three cubs are very rare in Ship Creek. These are only the second and third brown bear sows I have observed with three cubs in Ship Creek while conducting surveys since 1985. Brown bears in Ship Creek usually have two cubs. One other brown bear was located on the western slopes of Ship Creek near the north end of Temptation Peak. This completed the bear survey.

4. This is one of my most productive bear surveys in Ship Creek over the years. A dozen bears were found on the survey. On many surveys no bears are found! Finding the black and brown bear sows, on the same day, both with 3 cubs, is rare and so very special.

MEMORANDUM 68
SUBJECT: Aerial Black Bear Survey in Ship Creek and Eagle River

June 25, 2001

1. An aerial back bear survey was conducted beginning at 11:35 AM on June 24, 2001 in the upper parts of Ship Creek and Eagle River. The area surveyed in Ship Creek includes the watershed upstream from the High Dam to the headwaters in the Main Stem and the North Fork. The area surveyed in Eagle River includes the watershed upstream from the Gates (opposite Mt. Yukla) to Eagle Glacier. The survey was flown in my Arctic Tern taildragger based at Merrill Field in Anchorage. The temperature was in the low 60s Fahrenheit. The skies were obscured with a thin overcast at 5,000 feet ASL. Isolated fog patches were present in the valleys. Light rain was observed approaching Eagle Glacier.

2. A total of 10 black bears were observed on the survey. Nine of the black bears were observed in Eagle River and one in Ship Creek. All sightings were in the subalpine and alpine vegetation zone from 2200 to 4200 feet ASL. The bears observed near the Mountaineering Club of Alaska hut on a small rocky ridge protruding out of Eagle Glacier at over 4,000 feet ASL were a surprise. They had to cross a half mile of glacial ice on a lobe of Eagle Glacier to get to the cabin site. Figure 1 shows the location of the black bear observed in Ship Creek. Figure 2 shows the location of the black bears observed in Eagle River.

3. It was very unusual to see this many black bears on a single survey. It was obvious that the climatic conditions were unusual at the time of the

flight and many of the black bears in the area flown were out and about on mountain slopes in the subalpine where they could easily be sighted. When unusual conditions such as this are apparent, it is important to take advantage of the opportunity and conduct comprehensive surveys.

4. A sharp contrast to seeing so many black bears is that no brown bears were observed on this survey. The few brown bears that have been observed in June this year have been in the valley bottoms in forested areas. They are very difficult to locate and observe under these conditions. Sightability will not improve for the brown bears until they move onto the subalpine mountain slopes in September and October as they prepare for winter hibernation.

MEMORANDUM 69
SUBJECT: Black Bears on Fort Richardson/Ship Creek in 2003[*]

December 28, 2003

1. The number of black bears observed flying over Fort Richardson and the upper Ship Creek drainage during the past 15 years has been approximately 8-12 bears per year. Rarely do I remember finding more than a dozen in any one summer. The summer of 2003 has been exceptional due to the large number of sightings of black bears on aerial surveys into these areas. Several sightings by other pilots and surveys on the ground by fellow employees have greatly helped to boost the number of bears sighted in 2003.

2. In 2003, a total of thirty-five (35) black bears were observed on Fort Richardson and upper Ship Creek drainage (Table 1). Footnotes 2, 3, 4, and 6 in Table 1 denote black bear observations by others than the author. Of the 35 black bears observed during this time period, twenty-eight (28) were observed on Fort Richardson, one (1) on Elmendorf AFB and six (6) were observed in upper Ship Creek drainage (Chugach State Park). The site locations of the black bears that were observed during this time period are shown in Table 2.

3. The minimum number of black bears observed in 2003 in the areas surveyed was thought to be thirty-two (32) black bears. The only obvious

---

* Memorandum and aerial flights by William A. Quirk, lll, Environmental Scientist / Biologist, Department of Defense, Fort Richardson, Alaska. The author is a seasoned Alaskan pilot with his Arctic Tern taildragger based at Merrill Field in Anchorage. The views expressed here are his own.

repeat observations were, as follows: (1) Sub adult bear observed on May 19 down slope from the Army Ski Lodge parking lot which was sighted again on June 22 in the same area; (2) Adult bear observed on Oilwell Road on the South Post of Fort Richardson on August 24 and observed again on September 26 near the Ship Creek Bridge off of Arctic Valley Road; and (3) Sub adult bear observed on May 22 near the Ship Creek Dam and sighted again on June 22 on a bench near the Biathlon Range. All of the repeat bear sightings were on Fort Richardson.

4. Other black bear observations by the author during aerial flights in the summer of 2003 that were not on military land or the upper Ship Creek drainage include the following sightings: (1) Adult bear at 3,000 feet elevation on Bear Mountain (above Mirror Lake along the Glenn Highway); (2) Female with three spring cubs in an alpine bowl at 3,400 feet elevation on the north side of Pioneer Peak; (3) Two sub adult black bears along the mountain slopes of the Chugach Mountains north of Knik River; and (4) Numerous (six to eight) black bears observed in the Lake George Basin south of Knik Glacier.

5. In all of the flights over Fort Richardson in summer 2003, the author did not observe a brown bear. This is the only year I can recall not seeing two or more. Several brown bears (approximately 3) were reported to have been observed from the ground along roads and trails on Fort Richardson in 2003. The author observed eight (8) different brown bears in upper Ship Creek Valley (Chugach State Park) on aerial surveys in 2003.

6. The minimum number of black bears observed on Fort Richardson during the summer and fall of 2003 was twenty-five (25) bears (Table 3). Composition of the minimum number of bears on Fort Richardson is, as follows: 4 females with offspring; 5 Spring Cubs; 5 Yearling Cubs; 7 Sub Adults; and 8 Adults for a grand total of 25 bears. A Pie Chart is attached that shows the black bear composition on Fort Richardson according to age. The cub litter size was 2.5 which is close to Bostick's[*] litter size of 2.6.

7. It is always very difficult to estimate the total population of bears in a defined area from survey data. A Correction Factor is needed to fill in the number of bears missed during the surveying effort. In Bostick's black bear

---

[*] Bostick, D.P. (1997). A Preliminary Report on the Ecology, Behavior, and Management of Nuisance Black Bears on Military Lands within the Municipality of Anchorage. Joint Black Bear Study, Elmendorf Air Force Base and Fort Richardson, Alaska.

study on the two military installations, he found that the bears are highly mobile, especially the males and other bears without cubs. This means that bears moving onto and off of the military reservations occur frequently. This creates difficulty in determining a realistic Correction Factor. Nevertheless, the bountiful survey data collected during the summer of 2003 may not be so easily repeated any time in the near future. This may be the best opportunity to estimate the total number of black bears occupying the Fort Richardson Army Reservation.

8. Although some of Bostick's techniques were not according to the Scientific Method, his study is the only one which has attempted to estimate the actual number of black bears on the two military installations. His population estimate technique involved identifying known family groups of radio-collared sows with cubs and extrapolating these numbers to account for areas of suitable habitat occupied by family groups which had not been captured and collared. This was based on consistent sightings of uncollared bears with cubs in these areas. Bostick then added a certain number of males based on the male / female ratio reflected by the known collared animals. Using this technique, Bostick calculated a black bear population for the two military bases of 30-42 animals excluding cubs of the year (COY). Adding COY to Bostick's estimates would equal a total population in the neighborhood of 38-50 black bears on the two military bases.

9. The projected or estimated population for the Fort Richardson black bears was calculated by using a conservative Correction Factor of 30% added to the survey results of 25 bears (Table 3). Calculations show the projected population on Fort Richardson to be 33 black bears in 2003. For all the years of flying surveys over this area, I did not suspect the numbers would be this high. It is likely that the year 2003 is showing a spike in the black bears population in this area and that this is the reason for the large number of black bears on Fort Richardson.

10. Although it is widely known that black bears go back and forth between the military installations, especially between Sixmile and Otter Lakes, the author did not fly any surveys in this area in summer 2003. This area is difficult to fly because it is in Elmendorf's Flight Pattern when aircraft take off from Runway 5. With the bears missed in this area added to the totals, the estimates for Fort Richardson's black bears do seem to substantiate the number somewhat closely with the results in Bostick's study.

TABLE 1. BLACK BEARS ON FORT RICHARDSON AND SHIP CREEK 2003

Date	Females & Cubs	# of Cubs/Age	Sub Adult Bears	Adult Bears	Total Bears
May 19			1		1
May 22			1		1
May 24			1[1]		1
May 29	1[2]	4 (Yearling Cubs)		1	5
Jun 2				1	1
Jun 6				1	1
Jun 8			1		1
Jun 8				1	1
Jun 8	1	1 (Spring Cub)		1	2
Jun 12	1[3]	2 (Spring Cubs)		1	3
Jun 16			1		1
Jun 18	1[4]	3 (Spring Cubs)		1	4
Jun 22				1[5]	1
Jun 22				2	2
Jun 22			1		1
Jun 22			1		1
Jul 6				1	1
Jul 28			2[6]		2
Aug 24				1	1
Sept 26				1	1
Sept 26	1	1 (Yearling Cub)		1	2
Oct 18				1	1
Total	**5**	**11**	**9**	**15**	**35**

[1] Sub Adult bear observed on Elmendorf AFB during an aerial raptor survey.
[2] Reported by Joe Mets on an aerial flight. Images of the bears were recorded on a Digital Camera. Cubs were very large and may have been 2 year old cubs instead of yearlings.
[3] Reported by Brandon Berta from a lookout onto Eagle River Flats.
[4] Reported by Paul Woodward on an aerial flight.
[5] A very large and dominant black bear was observed pressuring a female brown bear in upper Ship Creek. Author circled overhead for 40 minutes while black bear forced brown bear up slope to about 2,200 feet in sub alpine habitat. Then they both disappeared into the alders. Images of the bears were recorded on a digital camera.
[6] Two sibling black bears observed by Chris Garner while driving on Arctic Valley Road. Images of the siblings were recorded on a digital camera.

TABLE 2. BLACK BEARS ON FORT RICHARDSON AND SHIP CREEK 2003

Date	Elevation (Ft)	Location of Black Bears
May 19	1,900	Sub adult down slope from Army Ski Lodge
May 22	800	Sub adult on gravel road near Ship Creek Reservoir
May 24	200	• Sub adult east of Boniface along Ship Creek on Elmendorf AFB
May 29	400	Sow+4 Cubs on Helicopter LZ 71 (South Post of Ft. Richardson)
Jun 2	330	Adult killed on Glenn Highway (NE of Muldoon Interchange)
Jun 6	220	Adult crossing Route Bravo east of Eagle River Flats
June 8	320	Sub adult in Chester Creek wetlands on Army South Post
June 8	1,200	Adult near Biathlon Range on Fort Richardson (Arctic Valley Road)
June 8	1,420	♦Sow+1 Cub on east slopes of Ship Creek in cottonwood forest
June 12	10	Sow+2 Cubs on northeast side of the Eagle River Flats.
Jun 16	1,350	♦Sub adult in wetlands in bottom of Ship Creek (east slopes)
Jun 18	620	Sow+3 Cubs on lower end of 5-Mile Trail near Arctic Valley Road
Jun 22	1,500	♦Dominant black bear on west slopes of Ship Creek (Temp. Peak)
Jun 22	1,360	♦Two adults on west slopes of Ship Creek
Jun 22	1,950	Sub adult down slope from Army Ski Lodge parking lot
Jun 22	1,160	Sub adult on bench near Army Biathlon Range
Jul 6	580	Adult ¾ mile north of Cochise Lake (South Post of Fort Richardson)
Jul 28	470	Two siblings east of Moose Run Golf Course on Arctic Valley Road
Aug 24	510	Adult on Oilwell Road (South Post of Fort Richardson)
Sept 26	490	Adult on Oilwell Road north of Ship Creek
Sept 26	1,960	Sow+1 Cub down slope from Army Ski Lodge parking lot
Oct 18	2,100	Adult on western slopes of Chugach Mountains above Cochise Lake

• Black bear observed on Elmendorf AFB
♦Black bears observed in the upper Ship Creek Valley (Chugach State Park)
(All other entries are black bears observed on the Fort Richardson Military Reservation)

TABLE 3. MINIMUM NUMBER OF BLACK BEARS ON FORT RICHARDSON—2003

Females with Cubs	# Cubs/Age	Sub Adult Bears	Adult Bears	Total Bears
1	4 (Yearling Cubs)[1]		1	5
1	2 (Spring Cubs)		1	3
1	3 (Spring Cubs)		1	4
1	1 (Yearling Cub)		1	2
		7		7
			4	4
Total 4	10	7	8	25

[1] These cubs were very large in size and may have been 2 year old cubs.

MEMORANDUM 70

SUBJECT: Trumpeter Swan Survey—Palmer, Alaska Region

October 19, 2010

1. This was the forty-first trumpeter swan survey in the Knik River Drainage (KRD) and the Palmer Hay Flats (PHF) in 2010. This was the seventeenth fall survey for migrating swans. The survey began at 2:40 PM on October 19, 2010. The weather was overcast. Winds in the KRD were blowing 30 to 45 miles per hour from the southeast. The Arctic Tern was experiencing moderate turbulence while flying into the KRD. The flying was difficult and was at the maximum tolerance level. Ambient temperature was 45 degrees Fahrenheit.

2. The total number of swans in the Duck–Swan Lake staging area on October 19, 2010 was 1,191 (Table 1). There were 1,175 swans in the KRD whereas only 16 swans were found in the PHF. There were 1,175 swans in the Jim Creek basin lakes. The largest number of swans in the Jim Creek basin lakes was found on Swan Lake with 540 swans.

3. No power boats were found in the Jim Creek basin today. The spatial distribution and number of migrating swans in the various lakes shows the swans' preference for the Jim Creek basin over Duck Lake and the PHF. The lakes in the Jim Creek basin with the highest swan use were, in the following order: Swan, Leaf, and Mud. Swans are normally not found

in large numbers in Mud Lake because of the boat launch and the many power boats traveling through the lake to Jim Creek. The total of 1,191 swans on October 19, 2010 was the peak number during the fall 2010 migration period.

TABLE 1. TRUMPETER SWAN SURVEY-KRD/PHF ON OCTOBER 19, 2010

Location	Swans Observed
Gravel Pit Pond	
Barbel Lake	
Foot Lake	
Total Knik River Road	
Finger Lakes	
Chain Lakes (West)	95
Leaf Lake	260
Little Leaf Lake	
Swan Lake	540
Jim Lake	55
Gull Lake	
Mud Lake	225
Knik River Gravel Bars	
Total Jim Creek Basin	**1175**
Total Knik River Drainage	**1175**
Duck Lake	16
Ponds in Marsh West of Duck Lake	
Total Palmer Hay Flats	**16**
Total KRD/PHF	**1191**

MEMORANDUM 71

SUBJECT: Trumpeter Swan Survey in the Palmer, Alaska Region

September 8, 2012

1. This was the seventeenth swan survey in the Palmer Hay Flats (PHF) and the Knik River Drainage (KRD) in 2012. The survey commenced at 1:25 PM; sunny day with thinly overcast skies and light wind. The ambient temperature on the Knik River was 48 degrees Fahrenheit. The survey was conducted in my Arctic Tern taildragger based at Merrill Field in Anchorage, Alaska.

2. Thirteen nesting pairs of trumpeter swans were monitored on September 8, 2012 (Table 1). All nesting swans and their broods of cygnets were found although the moose and waterfowl hunting seasons had opened. The hunting seasons are very stressful for the swans—air boats and motorboats coming too close. They get chased and often move to more tranquil environs. The Gull Lake swans moved from their primary feeding grounds on the east side of Gull Lake to the west side of the lake. The Jim Creek swans were in the east end of the lake. A motorboat was moving toward the swans. I did not wait to see what happened. Fresh all-terrain cycle tracks were observed near the Chain Lake swans. One cygnet was missing from the last count on August 29, 2012. The Foot Lake swans were still in Barbel Lake. The lower Knik River swans were 1 mile from their nesting grounds on an island in the Knik River. These swans were shielded from human disturbance.

3. The Cabin Lake swans were back on Cabin Lake. The Wasilla Creek swans (three pairs; all pairs with broods of cygnets) don't have any human motorized disturbance and were doing well. The swans west of the Matanuska River Bridge were still on the east side of the Glenn Highway in the Ducks Unlimited ponds. They had a limited amount of human disturbance this summer. Most of their summer was in the Duck Unlimited Ponds (since late June).

4. Fifty Dall sheep were on the Chugach Mountain slopes at Wolf Point. This is winter habitat for the sheep. Sandhill cranes were flying over the Chugach Mountains at 5,000 feet above sea level on their outward migration from Alaska. They were flying toward Prince William Sound.

TABLE 1. NESTING SWANS PALMER REGION—SEPTEMBER 8, 2012

Location of Nesting Pairs	Swans with Cygnets	Other Swans	Total Swans
01. Cabin Lake	Pr+4		6
02. Wasilla Creek (Lower)	Pr+4	Flk 12; Flk 3, S	22
03. Wasilla Creek (Upper)	Pr+3	Pr	7
04. Wasilla Creek (Head)	Pr+5		7
05. Matanuska Bridge (West)	Pr+6	Pr; Flk 3	13
06. Gull Lake	Pr+4		6
07. Jim Lake (Slough)	Pr+2		4
08. Chain Lake (East)	Pr+6	Pr	10
09. Lake George Basin	Pr+2	Flk 3; Flk 4; Pr	13
10. Hunter Creek (East)	Pr+5		7
11. Hunter Creek (West)	Pr+3		5
12. Foot Lake	Pr+5		7
13. Knik River (Lower)	Pr+5	Pr	9
Total Swans	**Cygnets: 54**	**36**	**116**

Pr (Pair); Flk (Flock); S (Single)

MEMORANDUM 72
SUBJECT: Trumpeter Swan Survey in the Susitna Flats

August 22, 2012

1. This was the seventh trumpeter swan survey in the Susitna Flats in the year 2012. The survey area included the Cook Inlet coastal marsh (1-2 miles inland from salt water) from Point MacKenzie (junction of Knik Arm and Cook Inlet) west to the Susitna River, southwest to the Beluga River, and including the lower Susitna River north to Flat Horn Lake and Susitna Station. The swans in this area were found in freshwater bodies that are inland from the coastal saltwater marshes. The goal was to fly surveys during the summer months to monitor nesting pairs of swans and their cygnets. The survey began on August 22, 2012 at 11:10 AM and required 2.1 flying hours. The weather was sunny with thin overcast skies and light winds. The ambient temperature was 56 degrees Fahrenheit. The survey was conducted in my Arctic Tern taildragger based at Merrill Field in Anchorage, Alaska.

2. Seventeen pairs of nesting swans were monitored in the Susitna flats on August 22, 2012 (Table 1). One pair of nesting swans could not be found on

this survey. These were the Susitna River (Island) swans. Point MacKenzie swans had moved 3 miles west from their nesting site. The Little Susitna East swans had adult mortality on July 6. One adult swan was found dead on the bank of an unnamed creek near the power lines. The other adult swan and two cygnets remained here until early August. On August 9, the two cygnets and a pair of adults were found back on the Susitna Flats 2 miles southwest of the creek. Evidently, the one adult picked up a mate on the Susitna Flats after a one-month residency in the creek area. The Susitna River West swans spent most of the summer 2 miles west of their nesting site on Maguire Creek. Now they had moved to a creek on the east side of the Little Susitna River. The Figure Eight swans had been found only three times since the cygnets hatched on a small lake near Figure Eight Lake. They were found on this survey on the south end of Figure Eight Lake.

TABLE 1. NESTING SWAN SURVEY SUSITNA FLATS AUGUST 22, 2012

Location of Nesting Pairs	Swans with Cygnets	Other Swans	Total Swans
01. Point MacKenzie	Pr+3	Pr	7
02. Little Susitna River (East)	Pr+2	Pr, Flk 3	9
03. Little Susitna River (West)	Pr+5		7
04. Figure Eight Lake	Pr+3		5
05. Susitna River (East)	Pr+3		5
06. Susitna River (Island)	Not Found	Pr, S	3
07. Susitna River (West)	Pr+2		4
08. Ivan River (Upper)	Pr+5	Pr	9
09. Ivan River (Powerline)	Pr+2		4
10. Chedatna Lake	Pr+3	Pr	7
11. Beluga River (North)	Pr+2	Flk 10	14
12. Beluga River (South)	Pr+3		5
13. Susitna (West) N of PL	Pr+3		5
14. Fish Creek (Lower)	Pr+3		5
15. Maid Lake	Pr+2		4
16. Fish Creek (Upper)	Pr+4		6
17. Flathorn Lake (West)	Pr+3	2 Pr	9
18. Susitna Station	Pr+4		6
Total Swans	**Cygnets: 52**	**28**	**114**

Pr (Pair); Flk (Flock); S (Single)

MEMORANDUM 73
SUBJECT: Swan Cygnet Success Palmer, Alaska in 2012*

November 20, 2012

1. Thirteen pairs of trumpeter swans nested and reared broods of cygnets in the Matanuska-Knik River in the summer of 2012 (Table 1). The total number of cygnets from the nesting swans in late June was 58. The total number of cygnets fledged was 49, resulting in a cygnet loss in summer 2012 of 9. Survivability for the cygnets in 2012 was 85 percent. The number of nesting pairs of swans in the Palmer, Alaska Region in 2012 was the highest recorded in the past six years. No attempt was made to count the total number of cygnets hatched from the nest as the cygnets cannot be accurately counted from aerial observations at this time of year.

2. Cygnets die from natural causes such as injuries, chronic health problems, and predator attacks. Humans in the Matanuska-Knik River disturb the nesting swans and their broods of cygnets especially during the moose- and duck-hunting seasons in August, September, and October. Human disturbance of swans by operators of power boats and all-terrain cycles (ATCs) would tend to contribute to the loss of cygnets as nesting pairs are likely to abandon their traditional nesting grounds and move overland to a more protected site. These long movements across marshes, wetland tussocks, alder and willow thickets, and forested areas can stress out and greatly reduce the stamina of the cygnets, can cause injury to the young cygnets and can also exposed the cygnets to predator attacks.

3. Two adult swans from the nesting pairs in Matanuska-Knik River were killed this summer. The Wolverine Lake nesting swans suffered a death in mid-June near the time the cygnets were hatching. The owners of Wolverine Lake Chalet informed the author of what happened. They said two boys escorted dogs to the swan nesting site on the east end of the lake and then turned the dogs loose on the swans for the amusement. One adult swan was killed and was observed floating on the vegetation mat on the lake. No cygnets were observed. The lodge owners said the same two boys killed all the beavers in the lake. The other adult swan found missing was from the Jim Lake nesting pair with a brood of two cygnets. This was first observed on October 1, 2012 when only one adult was with the cygnets. The single swan with the cygnets was found again on October 6 and October 9. There

---

* Memorandum and Surveys by William A. Quirk, lll (Pilot, Biologist, Ecologist)

is no information on what happened to the missing swan. Jim Lake has a road to the north lake shore and many people arrive here for boating on the lake. The other nesting swans on Jim Lake in past years never succeeded in rearing cygnets to fledging. A pair of nesting swans was shot and killed on Jim Lake a few years ago.

TABLE 1. SWAN CYGNET SUCCESS PALMER REGION—2012

Location of Nesting Swans	Cygnets in June	Cygnets Fledged[1]	Cygnet Loss
01. Knik River (Lower)	5	5	0
02. Foot Lake	5	5	0
03. Hunter Creek (West)	3	2	1
04. Hunter Creek (East)	5	5	0
05. Lake George Basin	2	2	0
06. Chain Lake (East)	7	7	0
07. Jim Lake	3	2	1
08. Gull Lake	4	3	1
09. Wasilla Creek (Head)	5	4	1
10. Wasilla Creek (Upper)	5	3	2
11. Wasilla Creek (Mid)	4	4	0
12. Cabin Lake (West)	4	4	0
13. Matanuska River (Lower)	6	3	3
Totals	**58**	**49**	**9**

[1] Cygnets fledged (able to fly) in late September to early October

Average brood size for newly hatched cygnets in June 2012: **4.46**
Average brood size for newly fledged cygnets in 2012: **3.77**
Cygnet survivability in 2012: **85%**
Nesting surveys flown in 2012: **15**

MEMORANDUM 74
SUBJECT: Swan Cygnet Success Susitna Flats in 2012*

November 20, 2012

1. Eighteen pairs of trumpeter swans nested and reared broods of cygnets in the coastal marshes of the Susitna Flats in 2012 (Table 1). The total number of cygnets from the nesting swans in late June was 57. The total number of cygnets that fledged was 53, resulting in a cygnet loss in summer 2012 of 4. Survivability for the cygnets in 2012 was 93 percent. No attempt was made to count the total number of cygnets hatched from the nest as the cygnets cannot be accurately counted from aerial surveys. There was no indication that human disturbance negatively affected the nesting swans in the Susitna Flats in 2012.

2. One adult from the pairs of the nesting swans in the Susitna Flats died in early July 2012. This was the Little Susitna River(East) pair of nesting swans. The dead swan was observed on July 6, 2012 on the bank of a creek near the power lines, east of the Little Susitna River. The single swan and her two cygnets moved down the creek into the Susitna Flats marshes near the Little Susitna River. A survey on August 11, 2012 confirmed her presence and also showed that she had picked up a mate. These newly paired nesting swans with two cygnets were observed several times after the first sighting to confirm this finding.

3. Massive flooding of the Lower Susitna River and Flat Horn Lake occurred in late September 2012. A survey on September 27, 2012 showed the flooding of the river and sloughs. Flat Horn Lake was expanded in size by about 40 percent by backup water from the Susitna River. The flooded waters from the Susitna River were heavily laden with silt and clay. The swans don't like the muddy water—most of them moved away from the river into marshes with clear water.

---

*Memorandum and Surveys by William A. Quirk, III (Pilot, Biologist, Ecologist)

TABLE 1. SWAN CYGNET SUCCESS SUSITNA FLATS—2012

Location of Nesting Swans	Cygnets in June	Cygnets Fledged[1]	Cygnet Loss
01. Point MacKenzie (West)	3	2	1
02. Little Susitna River (East)	2	2	0
03. Little Susitna River (West)	5	5	0
04. Figure Eight Lake (SE)	3	3	0
05. Susitna River (East)	3	2	1
06. Susitna River (Island)	2	2	0
07. Susitna River (West)	3	3	0
08. Ivan River	5	5	0
09. Ivan River (Powerline)	2	2	0
10. Lewis River	3	3	0
11. Beluga River (North)	3	2	1
12. Beluga River (South)	3	3	0
13. Alexander (Southwest)	3	3	0
14. Fish Creek (Lower)	3	3	0
15. Maid Lake	3	2	1
16. Fish Creek (Upper)	4	4	0
17. Susitna Station (South) #1	3	3	0
18. Susitna Station (South) #2	4	4	0
Totals	**57**	**53**	**4**

[1] Cygnets fledged (able to fly) in late September to early October

Average brood size for newly hatched cygnets in late June 2012: **3.17**
Average brood size for newly fledged cygnets in 2012: **2.94**
Survivability for cygnets in 2012: **93%**
Nesting surveys flown in 2012: **10**

MEMORANDUM 75
SUBJECT: Abstracts of Trumpeter Swan Papers

February 20, 2013

1. I have written four papers in the past several years on the Trumpeter Swans in Southcentral Alaska. Three Trumpeter Swan papers were written in 2011. Two of these papers were presented at the Twenty-Second Conference of The Trumpeter Swan Society held in Polson, Montana on October 13, 2011. These two papers will be published in North American Swans, Special Edition, Proceedings and Papers of the Twenty-Second Swan Society Conference. This is a Bulletin of The Trumpeter Swan Society, Plymouth, Minnesota. A copy of my third Paper was provided to John Cornely, Executive Director of The Trumpeter Swan Society. He will review it and decide whether to publish it in the Proceedings. A fourth paper was written in 2014 and was presented to the 5th International Swans Symposium in Easton, Maryland on February 6, 2015.

2. Below are the Abstracts for my four Trumpeter Swan papers.

A Summary of the Status, Nesting Success, and Cygnet Survivability of the Resident Population of Trumpeter Swans in the Knik River Drainage and the Palmer Hay Flats State Game Refuge, Alaska

William A. Quirk, III, P. O. Box 212545, Anchorage, Alaska 99521-2545

ABSTRACT

Comprehensive aerial surveys of Trumpeter Swans (*Cygnus buccinator*) were completed during May through September 2008-10 in the Knik River Drainage and the Palmer Hay Flats State Game Refuge, Alaska to determine the population status, nesting success and cygnet survivability. Results show a resident population of 62-91 swans during the three year survey period. The average resident population was 40.7 white swans including an average of 10.0 pairs of nesting swans. The nesting swans reared an average of 39. 0 fledged cygnets. Nesting success for the swans well into the incubation period is very high (90-100%). Cygnet survival to fledging averaged 81% for the 3 year period and reached a remarkable 94% in 2008. Disturbances by humans and motorized recreational activities appeared to be limiting swans choosing nesting sites in this region.

Staging Strategies of Trumpeter Swans in the Knik River Drainage and the Palmer Hay Flats State Game Refuge, Alaska

William A. Quirk, III, P. O. Box 212545, Anchorage, AK 99521-2545

ABSTRACT

Aerial surveys of migrating Trumpeter Swans (*Cygnus buccinator*) in the Duck-Swan Lake staging area of the Knik River Drainage and the Palmer Hay Flats State Game Refuge, Alaska were conducted during 2008-11 to better understand temporal and spatial use in the region. Twenty-nine daily autumn surveys in 2010 (28 September and 4-31 October) and eight bi-weekly spring surveys in 2011 (9 April through 8 May) showed differing preferences for staging lakes by season. Autumn staging numbers for swans peaked at 1,240 on 21 October 2010. The Duck-Swan Lake staging area provided 18,360 total swan-use-days in the autumn migration in 2010 with swans preferring Swan Lake. Peak spring swan numbers in 2011 approached 1,500 swans on 27 April with a preference for Duck Lake. Disturbance levels by humans and food availability appeared to dictate the staging preferences.

Trumpeter Swan Disturbances from Motorized Recreation and Hunting in the Knik River Drainage and the Palmer Hay Flats State Game Refuge, Alaska

William A. Quirk, III, P.O. Box 212545, Anchorage, AK 99521-2545

ABSTRACT

Monitoring motorized recreation and hunting disturbances negatively affecting Trumpeter Swans in the Knik River Drainage and the Palmer Hay Flats evolved out of completing basic aerial swan surveys. The data collected on these basic swan surveys was used to write and submit two swan papers for publication. Surveys to collect the basic swan data in concert with monitoring motorized recreation and hunting swan disturbances have been flown by the author in the region near Palmer, Alaska for more than 15 years. Findings show consistently widespread and high swan disturbance levels by motorized recreational users and hunters which negatively impact the resident swans including nesting pairs of swans with cygnets and several thousand migrating swans that make use of the important Duck-Swan Lakes staging area. The author is recommending responsible land managing agencies in the region support a collaborative effort to regulate motorized recreation and hunting activities that are negatively impacting the swans.

Density and Productivity Comparisons between Two Populations of Trumpeter Swans in Southcentral Alaska

William A. Quirk, lll, P. O. Box 212545, Anchorage, Alaska 99521

E-mail: akquirk@gci.net

ABSTRACT

Trumpeter Swan (*Cygnus buccinator*) surveys were flown in the Matanuska-Knik River and the Susitna Flats geographic regions near Anchorage, Alaska for a 3 year period ending in 2013 to capture data for density and productivity comparisons. Swans exhibited dissimilarities in density and productivity in the two regions apparently influenced by habitats, climate, and human disturbance. The density of swans summering in the Matanuska-Knik River is denser than the swan populations in the Susitna Flats. Productivity of the nesting swans in the Matanuska-Knik River over the three year period showed average brood sizes that were 38% larger when compared to brood sizes in the Susitna Flats. Although density was higher and brood sizes were larger in the area with high human disturbance, those results reflect the generally higher quality habitat and the earlier spring break-up of the Matanuska-Knik River. The author recommends restrictions in the Matanuska-Knik River drainages on motorized recreation and hunting activities during incubation and brood-rearing periods for nesting swans and spring and autumn periods for migrating swans. Public education efforts should be employed to promote the value of these habitats for Trumpeter Swans.

KEY WORDS: Aerial Survey, Alaska, Nesting Success, Swan Disturbance, Trumpeter Swan